American Canto

Olivia Nuzzi

Avid Reader Press

NEW YORK AMSTERDAM/ANTWERP LONDON
TORONTO SYDNEY/MELBOURNE NEW DELHI

AVID READER PRESS
An Imprint of Simon & Schuster, LLC
1230 Avenue of the Americas
New York, NY 10020

Some of this reporting appeared in different form in *New York* magazine. One of the interviews with Donald Trump was conducted for a different book project.

First Avid Reader Press hardcover edition December 2025

AVID READER PRESS and colophon are trademarks of Simon & Schuster, LLC

Manufactured in the United States of America

1   3   5   7   9   10   8   6   4   2

Library of Congress Control Number has been applied for.

ISBN 978-1-6682-0985-1
ISBN 978-1-6682-0987-5 (ebook)

For the women who have mothered me.
And for my brother, Jonathan, to whom I owe my life.

Author's Note

It is inevitable that some of the people discussed in this book will disagree with or dislike what I have written. It is unnatural to see oneself filtered through another's perspective; I know that experience well. Direct quotations are from recordings or contemporaneous notes, including many hours of conversations with Donald Trump, beginning in 2014, when I was first assigned to write about him. This is not, though, a book about the president or even about politics. It is a book about life in America as I have lived and observed it, and about the nature of our reality, and about character; his and my own and that of the country he has so affected. It is also a book about love, because everything is about love, and about love of country.

American Canto

On the steps of the Met, the Politician on the phone. "You didn't do anything wrong," he said. He did not understand how I could be in any kind of professional trouble over a personal relationship. "If we got married, it still wouldn't be wrong," he said. "My aunt married my uncle after she interviewed him." This was different, I said. For one thing, I was not Jacqueline Bouvier and he was not John F. Kennedy. For another, he was already married, and I had been engaged until several weeks earlier.

I looked down at the granite. Cockroaches. Dozens and dozens of them. Crawling everywhere. A parade, a stampede, a rally, a rave. I eyed them curiously. I did not flinch. When your world is falling apart, you walk forward. The cockroach, six legs and six claws, understands this. Down Fifth Ave, across Seventy-First Street, down Lex. Plastered on the glass door of the bodega, a magazine cover with my name on it. Advertising not my life, not disfigured public narratives about private matters, but my work.

I walked past the place where I was born. It had been a blizzard, my mother always told me. The date would later become shorthand for the occasion of that riot at the Capitol over which more than a thousand people were arrested and for which the president was indicted by a grand jury in the District of Columbia and charged with conspiring to defraud the United States and obstruct an official proceeding. He pleaded not guilty. When he returned to office, the government dropped the case and he pardoned the prisoners. He called them patriots.

Strange symmetry. Circular. On this humid night, a last gasp as the tail met the jaw. I did not yet grasp this.

I cannot tell you the first time I heard about Donald Trump because he was always there. As sure a part of the architecture of my world as the Fifty-Ninth Street Bridge and the Twin Towers. Six years old, in my father's truck, idling on Central Park South. He gestured to the town car in front of us. "That's Donald Trump," he said. I knew who he was.

I knew that he owned beauty pageants, and I knew about beauty pageants because of JonBenét Ramsey, and I was frightened by beauty pageants because of JonBenét Ramsey, because she was the first girl through whom I learned that if you are beautiful you may get killed, and once you are killed you will become the property of the country, and the country will resurrect you so that you can be killed again and again in ecstatic detail on the national altar of television; JonBenét Ramsey said that if you are beautiful you may get killed in service to your country.

In 1996, the year that Donald Trump acquired the Miss Universe Pageant, I turned three, and JonBenét Ramsey, who was six, was murdered. Sitting in the truck behind Trump's town car three years later,

I was as old as she would ever be, and her face was still everywhere, in the same papers where I saw Trump; the ones my father brought home each day, the *New York Post* and *Daily News*. The great monster of ephemeral newsprint, stalking through tabloids as other monsters stalked through fables. I filed him into this category of character. All the monsters seemed to me the same.

The mind is an idol-making machine.

—Saint John of the Cross,

paraphrased by Bishop Robert Barron

There are no lines in nature, only areas of color, one against another.

—Édouard Manet

On Deane Way, near the Navesink River, I was raised in a small gray ranch with a yard of hydrangeas and forsythias and tomato plants and a three-foot-by-five-foot American flag waving over the door.

One house over were the Murray girls. There were five of them, and I spent the most time with Hannah, two years older than me and thus an authority figure, the only such figure I would ever really respect. She was wise and mischievous and discreet. Trusted by other children and adults alike.

When I was very small she pulled me between two big white oak trees and told me there was no Santa Claus. This was not an act of cruelty in the manner that some older children inflicted this knowledge on their younger marks, but a favor. She thought I needed to know, that I deserved to know, that it seemed impossible I did not already suspect as much, and that it would be a kind of insult to my intelligence to not loop me in just because I was the baby of the group. She had assembled on the grass a council of the older neighborhood children to discuss the matter before she made the disclosure. She was thoughtful that way, a natural democratic leader. As the fourth of the five sisters, she had an innate sense of justice. I revered her.

As time passed and my world wobbled into uncertain shapes, I thought often of Hannah's face, and in that way I thought, really, of all the Murray faces. To know one Murray face was to better comprehend all the others, beautifully marked as they were by wide-set eyes and ivory skin and framed by bows in their red, brown, blonde, blonde, and blonde hair.

I recalled one afternoon in particular, when I was lying on the carpet of her bedroom and I looked over at her face, and it occurred to me that I had seen her face for so many hours and days in every year of my life, and in so many places, in so many lights, and in this place more often than any other place, in this bedroom near the staircase, lambent against these pale walls and floral linens, but I could not see her as clearly as I once had.

It seemed she was too close an object. Her face had transformed into a blur of colors, into flashes of ivory and blonde and blue and pink, and I could not tell if it had happened just then all at once, or if it had been changing in subtle ways over time and I was only then noticing.

Lines recede, borders dissolve, when you look very closely for very long at anything. The familiar fades into the foreign. You do not know and then you know so well and then you walk through the door of your life for the first time again.

I woke the morning after Election Day on the wrong coast of the right country. A brush fire had come charging across the road, through two houses, and onto the cliffs above the sea. But I did not know that yet.

All I knew was that my phone was ringing, and when I picked up it was a friend, walking along the Atlantic in Palm Beach, where I was supposed to be, and she was dodging sources and subjects, like I was supposed to be, and when the conversation turned to a sensitive topic, right around the time I was wondering why my coffee was not brewing, the call dropped. The power was out.

A few minutes later, the planes swooped down to spray the flames in the bluffs. I watched from the Pacific Coast Highway, as far away from my problems as I could get on land, which was not far enough.

You cannot outrun your life on fire.

In the little house at Zuma, I light candles in every room. I never turn on lights. For this reason, I often do not notice for a while when the power goes out. The power is usually out. I do not mind.

The sun boils red into the water. Ball of fire at Point Dume. Clear. From Boney Ridge, the San Gabriels, the Topa Topas, the Channel Islands. Below us, fire, above us, fire. That we came from fire and return to fire, that we move forward only because we have learned to tame some fires, that here at least untamed fire is the greatest present threat to life.

Around Saddle Peak, the earth is the rich color of the raven, and on the dirt here and there are brushstrokes of hot pink and fuchsia, the expressionist chemical aftermath of the fight against the last wildfire.

When I smell the burned-up earth, my mind turns east to spring, to an afternoon outside the Manhattan criminal court where Donald Trump was on trial, when the boy who missed his mother and could no longer bear to be here doused himself in gasoline and lit a match. When I learned what burning flesh smells like. Strange and sweet.

I think of the police officer staring into space and lighting a cigarette, taming fire to sustain his sanity, looking like he had seen a ghost. I suppose he had.

I think of that boy—his name was Max—his flesh in the air, his flesh on our tongues, how the rest of the day, the rest of the court proceedings, and then on the drive uptown and then on television, I tasted him. In those moments I could think of little else. That he was in my mouth as I spoke about the trial, that my words were formed by pieces of his body, that I spoke him out loud.

It had taken about a month for me to begin to understand what people mean when they say Los Angeles makes you go insane. The monotony of the beautiful sunshine, day in and day out. When I heard this before, in New York, spoken by a certain kind of actor/producer/model/DJ/trust-fund-lifetime-sweepstakes-winner, I did not take it very seriously.

It was after three or four weeks of my exile, when I was staying in Nichols Canyon, and I was driving west on Sunset early in the day, that it occurred to me that my life was completely different than it had been when I arrived here, and yet it did not feel that more than a day or two had passed, because the passage of time was hard to register, because of all the sunshine.

The days were still long when I arrived in a whirl of external scandal and internal confusion. Every hour, it seemed, there was a new headline, a new threat. There are two types of men who are the most dangerous.

The first are those with everything to lose. The second are those with nothing to lose. I knew them both.

My work had been what I retreated to when everything else seemed in doubt. Now a monumental fuckup had collided my private life with the public interest. My work could not be retreated to because my career was in doubt. I still had something to save then, or I thought that I did, though I had nothing in particular to do besides shelter in place. Wait for the collapse of my life to conclude. Wait to assess the wreckage.

The paradox is that the place in America where people migrate when they wish to become known is in fact an ideal place to disappear. I made my way further up the coast to make my disappearance more total. In Malibu I did not feel as I felt in the canyon or the hills. I did not feel the country was closing in. In Malibu life was solitary and surreal and my days were lost and I was trying to sort out whether I liked that. I liked lost compared to the verge of found; I worried about being found.

From the deck, I could see miles of shoreline to the south, hills to the east, and to the west the never-ending blues. Still I looked north over my shoulder through the arch of elms and the groves of palms. I had the sense, hard to shake because it was true, that I was being hunted.

Above the Pacific, I threaded along a blonde hillside. Past the caution tape, a few yards down the charred ground, I came upon a rattlesnake, maybe four feet long. Silver in the sun, tail coiled, belly shedding skin, eye a miniature eight ball. So harmless now. The fire had been out for days but the winds were still raging. They blew the tears right off my cheeks. Tough love; another insult, however justified.

I inched closer to inspect his lifeless form, thinking all the while that

I would rather be scared. I would rather venom lurk someplace beside me. Range of original error. Leading me, yes. And I was thinking about how one man's revolution is another man's invasion. How another's freedom is my captivity. You know that power corrupts. Did you know that power corrodes?

An old man stepped off the trail and into the brush. He waved me forward. "You go ahead, you're younger than me," he said. "No, it's okay," I said. He shook his head and gestured at the terrain, steep and rocky in this section. "No, you go," he said. "I've gotta make sure I don't fall on my ass." He had a kindness about him. As I wove on I looked over my shoulder and remarked that if he did fall, it would probably be onto his face, not his ass. He laughed. "I haven't done that in a while," he said, "just in public in other ways." I smiled. "Yeah, me too."

Down the road at the gallery, Eamon Harrington showed me a painting. It was a television news screen. Cluttered as such screens are with blocks of banners that scream out the headlines of the moment. WILD-FIRES IN MALIBU. YOUNG VOTERS BOYCOTTING. MAYHEM IN GAZA. NEW ALZHEI-MER'S RESEARCH. He had painted it sixteen years ago. We laughed. So much happens, so little changes.

He told me the winds would be returning that night. Certain winds meant certain fire. It felt here more than most places I had been that you were always at risk of extinction. That people elsewhere, if they felt otherwise, were merely too distracted to see how fragile their civilization was.

When I was elsewhere.
When I felt otherwise.

Here I paced for hours while the sun burned hot. The cold came on quickly. The waxing crescent moon hovered low over the hills, winked above the sea. A scalpel, it lanced my chest, rooted around, found little of value, tossed me aside, then disappeared behind the curve of the earth to taunt someone else. Land of my idle, my idyll. The hand of God reached down to swat me off the path I was on. God struck a match. God struck me again.

In the news, the Politician offers a united front and a rewritten history. My vow of silence does not feel like enough. I wish to fall silent on myself, too. I wish to sink into the sea. To flee behind the curve of the earth. To emerge a new shape, a stranger. To stop giving fake names in coffee shops. To never see myself, the character of myself imagined by others, viral allegory of hubris, female avatar of Icarus, stripped and left for dead in a pool of wax. I do not wish to be understood, which no one seems to understand.

Birds of prey circle. It is inconceivable, it seems, that someone would choose to allow a crisis to go to waste, would not want to make of their attention more attention, would not want to reap some kind of short-term profit from the mess of their life.

The paparazzi, the calculating ones, write to tell me where their colleagues are staking me out. New York. Washington. Outside my brother's house, where they get into an altercation with a neighbor. Never anywhere I am. They think that if they do me this favor, I will cut a deal and agree to be photographed by them in exchange for what they advertise as control over my image. *My Image*, a ship that has sailed and sunk. The offer includes a promise that doubles as a threat: If I accept their terms, I will be left alone the rest of the time, which means that if I do not accept their terms, I will not be left alone.

They are outside my parents' house, one of them said. I asked him to let me know if he finds my parents; I have been looking for them for years. For the first time in a while, I feel with some frequency grief's phantom limb. I should call my mother. I should see my father. I am always forgetting to do something, that is how their absence registers. Was I not somebody's daughter? Did I not mean to check in today? I vow to call more often in my next life.

In the discourse someone I have met before jokes about my murder. Others contact me to warn me that such a thing is not a joke but a possibility. I was not going to sleep anyhow.

People often, often people I do not know very well, reach out to tell me that I have appeared in their dreams. I wonder if this is because I sleep so little. If the version of me who lives on the plane of dreams tires of waiting for me to release her to action, if she goes out searching for places where she may exist without my permission, if she identifies the minds of those who have felt any kindness toward me, if she thinks that within their dreams she might get to live freely instead. I wonder, too, if this is a function of being a visible face but a veiled personality. If my impression contains empty space that renders me an adaptable idea and thus a useful device for subconscious minds. It is nice to think of this, that I might still be in some way, to someone, of use.

———————

At the home of a friend in the hills above the Tower, there are mushrooms on the wallpaper in the powder room. I catch a glimpse of myself in the mirror and am startled by how young I look. As though I just arrived here. I used to feel very old. The night before, a high school girl had told me that I reminded her of a baby deer, and this would not have meant much to me had a woman not described me earlier in the week as looking like a deer in headlights, and had a psychic not remarked that she saw me as "half fawn and half mustang," by which I assumed she meant the horse and not the car that I drive out here. The driver's side door sometimes pops open on the freeway, a minor thrill. The psychic would not reveal more, she said, because she sensed I doubted her powers. She was correct. I thought of the occasions, most often on the East Coast, when I saw dead deer on the side of the road, made the sign of the cross, said a prayer that they had not suffered, and drove on. Hit and bloodied off a boneheaded sprint to death, I agreed, I could see myself, a deer. In the powder room, I turn away from my reflection to look at the fly agarics. Red capped, white polka dots. The *Alice in Wonderland* mushrooms that, when taken, distort your perception of scale, making you feel very large or very small. I feel that I have swallowed some of those. I feel that the world around me is so big and I am so puny.

The sun begins to set just when I accept the day. A horror. A beautiful light. I thought of what I would do in a normal world. If I was who I was before, what I would do.

Green fire of grass,
Blue flame of lupin bloom,
And poppies burning on the bare hillsides.

—Madeleine Ruthven

Ruthven was a screenwriter in the silent era. Hauled before Congress in the McCarthy hearings, she pled the Fifth; she was in fact a communist.

She wrote in poetry of the Santa Monica Mountains. Forty miles, from the Hollywood Hills to the sea. I live now in these mountains. I like these mountains, like that they connect the center of a world to the end of a country, like that from here you see how you can never see the end.

It was one hundred million years ago, give or take, that the North American tectonic plate triumphed over the Farallon tectonic plate and through the mega-anna surfaced peaks of granite, sandstone, serpentinite, marble, chert, limestone, basalt, dolostone, and quartz that sculpt this part of the westernmost edge of the landmass. In this peripheral territory within the visible context of rock, I found it was possible to discern scale and shape otherwise blurred.

I looked east and back. That is what it felt like: east and back, away from the water and to the valley, where I saw not the slope of the earth but what had been, what I was, what continued on. It was true that my life had skidded to a stop on the cliff at the end of the country. Yet this phenomenon did not seem a function of just distance or stillness. From the hill, I accessed a parallax view within an overview effect that amounted to what I came to consider *apospection*, from Greek, *apo*, as in *away from*, and Latin, *specere*, as in *to observe*.

From the hill, I saw fire all around, saw fire in my wake. From the hill, east and back, I saw the wildflowers as Ruthven did: Emersonian expressions of gentleness derived from violence. I fixated on these flags of surrender. We get caught up in beginnings and ends, but far afield in the belly of the horseshoe theory, the poppy burns and the lupin flames and life and death braid together in the blaze.

On Backbone Trail, rock to rock, a friend in town from Washington told me about something her pastor had said in a recent sermon: Sometimes in life you will arrive someplace to find that God has already been there.

———

Whoever fights monsters should see to it that in the process he does not become a monster. For when you look long into an abyss, the abyss also looks into you.

—Friedrich Nietzsche

Hannibal Lecter was in Silence of the Lambs. *You saw the movie, Olivia, right? One of the greats, in your opinion? One of the great movies?*

—Donald J. Trump

———

It was the flag. When I close my eyes in search of the end or the start, the place at which *before* stopped and beyond which *now* began, that is what I see. The blur of colors, the flash of red, of blue, of white, stretched and folded, pulled apart, undefined yet unmistakable, the flag. There was no one day, one moment, one event, one decision, one word that marked the change. There was the flag as it mutated from metaphorical to literal weapon, as it was marred by a corruption of the American character that could not be understood or even fully observed through the prism of the partisan binary. Which is to say that it was the flag, but it was not about the flag, not about notions of patriotism or nationalism or idolatry. It was the flag that thrashed in psychedelic distress, suggested a bend in lanes of reason, a tear in the fabric of consensus reality.

In this period of now, from 2015 to 2025, in which the man through whom the culture was synthesized achieved dominance, I found myself fixated on the flag, on the way the flag expressed how the country was warping, and yet the magnitude of this change could not be categorized appropriately or catalogued completely amid such amnesia. At the southern border or the White House or the Midwest auto factory or the boat in the Atlantic or the truck rolling beside the Pacific, the very flag that had been clutched like pearls at the turn of the century was refashioned as costume jewelry. Red, white, and blue asphyxiated blue, gray, and black. Stars and Stripes a backdrop for the star of the country. One stripe remade a banner across which his campaign slogan crawled.

That it looked so unserious, the manner in which the symbol of a country was seized and perverted in violation of code and good taste to communicate tribal allegiances at once camp and seditious, was a sleight of hand. That those who did not participate in the process by which it was edited or did not dwell in places where such flags were flown were not inclined to be offended by the sight of them prevented their inclusion in the broader culture wars. Yet even the flags about which nothing seemed amiss were tricks of a kind, most of them made of plastic parts imported from a foreign adversary and assembled by low-wage immigrant workers and offered for pennies wholesale to mega-chains who advertised them as MADE IN AMERICA at markups of 15,000 percent.

As the edited flags waved strange and ominous, my job was to bear witness to the processes of American presidential politics, to travel the country and attempt to understand those who sought or wielded or influenced executive power. I had never been interested in politics, exactly. I was interested in characters, and as it happened there were lots of them in politics, and like all great characters they wanted something, would do whatever they had to in order to get it, and often they were delusional—but often enough to encourage delusion, delusions manifested in America. Almost as soon as I entered the profession, I was assigned to cover the dominant force, the president, the greatest character of all.

I came to see him as the mirror through which the country was reflected back at itself. The mistake was to think it possible to opt out of the picture he revealed. Those who tried found his concave surface made light into flame, that the heat warped even that which the flame did not burn as the field of his distortion sprawled ever wider, its imperial expansion across territories not a hostile takeover but a series of terms and conditions to which we had repeatedly and emphatically agreed.

We were primed to participate in the farcical parable in which the son of a businessman dreams of making movies, goes to Hollywood, comes home, becomes a businessman who thinks, still, of the screen, thinks of Hollywood, who makes himself a star as consolation, becomes the skilled practitioner of a screen art that perverts notions of truth and make-believe, who like many stars succumbs to tyrannical impulses and authoritarian fantasies because the compromise of his life feels like a loss of control, an expression of weakness, because it is, and whose fantasies, in a pretty good twist, are not his alone but are instead woven into a mass delirium that splits us into a Gemini nation under a Gemini ruler.

Everything seemed suddenly flexible. With all information available at all times to all people, all matters appeared potentially negotiable. Fine fractures splintered deep, fanned out far, cracked up for good. The parties were over. The system was moot. Vast interconnectedness and mass overstimulation gave way to individual isolation and nihilistic boredom so total that it all but invited the ascendant mob-mentality politics of comic relief and sadistic catharsis.

Our more flammable world. Arson, the national pastime. Self-immolation, well.

Events lost context. Words lost meaning. *Denier*. Nothing could be believed because everything was subject to change. *Truther*. Everything could be believed because anything was possible; this was at once inspirational slogan and active threat.

The man who cried dictator yesterday might be his deputy tomorrow. The man who condemned the violence might soon tell you there had been no violence at all. The woman might make official her concession but then refuse to concede the point. The man might refuse all concessions, and for his more total commitment to His Truth, be rewarded with a prophecy fulfilled.

A promise was only a suggestion. A suggestion was only a joke, unless you were not moved to laugh; then the joke was on you.

In this reality, reality ceased to feel real.

I mean to tell you as best I can what it was to face this unrealness, to stand so close that it seemed at times almost plausible, to tiptoe along the edge of the abyss, and to balance there just long enough to forget that the plates would soon shift.

I mean to tell you of the canyon where voices carried. The place where monsters spoke to me. Where I listened. Where I found that, as fortune or curse would have it, I knew the language of monsters. Where, with news on my tongue and tears in my eyes—the role of town crier, I interpret literally—I ran back over the hill to translate for those who could not stomach the thought of standing face-to-face with monsters but who required knowledge of monsters as the monsters accrued ever more power, as they revealed or converted ever more monsters among men.

I mean to tell you that, as it relates to monsters, little can be assured beyond their ceaseless want. That you feed the monster, and the monster wants only more. That here you have surrendered to the endless transaction, and through the terms on which you meet the monster you are transformed monstrous, too, for the day that the monster is done wanting is the day that the sun does not rise; want makes the monster as sun makes the day.

I mean to tell you that as I studied them, I was sometimes fooled. Fooled about their power. Fooled about my own. Fooled about the nature of power. Fooled most of all into thinking that anything was ever about anything other than power, which is to say the misconception of control, which is to say the misdirection of fear, which is to say the misprocessing of love and its absence.

Certain dramas you can count on. Empires fall at last. Heroes fail at first. And here I mean to tell you that character is not what you are in the end; character is the thing you cannot outrun or outgun that spars with fate all along. I refer now to my own. Witness and witnessed. When I slipped, I was swallowed whole. Straight through the plot, under the blade of the devices, and out the other side.

I mean to tell you that this is more meaningful and more meaningless than you might think.

I mean to tell you that, before I was consumed by it, I could not have told you what it was.

The flag winked beside lanes that bent to borders that faded to barriers that fell to the lines I crossed. I am talking, of course, about how it happened between me and the Politician. I am talking, of course, about how it happened between the country and the president. I cannot talk about one without the other.

When I open my eyes I see, still, the blur of colors, the flash of red, of blue, of white.

I mean to tell you now as best I can.

———

In the little house at Zuma, a single gust of hot wind broke through the window, cracking it open, enveloping me. The chaotic visitor. The Santa Anas. The property had been destroyed in the Woolsey Fire. The owners rebuilt. I lived now within a resurrection.

Dust and debris formed cyclones on the road. People drove recklessly. People swerved to dodge those people. The artist was nice, but by the time I made it down the coast she had already had one martini, and by the time I was able to leave, she had had several more, plus a few tokes of a joint, and she was leaning in too close for my liking, and she kept grabbing hold of me for emphasis while talking.

I wonder if I would recoil from people who grab hold of me if I did not feel that I had been grabbed by the hands of the country. I wonder if I would recoil from women who drink several martinis were it not for my mother. Were it not for her, perhaps I would be one of them.

INTERVIEWER: *Would it have been a different album if things were different?*

LEONARD COHEN: *Oh, yeah. Everything would be different if everything was different.*

—MTV, 1993

Cohen had finally lost his patience with the interviewer, young and earnest, who peppered him with the well-intentioned but simplistic questions that young and earnest interviewers ask. Then, just as quickly as he had snapped, he assumed a more generous posture, not condescending but gentle, as if he was crouching down to speak to a child.

It is easy to mistake force or scale or scope for power when what it really is is grace, by which I mean restraint.

I called the president. He picked up. He sounded odd. His voice was liquid. He said, "Hello," but he said it like *Huhhllllll—oHOoooooooooh.* The *Huhh* a deep huff, the *llllll* elongated, as though his tongue might be stuck on the roof of his mouth, the *oHOoooooooooh* exaggerated into two parts: *oH*, emphasis on the closing of the vowel, and *Oooooooooooh*, emphasis on the opening of the vowel again.

I paused. This was his phone number. He had called me on the number recently. But he sounded so unlike himself. Was it someone else?

Finally, I said, with some doubt, "Mr. President?" There was a pause and he said, "Yeah," but he said it like *Yyyyy-AH-awwww.* Deep, slow. Goofy, really. The *Yyyyy* suspended for a touch too long, the *AH* a very big sound, like he might swallow up the phone, and then the *awwww*, a cartoonish vocal gesture, somewhere between *Duh, of course it's me, your president* and the empty cooing of the Valley Girl of late-twentieth-century stereotype.

I zoomed out on the subject of his phone comportment, an unusual and unusually central facet of his character.

Long after they had fallen out of fashion, if not manufacture, he held on to a flip phone because he preferred the way that the device hinged along his face so that its microphone was positioned close to his mouth—all the better to transmit an accurate reverberation of his speech in word and spirit. He could fight the march of technological innovation for only so long. He adapted.

In the early days of his first administration, he kept a large photograph of himself holding a smartphone to his ear framed on the wall of the West Wing, an artifact of some amusement, since the make and model of the device in question was considered difficult to secure when compared to other similar devices.

His first impeachment had taken place over the matter of a phone call in which he had sought to compel the president of another country to action that would have harmed his opponent in the next election. He denied wrongdoing; it had been, he maintained, "a perfect call."

Later, he placed a call to the secretary of state in Georgia amid his frantic assertions that widespread fraud was to blame for the results of the election he pretended he did not lose. "What I want to do is this: I just want to find, uh, 11,780 votes, which is one more than we have, because we won the state," he said, according to a recording of the conversation.

In the same period, he placed a call to an official tasked with investigating his fraud allegations, and that call, too, became the subject of controversy and claims of obstruction. "I had a very good conversation. They made the conversation look like it was a false conversation," the president told me. "It was a very good conversation talking about fraud in our country and 'Thank you very much for looking at fraud in the country.'"

He was defensive about efforts to cast in a perverse light what he insisted were his always-appropriate telecommunications overtures. "It was a phenomenal call, it was a perfect call—I like to use the expression *perfect call*," he went on. "I did a lot of perfect calls. I'm the only guy who does perfect calls and gets impeached. But that was impeachment hoax number one."

It was also among the articles in impeachment number two, and central to one of his four indictments, for racketeering.

More recently he had acquired a new kind of smartphone, and a Palm Beach number, and compelled perhaps by mounting evidence that he was divinely protected from mortal and legal danger, he had begun texting more often, a practice he had largely avoided to this point along with email and other forms of written communication on the wisdom that no good could come from a paper trail.

He did not commit thoughts to the cloud at all, really, until after he was defeated in the 2020 election and departed the White House a sore loser, having incited a mob that attacked the United States Capitol and threatened to hang his vice president in a failed attempt to stop the certification of the votes, and then having refused to attend to the rituals of the democratic transfer of power.

People do change. One longtime friend of the president, a shallow thinker and—and it was hard not to see this as connected—a perma-optimist on the subject of his morality, woke each morning and transmitted to him via text message a Bible verse. As he related this to me, the longtime friend said, in all earnestness, that he was sure the president read the passages and that he absorbed and appreciated them. Another longtime friend told me that the president's relative unfamiliarity with the medium sometimes presented challenges, as when he did not seem to understand the concept of a group chat, and as a result unknowingly sent a message mocking his own cabinet secretary to, among others, the cabinet secretary.

Still he was always more likely to call and to answer a call. He seemed to answer all calls, in fact, whether or not he recognized the phone number, and whether or not he was in the middle of something. He was always more himself while talking on the phone, as if dividing his physical being from the target of its expression made the whole of him a less fraught force.

On the line I hesitated. Then I said, "It's Olivia Nuzzi."

I said my name in my wonted manner of speaking, a near whisper that the president had remarked on over the years.

In Nietzsche's novel about a prophet who returns from isolation in the mountains, *Thus Spoke Zarathustra*, the titular narrator describes his own soft voice as a reflection of his conflict with his consciousness: "Thus did I speak, and always more softly: For I was afraid of mine own thoughts, and the thoughts behind mine own thoughts."

The softness of my voice seemed less a psychological phenomenon than a physical one—related, I assumed, to more general audial oddities that were the effects of ear surgery I had as a baby and that functioned as a peculiar performance enhancement in my role as witness. In crowded rooms, I could isolate conversations, listening in one ear to someone speaking to me and in the other ear to what was being said between parties a table or two or three or five away. The more distant noise might at intervals sound nearer. Very loud noises might not sound loud at all, while whispers into ears several heads away rang clear as if spoken into my own.

What I heard was recorded and filed away whether or not I was actively listening, a party trick of my mind that permitted me in childhood to wriggle out of trouble related to my space cadet tendencies. A math teacher once loomed over my desk, where I was drawing lilacs in a notebook, and demanded that I tell him what he had just explained to the class, and I repeated a monologue of his speech that I did not quite recall even hearing moments before, but that I was certain was correct. He affirmed this with a respectful nod in my direction. I possessed a special skill that would allow me to get away with a lot, he said, and it was my responsibility to use it wisely.

It was this special skill that permitted me later to walk through the scene of a rally or forum or debate or diplomatic summit and transcribe in real time the words uttered by a politician while making in real time observations about his or her physicality or the reaction in the crowd to this or that word or phrase or the eyes contracting in boredom or expanding in awe or the quality of the sunlight in the East Room at that very moment or the knot forming in the flag as it snapped in the wind tunnel in the hangar.

My voice was ruled a few decibels lower than standard settings by, besides the president, technicians at radio stations or television producers testing sound levels or customer service representatives or members of the House of Representatives or anyone else at whom I might direct speech. It sounded loud enough to me, but I deferred to the external consensus. Across the Resolute Desk, the president once interjected as I formulated a question to pose one of his own: "Has anyone ever told you that you speak very softly?" He seemed hung up on this detail. He looked at a member of his staff. "She speaks very softly," he said again, adjusting his speech mid-sentence to deliver the words *very softy* very softly.

Now, as the line remained silent, I wondered for a moment if I should have made an effort to be louder, or if I should have mimicked the president in his oozing manner of speech in order to meet him on whatever plane he was presently living on. What would that have sounded like? It's *Ohhhhhhhh-lihhhh-VEE-ya-Ahhhh Nooooohhhhhh-TOOT-zzzeeee?*

As I contemplated this communication, it ended. The line went dead.

Blondes make the best victims. They're like virgin snow that shows up the bloody footprints.

—Alfred Hitchcock

You can manipulate any dataset to conform to a narrative. For instance, if you do not count strawberry blondes or dirty blondes (a stretch, but I could make an argument), and if you do not count Gerald Ford (easier), Donald Trump is the first blonde president. Is it any wonder then that he can so easily fetishize his own victimization?

Britney Spears appeared in a cavernous room dimly lit by fire. She had a feral look. Bleach-frayed hair. Pharmaceutical stare. She wore a flimsy leopard-print leotard, brown leather boots, a band of red fabric on her left wrist, and nothing else.

The purr of her voice was unmistakable at 100 bpm, even as the recorded music flitted in and out in staccato cuts. She stalked up to the eye of the camera, her own eyes wide and accusatory. She turned on her heel and with one hand smacked her ass. She tossed her head from side to side. Her artificial mane, pale at the ends and dark at the roots, shot up to the ceiling and crashed around her breasts.

She strutted a few steps more, bent over, and smacked her ass again, with both hands this time to emphasize the point. Her skin was slick. She kept moving to the fire. Stood there swaying, dropping to the wood, bouncing up again, bouncing in and out of frame.

Her movements were quick and deliberate and inexact. She communicated something unidentifiable but urgent.

Mostly, she twirled and twirled and twirled. Rapunzel or Mowgli. Prisoner or recluse. Inside the house yet somehow on the loose. America's dancer trapped in its jewel box. On a tour called Dream Within a Dream, she performed this way. Emerged from the center of the stage, arms stretched overhead, in a tulle skirt. At the time the country was at war and she was in a different kind of captivity. I loved her then and love her now. She is all heart. She is all broken heart.

———

The birth of Donald Trump's movement is the aftershock of the so-called birther crusade, a racist conspiracy against the forty-fourth president, the first Black man elected to the office. The notion that he had not been born in the country and was thus constitutionally illegitimate had entered the ether during the Democratic primary for the 2008 election. It was formed on no basis at all by fervent supporters of the woman who would lose that contest, win on her next shot, then lose the big one.

What had been confined to the political fringes was urged into the mainstream by a mainstream celebrity who appealed to the fringes as he contemplated a campaign of his own. He vowed to send investigators to search for answers in Hawaii, where the forty-fourth president had, in verifiable fact, been born.

"That was bullshit," an adviser who worked for Donald Trump during the period told me, "He never sent anyone there. He never planned to, never tried. It was just, you know . . . He was performing."

The birth, too, of my time as witness.

Atlantic City was a graveyard, and the Taj Mahal, conveniently located a few yards east of a funeral parlor, was next in line to be buried, the fifth casino to close in the last year. It was already half-dead when I arrived.

I watched the sunrise from my room on the thirty-ninth floor. It was about to be a frigid and wet December day. Outside my window, seagulls cawed loudly and recently shuttered casinos, their neon signs dark—Trump Plaza, Revel, Showboat, Atlantic Club—rose from the empty streets like headstones.

The casino floor was scarcely populated. The card tables were encircled by vacant chairs. Vagrants wandered through the bare forest of slot machines. Elderly women played Triple Double Diamond and Tiki Magic while they chain-smoked.

Two grandmothers, Toni and Cathy, told me they had been coming to Atlantic City from their home in Gloucester County since gambling was legalized here in 1976. Well, Toni told me. Cathy's eyes were glued to Tiki Magic. She had been feeding quarters to the machine for several hours. She leaned with one leg on her walker. Her other leg had been amputated. She retrieved a cigarette from her purse and lit it without moving her face away from the screen. If she played enough, and she planned to, she would earn them a "free" night in the hotel.

"It's just terrible what's happening," Toni said. "We used to go to Trump Plaza, and then they shut that down, so we started coming here. Now we don't know where we'll go. Look at that!" She turned to Cathy's screen, which cried out a song of triumph and lit up with flashing images of hibiscus flowers. She had won two dollars.

Cathy was not the first person to walk away from this place richer.

"I made a lot of money in Atlantic City," Donald Trump told me. "I hope you can say in your article that Mr. Trump sold out a long time ago and did well. I made *a lot* of money.

"It's so sad to see what's happened," he said. "I left years ago. I got extremely lucky. My timing was extremely good—through talent or luck, I'm not sure. I made a lot of money in Atlantic City."

He kept repeating himself in this manner. For whose benefit it was not clear.

"Mr. Trump made a lot of money in Atlantic City," he said, as though the mantra might become a thought of my own. He said it again: "I made a lot of money in Atlantic City. I almost feel guilty about it, but I made a lot of money in Atlantic City and I got out."

There was a sadness in his voice that overpowered the energetic rasp he is known for.

"It was so vibrant," he added. "If I would have had you there fifteen years ago, you would have said, 'This place is hot.' Of course, you were two years old then, but the place was poppin'—you wouldn't believe it. Every one of those places were packed full. Now you look at it, and it's very sad what's happened."

———

They call it a spin room. It is the area near a presidential debate stage where representatives for campaigns go to *spin*, which is media jargon for lying, after the televised spectacle is over. The candidate himself does not go there unless he has had what the peanut gallery determines to have been a bad night. This was not that. Not quite. *Good* and *bad* were in an instant no longer quantifiable measures of political success and would not be again.

In Cleveland, after the first Republican debate of the 2016 primary cycle, there was adrenaline in the air. The mass had one heart and it was beating very fast. Like a hummingbird, but huge. *Yuge*, as he would say. That was the only measure that now mattered. Size. This was big. Big replaced good.

When he moved, the mass moved with him. Here I say *the mass* as though I was not a part of it. I was not a willing part of it, but I was part of it no less. Is that not a story found within any mob?

The mass lurched, we lurched, forming a circle around him, and as he walked, some people walked backward to keep their eyes trained on him as though he could vanish were they not looking, like they might cede some competitive edge to the others crowded in if they lost track of him for even a second, and some of them fell, literally fell over themselves, onto the floor, and then they got right back up and kept on moving with him, nudging as close as they could to the force within a mania fit for a Beatle or a Bieber.

Before I knew what was happening I was pinned between bodies, with no chance to escape, no place to go, and then, all of a sudden, I was pressed right up against him. My body squished into his body. I did not want to be there. Did not want to be so close. Did not want to touch him. I stopped breathing.

He is taller than you would think. He was even taller then. Six foot something. He is broad, too. This big creature. I turned so that I would not have my face shoved into the fabric of his Brioni suit. His padded shoulder pushed back as he spoke. I struggled for a way to angle my head away from him. The mob was packed too tightly. I looked up. I exhaled.

All around and above us, the boom mics, the recorders, the cameras, the lights. So much light trained on him, and here against his back, standing at my height, five foot eight, I could almost see the scene from his perspective. The sphere of plasma around the darkness. This was the moment from which we would not return. The last gasp. The break upon which all surrendered to the force.

Every spare wattage of light directed to reflect off the gleaming sculpture of hair on his head. For so long, it was about his hair. His hair was the thing about him. The thing people knew, the thing they mocked. Important men often possess important hair. Now, inches away, I squinted at it. A nest of metal. A spool of gold. The way it was sprayed into this improbable shape, God could not have wanted that, I thought, could not have intended for such a structure to exist in the natural world.

What I wanted was to leave. I looked around for an exit, for a way to untangle myself from the mass, to peel away from this unwanted contact with the Italian-wool-swaddled force itself, but there was nowhere to go. Trapped in the field of his distortion, I could feel it, the unstoppable start of the pulling apart and apart and apart and apart.

The plan for the 2016 election was to prove the haters wrong by running, to poll well enough to be able to say he could have won, or to rig enough polls to make it look as though he could say so, and then return to his pink marble palace to film the next season of his lucrative terrestrial reality television show.

He had registered as a Republican, then switched to the Independence Party, then the Democratic Party, then back to Republican, then independent, then the Republican Party again. In the 1980s, as he sought to expand his impression of empire, he started to talk about matters of foreign policy in the press. He offered to negotiate with the Russians. He began, whenever possible, to encourage the idea that others were encouraging him to run for president. In 1988, he quietly commissioned a poll about his political appeal. He toyed with an independent campaign in the 2000 and 2008 elections. He said he was "being serious" about seeking the Republican nomination in 2012. After a while, no one took him seriously.

By the time I met him, this was a source of angst. He was tired of being laughed off as the Boy Who Cried Presidential Campaign, dismissed as just an attention specialist who had deduced sometime around the millennium that threatening a run for office was an easy way to generate headlines every few years.

I was in a cab when we first spoke on the phone. It was November 2014. I was twenty-one years old. At the end of that conversation, he paused expectantly. I picked up that he was waiting for me to ask the question. I was not especially interested in the answer, but asking seemed only fair since he had politely entertained all the questions I had wanted to ask. "Are you going to run for president?" I said. I remember I was conscious of my tone, which rang false even as I tried to come across as believable. I am a bad liar. In response, he exhaled with a single note of laughter, as if he was sick of the question. This rang false, too. He was an insistent liar, not a good one. We were even.

He launched into his script: "I'm thinking about it. I'm certainly looking at it, and we'll see who runs, and we'll see how bad of shape the country is in," he said. "We just topped eighteen trillion dollars in debt, which is a very bad number—that's a record-shattering number. We just hit eighteen trillion dollars yesterday, eighteen trillion dollars in debt! Much of it to the Chinese and to people who are actually our enemies. This country needs really strong leadership and good leadership or it's gonna be in very big trouble. So, I'm certainly looking at it. A lot of people want me to do it." He cited his "millions of followers" on social media. "*Many* millions. Boy, they really want me to do it. But we'll see who runs. I'm going to examine what's going on, and after the beginning of the New Year, I'll make a decision. It's something that—it could happen. You know, look: I love the country, and I hate to see what's happening to it. It's run so poorly and so stupidly, beyond poorly. It's just run so stupidly. So, we'll see what happens. You'll be the first to know."

I did not buy it. This is how I reported on his statement then: "Few things in life are certain—but ahead of each presidential election, you can be sure businessman and TV personality Donald Trump will engage in a long flirtation with mounting a campaign for the White House."

To gain some credibility, to reset for the zillionth time the fifteen-minute timer, he would need to enter the contest for real, at least for a little while. Then came his announcement speech, and the outrage over his assertion that Mexico had been "sending rapists" over the southern border. The television network killed the deal. There was no show to return to. No vehicle for the attention he required. He had to keep running straight into his bluff. The fifth-floor soundstage at Trump Tower was repurposed as campaign headquarters. What followed would be not just the greatest performance of his life but the greatest of any entertainer yet this century.

Fifty-Seventh and Fifth. My first appointment at Trump Tower, twenty-one floors above the old set, in the candidate's twenty-sixth-floor office overlooking Central Park. The place reminded me of the Playboy Mansion as I had seen it depicted on a reality television show about Hugh Hefner and his three central girlfriends.

One of those women—my favorite, Holly Madison—remarked once, direct to camera, that her sister was so important to her in part because she was the only other person who knew what it was to grow up in her home. As observations about the nature of siblings go, this may seem obvious, but it struck me at the time as important. To establish consensus reality we require witnesses, corroboration. Consensus by definition cannot be determined in isolation. I filed the thought away.

Like the Playboy Mansion, Trump Tower was an eroding time capsule, a shrine to the man who built it and also to the tastes of the era in which he had reached this Midtown summit. The epic view of Manhattan offset by beige carpet that had frayed and wood that had dulled and glass covered in dust. The receptionist's desk was circular, made of wood and sun-faded leather, and there was a tear across the front of the fabric.

Standing face-to-face with me now for the first time, he was amassing political power; he had not yet secured the Republican nomination, but he soon would. I had the thought that it was not natural for a stranger to be such a part of the torn fabric of your existence that he did not seem, upon meeting, strange, even as he was immediately and overtly unusual.

Across his desk, I extended my hand to shake his. "This is Olivia. She's very young," his aide said. He looked at my hand as if this custom, the shaking of hands, was not practiced in business and show business and politics, as though my hand were an alien object, not born here and thus illegitimate. He smiled. He stayed like that, frozen, for a few moments. Then, all of a sudden, he appeared to remember the ritual, the shaking of hands. He nodded his head as if to say, *Oh, right.*

Much had already been made of his hands. In *Spy* magazine, of which I was an enthusiastic collector, Graydon Carter had dubbed him a "short-fingered vulgarian," kicking off a decades-long and still ongoing feud. His allegedly small hands had been the subject of considerable mockery, including during the recent primary debates, when a rival candidate who would one day become his secretary of state raised the subject as a means of calling into question the size of his anatomy.

Yet it was not the size of his hands that registered as remarkable. It was the texture of his skin. I had never felt anything like it. His hand was so soft that it felt almost wet. My father had just died. I thought of his hands. Rough, dry. In winter, the skin on his knuckles cracked and bled. He worked, every day; he worked, through the night; with his hands, he worked. Trump looked me up and down. "Very young and very beautiful," he said.

Down the FDR, almost ten years had gone by.

At the courthouse in Lower Manhattan, where for the first time in American history a former president was facing criminal charges, I was thinking about Aristotle. Not because the law is reason free from passion but because he theorized that eels spring into existence through a kind of mud metamorphosis. Scientists now believe the European eel is spawned in the Sargasso Sea, then swims across the Atlantic, and when it reaches maturity, migrates thousands of miles back there, to the location of its birth, to spawn and die. This trial was similarly disorienting. Circular.

What year was it?

He was again the candidate. From his penthouse, his relationship to his phone was compulsive and his output on social media prolific. He called into a right-wing television channel, his picture frozen onscreen as he offered rolling commentary on a breaking-news event in his familiar rasp. He fired off a remark in which he said a left-wing television host with whom he had a longstanding private rivalry over a woman that played as a public rivalry over politics "looks like shit." He emerged through the gilded doors of his high-rise dressed in his uniform of too-big suit and too-long red tie, trailed by security and yes-men and a beautiful assistant. He boarded an idling SUV. He delivered winding campaign speeches with asides about politicians from 2015 and 2016 and celebrities from the 1960s, and in exchange for the entertainment, his fans charged his life force with their attention.

His main strategist was around. His caddie, too. So was the woman he made a celebrity villain on reality television. And his most trusted aide. And the famed porn star with whom he had an affair. I was on the phone with his adviser. I was exchanging messages with his fixer, with his White House counselor, and with the man who considered himself the philosopher king of the always-shifting populist ideology the candidate had come to represent. One longtime strategist, his Trickster, was not speaking to me, and it was anyone's guess as to what he was upset about this time. I was sure he would get over it, whatever it was. He always did.

All this time later, the status of many of these people was upside down. His most trusted aide was no longer his spokeswoman but a witness for the prosecution; when she arrived on the stand, she had not seen him in about two years. His fixer was now a witness, too, after the president had turned on him and he had served time in prison, some of it in solitary confinement. The porn star was not defined by her bought-and-paid-for silence but by her testimony. And the woman he made a celebrity villain was still looking into a camera, as God intended, but when she sat down next to me for a Last Supper panel on primetime television, it was to spin against him, not on his behalf.

For all witnesses, the experience of reliving the first campaign was blurring. That was true for this witness in particular. Circular. In this little loop in which we live, in which history is repeating itself at hyperspeed, in which time seems to stretch and fold, in which we move not ahead or back but down.

He had been the president and by the laws of governmental honorifics, he would always retain the title, even if things did not go the way he hoped in the November election. *He had been the president.* At the moment now where the tail met the jaw, it seemed a faraway notion, this distant plot point in the belly of the story. I looked back. *He had been the president.* It had happened. I had been there.

The old man with white hair plus corresponding mustache is sitting a few feet in front of me. He has on glasses, and through them he is peering down at the desk, looking at photos. His daughter is a few chairs away working at a screen. She is a photographer at the White House. She brought him here with her today, March 28, 2019.

I have never liked his daughter—even though she just told me where to find the Wi-Fi password—because she is a loud talker and she talks even when there is nobody around for her to talk to. For reasons related to general antisociality and paranoia about government surveillance I rarely work out of this place. The governmentiest place of all. But when I do, her talking interrupts my train of thought while I am trying, halfheartedly, to write. Once, I was writing, and she was talking loudly about, of all things, a grilled cheese sandwich with lobster, which, first of all, is not really a grilled cheese sandwich. It is a lobster sandwich, technically, I think. And this went on, her talking about this, the matter of this sandwich, for half an hour. A lot of time for me to contemplate the integrity of the sandwich, to conclude for certain that in either formulation, I would not order one myself.

I never filed the story I was working on, if I am remembering correctly, though I probably would not have done so if she had never said a word about sandwiches or about anything else. It was not a very good premise and if I let something sit there for a while instead of finishing it right away I am likely to abandon it altogether. I can talk myself out of anything—a character flaw.

Outside in the Rose Garden, I am standing up against a bush, and a foreign photographer—who always tries to talk to me, but who I cannot understand beyond the vague comprehension that he is communicating approving observations about my appearance—bangs into me with his stepladder.

Reporters are behind me, in front of me, to my side, packed all around until we blossom as a bouquet of boom mics and cameras and recorders and phones, sprouting up from the pavement, or as a class of anchovies, stuck together, upright, having been freed all at once from a tiny jar. Someone is standing, somehow, *in* a bush, which seems unnecessary. It seemed a little rude, even, when I extended my toe into the mulch for a moment. Like it was disrespectful, that small act, even as this place remains occupied by a hostile actor.

I never know how to navigate scrums or gaggles. In fact I do not know for sure what distinguishes a scrum from a gaggle. I guess a scrum is a pack of reporters and a gaggle is a pack of reporters who are questioning an individual, which is why you can use *gaggle* as a verb, but not *scrum*. *The president gaggled,* you could say, *he was gaggling in the garden.* The informality of a gaggle, or the spontaneity, plus the fact that it is staged by the press and not by the person being questioned, distinguishes it from a press conference, I think, but I do not know.

The daughter taps me on the shoulder as we wait for the president. She will be shooting right through the space next to my head, she says. I offer to switch spots if she wants to be closer to get her shot, but she says that it is fine where she is. Her dad helps her with her equipment. He is a small man, wearing jeans and a striped blue-and-white dress shirt, his visitor pass draped over his neck. She introduces him to all of us, this section of the scrum, the flowers or the fishies, and we say hello and we wave. She stands on her ladder and points her camera down at him; it makes a shuttering sound.

The president steps out of the West Wing and trots along the walkway. You never know, in these scenarios, if he is going to come over and talk to us or head straight to Marine One, so observing the direction he moves after passing the large tree on the lawn is crucial. He moves left, and the reporters begin to, I guess, *clamor*. TV reporters are always in the front, and photographers and videographers are always hovering above from their aluminum perches. I just sort of pick a spot and stand there, craning my neck to get a look at him, which is the whole point, I suppose, of my attendance here, to bear witness.

Yep, that is him all right. Unmistakable. I have no idea what he is saying. All I hear is something about Russia and the Justice Department and the usual list of supposed accomplishments. I can make out his favored suffix—*est.* As in, *greatest* or *biggest.* Everything is like that in his characterization. The helicopter and all the feral shrieking from the reporters is so loud it is like, why not just hold this event next to the stage at Metallica or under the George Washington Bridge? I frequently joke, to editors and other relevant conversation partners, that he may have just announced that he found the aliens, for all I know, or Jimmy Hoffa.

I learn later the president told us that his "people" would be fixing an issue he had created in the first place related to the funding of some federal program. A lot of his existence here is like that, like hitting a woman and then kissing the bruise to make it better, and a lot of our existence is providing the color commentary for every blow, like he is Muhammad Ali. (You could not use this metaphor now, not in this *climate*. You would get a lot of angry feedback. *How dare you compare anything to domestic violence*, and so on.)

The old man, standing away from the scrum, is surrounded by petals from the cherry blossoms. They are scattered around him like confetti, like he just burst out of a cake. (This metaphor would be okay.)

I smoke a cigarette and I call my brother when I get back to the West Wing. I tell him about the old man with the white hair and the glasses. Then I walk back inside to the dark corner behind the briefing room, where the daughter is apologizing to her father. "Sorry, I know this is kind of boring," she says. "No," he says, waving her off, "I'm downloading the pictures." I wonder about this dynamic, so foreign to me, a parent helping his adult child. It occurs that I am watching these two interact as though I am watching a nature documentary in which the human species is narrated. *In the cavernous dwelling the adult male assists his kin.* It occurs that I am watching too intently, probably, and I ought to watch something else. I look down. I watch my fingertips as I type this sentence.

Two White House officials arrive to retrieve me in the briefing room. The interview is the reason I am hanging around late, and the officials lead me to a chair in an area of the West Wing that is empty at this hour. The more senior official is angry, meaner than usual, and the conversation quickly veers, you might say, *off track*, with one passive-aggressive dig after another until she is no longer passive at all.

Ordinarily I would just let this go, continue on topic without engaging with her outbursts, but I am not really in The Mood, and so I press the official, asking her to explain exactly what the problem is, what has made her so angry, making it so that, now, we cannot have a *productive* interview. People in Washington love to identify as *productive*. She talks in circles, claiming I had reported something false, but she will not say what that something was. I suspect this is because she is lying. My suspicion finds more support when, in her efforts to deflect from the question, she yells at me about my face, which she says is overly expressive when she talks. She does not like what it looks like when she yells at me. I say something to the effect of *I cannot see my own face, and so I do not really know what to tell you, aside from, perhaps you ought to stop yelling at me?*

This angers her more and she barks an order: "Everyone turn their recorders off!" By *everyone* she means me, chiefly, but I lock eyes with the junior White House official, who fumbles with his device as he seeks to follow her command as fast as possible, fearful that her anger could soon find a new target. I turn my recorder off, too. I do not mind. She does not appreciate that I possess a built-in tape recorder. Then she says, "You know, you got emotional once and shared something private with me, and I have never told anybody about that—except, I guess, now." She says this with a nod in the direction of the junior official, her tone dripping with phoniness and venom.

This is designed to be a taunt. Designed to somehow humiliate or threaten me. To remind me that this official knows I am a human being and not some kind of reporter-robot, just as I know things about this official. She was referring to a time when, during an interview, the subject of fatherhood came up, and my eyes had filled with tears and I had told her why. She then raises the subject of my weight, which has in recent months plummeted again. I respond this way to stress of any kind. What this has to do with my reporting about the government is unclear.

I am puzzled by these personal lines of attack, and I keep looking around the West Wing as though I expect the scenery to morph into something more fitting of an exchange such as this, a reality television set, maybe, or a school locker room. I wonder why she thought this strategy would work. It suggests that she sees crying as a kind of weakness, and it suggests certain complexes about female bodies and vanity more generally. All of which I find interesting. In my mind, she had been a different person when I first knew her. She had been so kind, for instance, about my father. Now she is unrecognizable as she sits before me vibrating with contempt and judgment.

She often makes miscalculations as it relates to acts of psychological warfare. She makes wild assumptions about the people she believes she must needle and frequently her assumptions, at least as they relate to me, have missed. For instance she tried to pit me against a television reporter who is one of my closest friends, tried to make me jealous about some sort of *news exclusive*, and when I realized what she was endeavoring to do I laughed and I said, *Oh. You have to try something else, because I do not care about news and am not competitive by nature.* In truth I consider news to be a burden and I would almost always rather someone else break it. And she said, literally, "Hmph!" and she, again literally, shrugged. And I was somehow charmed by this, by how transparent she was about her behavior, about how there was a kind of purity in her hubris, an evil optimism in her efforts to manipulate, and about how plainly her failed attempt to read me had instead revealed qualities I could read in her.

Now, yelling—still, she continues to yell, and I do not like it when people yell, and I do not like it when officials in this White House make me a party to their disrespect of the office of the presidency. I rise to leave because I do not see why I should sit here and be yelled at by anybody but she yells louder and she orders me to sit back down and I comply, reflexively, because she is my mother's age, and she sounds like my mother when she yells, and she shares with my mother what I can only describe as a borderline personality gaze. A particular mad sparkle in the eyes. A glint of the knife's edge.

Eventually I do leave. I walk outside again to smoke. More shaken by the encounter than I would like to be and smoking more often than I would if I did not need to flee from people who yell, who are yelling inside the West Wing. It is the magic hour, bright blue. I seem to be the only person left here. I missed my train to New York, the entire thing went on so long. I miss my father enough to cry out for him like a child, like there might be a chance he can hear me, like he might burst from a cake through a plume of confetti petals so that his daughter can show him around the place where she works. Then he did not like yelling, either, though he did very much seem to like crazy women.

When a man has a certain fantasy, another man may lose his life.

—Carl Jung

41

The moon is full in the sky and the sky is full of drones. In the valley, on Mulholland Highway, I see a soft light. Of every star I am these days suspicious. The sun has only just set. But it is not a plane. That much is clear. It moves in an unusual way. Its light has an unusual quality. I curve through the canyons, the towers of rock so close to the road, the road so narrow, and the foreign lights like big fireflies overhead. *Lucciole*—Dante called upon their image in twilight to relate the sight of flames shining in the skies of hell.

Human flight and human-less flight took off in tandem in the early twentieth century. Uncrewed aircraft, controlled by radio and remotes, were developed as tools of warfare by developed countries with hell to wage.

By the time the US misadventure in Vietnam had killed at least five thousand airmen, with another one thousand captured or otherwise missing, the air force's 100th Strategic Reconnaissance Wing was flying thousands such craft over what were determined to be the most perilous territories of Southeast Asia.

As with the war itself, the drones in question proved to be of questionable value. The air force deployed them without conducting adequate testing, and many of them were lost in avoidable mishaps related to insufficient fuel while the spying they conducted was sometimes thwarted by processing mistakes that yielded low-quality film.

The modern drone, with surveillance and armament capabilities compelled by miniaturized technologies, would not take flight until the Gulf War. "Drone war" would not become a central facet of our fatally interventionist foreign policy until the mid-aughts, when the number of robotic strikes in Pakistan alone ballooned from one in 2004 to a high of 122 in 2010. Across administrations, across the major political parties, by design, the phrase *drone strike* conjures an image of a high-tech apex predator, hunting and killing with precision. But in just that six-year period in Pakistan, drone strikes resulted in 235 confirmed civilian casualties. The strikes in Pakistan continued until 2017 while similar strikes across the Middle East and Africa continue still.

"The drone is killing tremendous numbers of people," the president said. "You hide behind a tree and the drone comes down and it circles you with fire. You don't have a chance. The tree comes down also, by the way. It's so intense. I mean, you see these trees being knocked down, like, they're being sawed down by a top-of-the-line, uh, timberman."

Years into the war with Russia, birds in Ukraine began building nests with fiber-optic cables left behind by exploded FPV, or first-person view, drones.

As the technology transformed the means by which we spy and kill, its extra-battleground capabilities found markets to impose distance between human beings and the results of their actions on farms and in mines, film crews, fire departments, police forces, and other commercial and government affairs. The documentary films produced during the streaming bubble are marred by the rote deployment of wide-angled establishing shots in which a drone soars over some landscape in such a way that would have been impossible or prohibitively expensive at any other time in the history of cinema but now feels utterly cheap.

And cheapness is a requirement for products that may be purchased for drone delivery by the digital everything-company; their vision of a Jetsons future in which the answers to the material needs of customers would sail down from the commercial heavens and land right in their homes ran into some logistics trouble: regulations stipulate the closest the drone can sink to the ground is fifteen feet, meaning deliveries must be dropped from such a height in special padded containers, meaning only items that are under five pounds and have been tested to prove that they can survive such a fall are available for such deliveries.

"1-hour drone delivery is available during the daylight hours and favorable weather conditions. We do not offer drone delivery at night, during heavy winds or unfavorable weather," according to company literature. "One eligible item per order will be delivered by drone. During checkout, please make sure that the drone delivery option is selected." Eligible individual items include a coconut-scented lotion called Brazilian Bum Bum Cream. "While you don't need to be present at the time of delivery, ensure that people, pets, vehicles, and objects taller than 5 feet (including plants) are at least 10 feet away from the selected delivery point . . . The drone will fly to the designated delivery location, check for obstacles and objects, descend to your delivery point, and release the package." *Release*, as though the package would be set free.

I was once gifted a drone. I named him Pistachio, since he was so tiny. I did not like it, the way he looked like a creature, the way it felt viscerally wrong to possess something with a point of view but no autonomy. I did not like the way that, in the White Mountains, he got stuck in a tree, and I felt that it was unfair, that human misdirection had injured his little propeller. I wondered if our Creator, watching us, felt similarly.

No place in America remains verifiably unwatched. The faithless eyes of personal devices are in our hands, the allegedly benevolent eyes of explicit surveillance devices peek out from every door, and eyes of unknown origin and motive may be flying overhead at any time. On Sunset Boulevard, a large sign is staked into the grassy median: WELCOME TO BEVERLY HILLS—DRONE IN USE.

The sightings of unidentified aircraft on the Atlantic shore multiplied soon after Election Day. A person close to the president-elect told me they were "spiritual beings." A former presidential candidate told me they were aliens. Others thought they were from China or Iran. I figured they were most likely the work of a domestic defense contractor, and that the government was well aware of what they were, and if the lame-duck president was read in on the matter, or at least read to about the matter during his intelligence briefings, that meant the president-elect would have the information, too, even as he called for the government to shoot them out of the sky. On the news, the outgoing secretary of Homeland Security had sounded so silly as he offered, by way of explanation for the uncharacteristic coolheadedness that kept them suspended above, the pesky matter of congressional approval, as if air strikes and whole wars have not been waged without meeting this constitutional requirement. With no official story being stuck to by officials, the truth about the drones was up for grabs—up to wonder, up to propaganda, up to conspiracy.

Before I watched the drones on Mulholland Highway, I had been talking about the drones on the East Coast over my brother's house, and I had felt a pang of regret that I could not go out there to report, that I do not now report. I find myself a lot of the time now absentmindedly interviewing strangers or friends. I miss that part of it. Relating to the world and everyone in it that way. Relating much less often to myself. My general curiosity is so great, and without that means to externalize it I feel the way I feel when I am forced to sit still for too long, tapping my feet, as if I might snap and shoot out of the chair at any moment. I have only a flight instinct, and reporting, I never had to consider it until now, is a way of fleeing yourself.

I had thought it a blessing and still do that when I entered the profession, at the height of what was determined the personal essay boom for young women writers, I could not participate because I did not care to write of my own life and experiences because I did not find any of it terribly interesting and certainly not more interesting than whatever I might learn about the world from other people and their experiences. Now as then, I write to establish what can be established. To assess through what can be established the scale of what remains up for grabs—up to wonder and faith that extends beyond reason. That I have made of myself what others have determined to be Good Copy is a horror.

The drones divert my inward gaze, and for that I am grateful to them. I look up.

Well, I'll be damned. Here comes your ghost again.

—Joan Baez

The first step is to get inside the drama. If you can't, you shouldn't be writing the music.

—Bernard Herrmann

A motorcyclist drove up beside me on the Pacific Coast Highway. Trying to get my attention. I had just seen an old David Letterman interview, just the day before, with a Playboy Playmate who told a story about a motorcyclist driving up beside her and trying to get her attention and then crashing into the car in front of him.

Please do not crash, I was thinking, and also, this: When my algorithm imitates my life, I find it odd, still, but I understand that is how algorithms work. Our devices listen to us. They listen to the devices of those around us. There is no telling what they hear, what they make of what they hear, what they do with the conclusions they draw. They are evolving all the time with all the information they absorb. But when my life imitates my algorithm, it gives me pause.

This motorcyclist did not crash. As the light turned, he turned to face me and blew a kiss.

At Will Rogers, where along the trail the leaves on the yucca trees look like little burned-up hearts, my phone rang, and when I answered, the Staffer said, "You're like a ghost," and I thought of how people have always said that. Earlier in the day, in the driveway in Malibu, the owner of the property remarked that having me stay there was barely perceptible. "It's like no one is here," he said. And he said it in a strange way, as if it was suddenly curious that my presence registered in this manner, this manner in which I do not register.

I thought of a friend, so many years ago in Washington, when I was still smoking, and I was smoking outside an office on M Street, and he was surprised to see me, and he said that same thing: "You're like a ghost." He never knew when I would be someplace and then he never knew when I left or for how long I would be gone and no one ever seemed to know where I was. I thought then it was a function of having secrets, that as the holder of secrets you become something of a secret yourself.

On the phone with the Staffer, she was telling me some matter of intrigue related to the forty-sixth president, and about a dozen boys, no older than thirteen, ran over in my direction and swarmed around me with their phones out and I was at first panicked by the sight of this, and still trying very hard to hear what the Staffer was saying, and the boys were asking me to pose for photos, and one of them said, "Naw, brah, she's on the phone," and another one said, "That's a fake phone call," and I appreciated his skepticism. I made my way through the pack of boys and the Staffer was asking what on earth all the commotion was and I did not really know how to convey exactly what it was, and she said, "Oh, they're just excited. They don't know anything," and I said, "No, they don't know anything."

The Staffer never believed in the forty-sixth president much, and so she is not all that broken up about the outcome of the election, because the results did not land with her as some kind of shock, and it is not that most others around her are broken up because they believed in the forty-sixth president so much; they are broken up because of their careers or the dimmer prospects for their careers, but she never liked all that the forty-sixth president represented, or what those other people represented, which amounted to this blob of Official Washington. "Bernie would have won," she said.

On a cliff back in Malibu, I climbed to my favorite rock and looked up for a while. I meditated on a phrase I like, written by Warren Zevon, "When you get up in the morning and you see that crazy sun . . ." *Crazy sun.*

When I rose I saw something out of the corner of my eye down to the right on the beach. It was a man in a white shirt and blue jeans, down on one knee. He was addressing a woman in a white sundress. I watched as she gasped and brought her hands to her mouth and then jumped in the air excitedly. I am no detective but it seemed to me she had accepted the offer. They embraced. A photographer ran across the sand in their direction. She pointed them to the water and as the tide came in around their ankles they posed for her. It was sweet.

On my finger was a phantom ring. My body had adjusted to the weight of the diamond over the course of the engagement, and for about a month after I left, after I left the ring on the counter and walked out, my finger maintained a hairline dent where the band had been.

It was beautiful, the ring. Almost comical in its exaggerated features, like something out of a cartoon. This big fat diamond from the 1800s on a thin gold band. I worried at first about what ghosts the stone might hold. Conflict is inherent to any diamond, forged as they are from pressure, mined by labor, and gifted with expectations. I knew so little about this object that I carried with me everywhere. Who did it belong to? Someone, or many someones. Had they been happy? Had the stone been part of stories that ended well? And how did I define *well*? Had it been only given or had it been stolen? Passed down civilly or fought over bitterly? I measured the idea it raised about my own life against its perfection. In fact it was not perfect by any technical standard, and I liked that about it most of all. Antique diamonds cut by hand form irregular shapes, sport little asymmetries, possess what you might call character, and its flaws achieved, to my eye, perfection.

I did not intend to do this, to make of the ring a crystal ball, but I could not refuse its invitation, could not ignore it, in a literal sense, as it got caught on things or caught the attention of passersby, young girls usually or old ladies, or as it lit up the wall of aircraft cabins with the storm of prismatic flecks projected from its facets. The ring intruded. I had in my mind thought of it, for about a year before I took it off, as the Diamond Albatross, and every time that phrase whispered itself into my frontal consciousness I had felt bad, that I felt that way, that I did not want anymore what the ring suggested, what I had agreed to by putting it on my finger in the first place, presented with the offer on a cliff on Capri after the sun had set.

He was sleeping with a woman who worked for the Democratic presidential campaign, and when he told me this, I was relieved; while still a betrayal, my behavior was not quite so egregious in light of this information. I had been her and so I did not blame her; I looked at her photo and remarked half in jest that she was the ideal person with whom to have committed such sins: She was pretty enough that I was not offended and not so pretty that I was offended. My calmness seemed to ignite further rage. The disclosure was made to hurt me. That it did not succeed was another injury. I pitied him.

I turned away while the couple on the beach was still embracing. It felt wrong to continue to watch. I climbed down from the rock and down the path. A few miles away at the grocery store, a voice called out: "I've been trying to listen to God." I looked in the direction of the sound. A young man in a white muscle car. I kept walking. He drove alongside me as I approached the threshold. "You weren't here and then I looked up and you were here and you're so beautiful, and that feels like God, you know? Maybe we could get coffee and talk about it?" *No, thank you.* I brought a Diet Coke to the cash register. The man working scanned me as he scanned the barcode on the silver can. "Girl Dinner?" he asked. I smiled as politely as possible. "I know Girl Dinner when I see it," he said.

Males intrude by their nature. It is not their fault entirely.

In Utah, the National Security Agency built its data collection mothership, known officially as the Data Center. Rated two stars on the digital search engine. "Every email every text every phone conversation that every American citizen has ever passed from one another safely kept here since 2014. For your protection at the expense of your liberty and privacy," per one negative review from an unhappy and, like all civilians, unwilling customer. Walter Kirn called the structure "as close as humanity had come to putting infinity in a box."

Writing in *The Atlantic* in 2015, he explained how, en route to the facility, his radio was tuned to a distinctly American sort of program:

> . . . one of those wee-hours AM talk shows whose hosts tend to suffer from a wretched smoker's cough and whose conspiracy-minded guests channel a collective unconscious understandably disturbed by current events. . . . To those who understand that fiction warps the truth in order to tell the truth, the literal meanings of such tales are beside the point. Nightmares are a form of news.

I think of driving off the road only at night, when the pearl moon spins in its cloudshell, when it casts a lane of light on the water, when it comes into view where the path zigs and zags as it does only up by Sycamore Cove.

L'appel du vide, call of the void. I would not do it. I tell myself this as I force my gaze away from the blackness and onto the white-lined center of the highway. I would not insult the angels. I would not interfere with their plans. I would not. I will not.

The Politician communicates an acid message through an intermediary. There are lemon trees in the yard. I did not plant them. There is a fist in my chest. It is not mine. I imagine a lemon, sliced through, bled dry. The fist squeezes the fruit, but there is nothing left, and the fruit heaves pits, and the pits lodge in my throat. *Quod me nutrit me destruit, what nourishes me destroys me.*

I think of the zigzagging road, think of swallowing the sea, think of salt, of acid, of angels. When I speed along the edge, the crucifix looped around my rearview mirror levitates. The bluffs wore a scab and the scab ripped open. The wounds of the first fire had stopped bleeding, the earth was still, and then the fire returned to burn what had survived, to make itself clear.

UNIDENTIFIED MALE: I was in my senior year of high school. Eighteen. It predated the camera phone. I don't know why I was even doing it because you couldn't send it anywhere. I had an Olympus point-and-shoot. I took it. A perspective shot. Hard. It was just kind of to look at. It was just for me. No one ever saw it, in part because I panicked immediately after.

OLIVIA NUZZI: Panicked how?

UNIDENTIFIED MALE: I worried, inaccurately, that I had done something illegal, and more questionably, if I had done something immoral. And so I took out the SD card and I tried to break it in half with my finger, but it had a kind of metal ribbon in it, and I slashed my thumb up. I still have a scar from it, this little half crescent right here—see?—on the tip of my thumb, where I just gashed so deep into my skin trying to destroy the evidence. It was a bad omen.

OLIVIA NUZZI: Did you get stitches?

UNIDENTIFIED MALE: No, I just suffered in silence. I don't think I even put a bandage on it. I think I just sucked on it until it stopped bleeding.

OLIVIA NUZZI: And what did you do with the SD card?

UNIDENTIFIED MALE: It was folded in half. It couldn't break. That was part of the problem: It fought back. I just threw it out.

OLIVIA NUZZI: What did you use the camera for before you took that photo?

UNIDENTIFIED MALE: My parents got it for me for summer camp and then I took it with me when I went to Europe after I graduated. It was to document very aboveboard, innocent activities with friends. I didn't take a nude photo again until I moved to New York in my junior year of college and I was working as a go-go boy. I had just turned cute maybe six weeks before I moved to New York and I felt confident in my body in a way I hadn't maybe ever.

OLIVIA NUZZI: Because you monetized it?

UNIDENTIFIED MALE: Yeah, I had commodified my body, my job was to do a step touch on a bar, so it was verifiable. At the same time, [the gay hookup app] came out. All of a sudden I had this mechanism whereby these nudes would not just be for my consumption, they would serve a purpose, and the purpose was immediately for validation, and less immediately, depending on how long it took to coordinate, for sex.

OLIVIA NUZZI: Were you ever concerned about privacy?

UNIDENTIFIED MALE: Never, no. It was not a fear. My father, we never really had "the talk," but he did tell me once when I was a teenager, "A stiff dick has no conscience." I was just thinking with my dick. There is no reasoning with it. You don't think about consequences, necessarily.

OLIVIA NUZZI: Did you keep the photos?

UNIDENTIFIED MALE: Yeah, I wouldn't have even thought to hide it. Privacy was just different at that time. I don't think I even had a passcode on my phone. I kept that attitude for a long time. Especially through my mid-twenties, I took plenty of photos that were fully identifying, stem to stern, in a way I never would now, and most people don't anymore. It wasn't until I moved to a more insular gay community where everyone talks shit, where knowing something, like that a couple is open or that someone in an established relationship is on [the gay hookup app], is a form of currency, that I first started to be conscious that maybe I should only send identifiable images to people I trust. But even then, that was a concern based solely on people I knew, on the nature of this community. There was no concern that it could get out to a wider world. I never considered myself a public person, or a person who anyone would be interested in talking about.

OLIVIA NUZZI: But you had become at least a public-facing person.

UNIDENTIFIED MALE: Yeah, but even then, I never thought about it. It wasn't until what I refer to as The Unpleasantness that it changed. I just never thought of myself as that. I had a presence, I had a profile, but I just thought always that I was an Also On Board. You know, "Tom Hanks and Others Die in Plane Crash."

OLIVIA NUZZI: Can you tell me what happened? The Unpleasantness?

UNIDENTIFIED MALE: It came in waves for a long time.

OLIVIA NUZZI: What was the first wave?

UNIDENTIFIED MALE: At first it was just relational to my husband. A friend sent me a message and said, "Hey, hon, have you seen this?" It was a forum that I had never heard of before, that I subsequently learned is probably tied to the government of a foreign adversary, and it was just the most held-together-by-duct-tape-looking thing, this rudimentary format, a bunch of rotating posts with people sharing a photo of someone and saying, "Anyone have anything?" Depending on the person in the photo, 90 percent of the replies might just be shit-talking, maybe some material, and then strategizing about how to bait the person to get more. It was like this digital public bathroom wall. In the post about my husband, there were some photos and videos he had sent privately, and then there were some images from a photographer he had posed for released without his knowledge. I was horrified for him, I was infuriated for maybe five minutes that he had been so stupid, but then I was just really, really sad for him.

OLIVIA NUZZI: Did you have to tell him?

UNIDENTIFIED MALE: Yeah, and we both had what retroactively was close to a panic attack. And then once you realize that there is a whole sub-basement of the internet that deals in trafficking this kind of stuff, it's hard to leave it, you get sucked into monitoring the ecosystem, because once it's shared in one place it finds its way to the other places, and you have to trace where it originated from, and you have to try to get the posts taken down one by one with DMCA complaints. It's Whack-a-Mole.

OLIVIA NUZZI: What's DMCA?

UNIDENTIFIED MALE: Digital Millennium Copyright Act. It is kind of the only mechanism that you have to get photos taken down that you have taken yourself, because it's copyrighted material that belongs to you, and when it's posted it's a violation of your copyright.

———

On the coast, the streetlights and traffic lights and the lights in the big windows of the big houses turned to black. It was not until I made my way up to Zuma that I saw the fire had been right behind me. The pink clouds puffed up to the south. Then the flames peeked over the hill. The sky grew lighter as the fire swelled and made its way to the sea. I watched from the deck as the night turned orange. How many like the rattlesnake, his little soul swallowed without ceremony in one breath? And where would the coyotes go? They did not walk across the deck and leap into the garden tonight.

12:40 a.m., one hundred acres burning.

I stand on the edge of the earth. I wander through the burned-up grasslands. Any fantasy of creation I understand as a fantasy of destruction, too. In every spark of life, an ember of death. A trillion little deaths a minute, collecting quickly around your ankles, tethering you to the beach, dividing you from the sea. Off the cliff over the Mediterranean and onto the cliff over the Pacific.

2:15 a.m., eight hundred and fifty acres burning.

As a child, I became convinced that death was not random, that life was the process of investigating what the point of it was, and as soon as you figured it out, in that very instant, you would ascend. God would eliminate you from this plane. He could not risk a leaker walking among the ignorant. The assignment was to crack the case for yourself. And when I would find myself thinking too hard about the central question, I would back away slowly, thinking, *Well, I will return to this matter some other time when I feel more ready to possibly meet my end.* What if I guessed correctly?

The unsolvable puzzle. Tripping once, on a balcony in Washington overlooking the National Cathedral. Smoking what I did not know was my final cigarette. Unless someone offers me a Capri, which does not count. The great cosmic riddle, I figured I had solved it. The joke was that the joke was never done being told.

4 a.m., eighteen hundred acres burning.

The wildfire is over my shoulder now, over the hill. The waxing gibbous moon is over my head. A thought bubble, it shines blankly. Across the country, the Politician is the guest of honor. Across the country with his wife. With Mike Tyson for some reason. People are mocking the photos, asking where I am, asking how she could stand there after all that.

I know how. The earth here is hot. Inside the bonfire, what evidence can I burn? I think of all I turned to ash in hotel rooms. I think of how you cannot burn a cloud. I think of the classified documents at Mar-a-Lago, how there were so many, how the officials did not know what to do with them, and how fire seldom seemed to occur, though the White House and the president's properties are studded with fireplaces. Too easy. I worry.

I worry about evil. If it is a force, if it is like the Santa Ana winds, if it may come on suddenly, if it may grab hold, if it may depart but not completely, if it may leave word, if the word might sound good, if I might again believe it. The snake charmer, the man-eater, the devil himself. Was it ever a question, that where there was a cloak there would be a dagger? A friend told me once, "Never trust anyone wearing a lapel pin." This politician did not wear one of those.

Midnight, three thousand acres burning.

A politician's greatest trick is to convince you that he is not one. And what is a politician? Any man who wants to be loved more than other men and through his pursuit reveals why he cannot love himself.

I arrived to the White House early. For weeks, rumors persisted that the president was about to fire his latest chief of staff, and though I had the official task of sorting out whether or not that was true, I had become more interested in the nature of such rumors themselves.

It had been an odd fact of his brief political career that the man known for the reality television catchphrase *You're fired!* did not enjoy firing people in his off-camera life. And for all the legitimate scrutiny over his financial mistreatment of those contracted by him at his private company, it was also true that the people in service jobs at his properties tended to stay there and seemed to have genuine affection for the boss and the members of his family. There was to me some poetry in the fact that he had tried and failed to get the catchphrase trademarked. "At the end of the day, he's a natural-born salesman and he likes people to like him," a senior administration official told me. "He's a conflict avoider. He hates firing people. He knows he's gotta fire every one of them, but he can't bring himself to do it. He's a Gemini. Do you know what a Gemini is? Those are two people in one body. There's always two faces with Trump." He avoided conflicts in which he might be compelled to feel pity, to feel like the bad guy. This was true even as he played a camp bad guy out loud, and even as his federal government was in a state of constant flux because of the musical chairs his fickle policy and staffing decisions inspired on a near daily basis.

It was always the case that rumors about the senior members of the president's team might be made up or urged along or otherwise molded into convenient delusion by their enemies internal or external. The leaks that defined the era were often aimed as lateral missiles, designed by one staffer or group of aligned staffers to kill off someone perceived as a roadblock to access to the president or as a psychic impediment to efforts to influence the president. The fish rots from the head down, and as he complained about the impression of disorder, which he blamed in public on the corrupt *fake news*, the environment was one the president himself determined. The porous nature of his White House was an invitation to anyone, anywhere, compelled to interfere to achieve goals personal or tribal.

As time went on, it became clear that the sickness was a feature, that anyone who entered the building became a little sick themselves, and no matter how dead any of the eccentrics or maniacs or divas appeared to be, how far away from the president their status as fired or resigned or never-hired-in-the-first-place should have logically rendered them, nobody was ever truly gone. The president abided by the Groucho Marx law of fraternization. He inherently distrusted anyone who chose to work for him and sought outside affirmation as often as possible from a vast and varied network of informal advisers whose advice he tended to overvalue. In practice this meant the people who were problems on the campaign or on the inside continued to be problems. The president's taste for the other and the new was so established that the most driven among them knew all they had to do was wait for an opening or shrewdly create one—a weakened staffer, a particularly demoralizing news cycle—and they could worm their way back in. The madness that plagued the White House was not just a matter of staff infighting over personality differences and factional philosophical rivalries, as it was often portrayed in the press, but also, in part, the result of manipulation from the fringes of what we—I— referred to in shorthand as *Trumpworld*. The term was supposed to describe the inner sanctum of power and the concentric ovals that surrounded the Oval. It began to feel like a description of the country unzipped, the state of disunion and delirium in the distortion field that engulfed the whole of us amid his rise.

There emerged distinct categories of personnel within his government: the True Believers, who require no elaboration; the Ideologues, who saw in the president's flexibility a chance to implement their philosophical will; the Nihilistic Opportunists, defined by greed and a zero-sum outlook; the Unthinking Opportunists, who were pleased to accept the ticket to ride and to whom cost of admission for themselves, for the country, or for the human race did not occur until much later or did not occur at all; the Unthinking Functionaries, operatives who shrugged their way through the transformation of one of the two major political parties and its implications for the republic; and the Establish-ment Guardians, human shields positioned between the president's whims and the levers of power, convinced their presence alone was a noble service, or at least convinced enough that they could get along unburdened by guilt that they were—in the Washington custom under-scrutinized before the arrival of the leader whose existence presented a juxtaposition with norms so stark that it revealed many norms as not normal at all—just striving for the sham power that accompanies prox-imity to the real thing.

While among them there existed a steady flock of Icaruses, the saf-est place for anyone who wanted to remain employed was near but not next to the hot center. If you were too far away, your enemies could insert themselves and turn the president on to their version of reality. If you were too close, you could be blamed by the president for anything that went or appeared to go wrong.

In the earliest days of the administration, competition manifested as a struggle for real estate inside the tiny West Wing. A perennial reality television contestant had gone so far as to steal an office that had been designated for a foul-mouthed hedge-fund millionaire because of its status-confirming glimpse of the Washington Monument. Both of them soon self-destructed along with a procession of others who failed to ma-neuver the chaotic status hierarchy the president seemed to cultivate out of boredom.

For weeks I had been fielding all manner of claims and accusations about the chief of staff from his many adversaries. Word of my assign-ment poked through the hornet's nest of the administration and its satellite chambers of influence. My interest was an opportunity for a highly motivated disparate class of haters, and my phone became a hive of nefarious activity, with one bad-faith "tip" after another coming at all hours through calls and messages delivered via encrypted channels. There was reason to believe the chief of staff was nefarious, too. There was no reason to believe the accounts of events or exchanges volunteered by anyone.

In the office of a senior White House official that morning, I expressed some exasperation. "Are we talking off the record?" the official asked. I said that if we could not talk *on the record*, it would be better if we could at least talk *on background*, industry jargon that means the words spoken in an exchange may be quoted with agreed-upon anonymous attribution, such as the variety I am using here, *a senior White House official*. The official frowned. That would not work for him. "Fine," I said. "Deep background." *Deep background* is industry jargon that means the information from an exchange may be utilized without quotations. The official thought for a moment. His aide chimed in. "Deep deep background," she said. "What is deep deep background?" I asked. *Deep deep background* was not to my knowledge recognized jargon of any ilk. "It's deep background, but, like, deeper," the official said, deadpan. I was becoming exasperated by this exchange, too. Everyone associated with this president was just as high-maintenance as he was.

A few hours later, the press secretary called and asked me to come to the area behind the briefing room termed *upper press*, where the constellation of communications offices are located. I complied. Once there, she asked me to put my things in her quarters and, wordlessly, led me to the Oval Office. I did not have a meeting with the president scheduled. As far as I could recall, I had not requested one. She gestured to an empty chair at the Resolute Desk and told me to sit. The president would be in soon, she said. He likes to make people wait, both to enhance the drama of his grand entrance and to emphasize his dominance.

Dominant as ever, he entered the room in grand fashion. "Olivia," he said, "I just heard that you were doing a story on . . . this stuff." He made a disappointed expression when he said that, *this stuff.* I always found the sight of him in the White House disorienting. He was a flash of Technicolor, deeply saturated, as though he had stepped out of a television, and in certain contexts his presence suggested a kind of glitch. In Midtown, he made perfect sense. In Vegas, even more so. In the snowbanks of New Hampshire, somewhat. In the cornfields of Iowa, less. In the White House, none at all, but in such a way that sense inverted; his realness was not a question, but the set of the White House seemed in doubt. I had first visited the complex during the forty-fourth president's administration, on the occasion of the visit of the pope. This president had carried on a feud with the pope during the campaign that ended in his election.

The chief of staff was "doing a very good job," he said. "We have a very good relationship. The White House is running very, very smoothly." He launched into his script. He talked so much and so fast that I did not bother to try to interrupt with a question for a while. "I want to tell you a couple of things. The chief is doing a very good job. I'm very happy with him, we have a very good relationship, number one. Number two, I didn't offer anybody else the job. I didn't talk to anybody about the job. And I'm not, I'm not looking. Now, look, with time, do people leave? . . . We have a very positive story going on at the White House. We have a very positive story for the country. We're doing a great job. We have the greatest economy in the history of our country. We have among the greatest job numbers. Among many groups, we have the greatest job numbers. We have things going on that are phenomenal on trade. China wants to make a deal—I said, you're not ready yet. But they wanna make a deal, and at some point we might. Iran wants to make a deal. They all wanna make a deal. We have great things going. We have a very smooth-running organization even though it's never reported that way. So the real story is that. It's really the real story. When you walk in here, you don't see chaos. There is no chaos. The media likes to portray chaos. There's no chaos. I'm leaving for Iowa in a little while. We're doing something that's going to be very exciting tonight in Iowa. A big, a big announcement, actually. Doing four rallies this week. I think the rallies have, frankly, built up our poll numbers very greatly. What am I now in Rasmussen? Fifty-two?"

He directed the question at the press secretary, who sat to my right, and she affirmed that the new polling, which had him at fifty-one, had him at fifty-two.

"Plus there's ten percent, they think, where people don't respond, unfortunately. I'm not sure if this is nice or not nice, but when they don't respond, that means it's an automatic Trump vote. But it's a fifty-two, and we're doing very well in the polls. You see what's happening with respect to the election, I mean, you know, to the midterms, even though—I know—historically, the president, you don't tend to do so well in the midterms, but we have, this is a different presidency and this is the greatest economy ever. So, we'll have to test that. But even the polls are saying that we have really come a long way in the last three weeks. I think we're gonna do well. And that's all I have to say. I want to just tell you that I'm very happy with [the chief of staff] and I get along very well with him. We have a very good relationship. And if we didn't, I wouldn't stand for it for a minute, and he wouldn't want it any other way. So it's just a different narrative than what you were saying. And with that, you're gonna have to write what you have to write, but the truth is, we have a really smooth-running White House and nothing and nobody has done more in their first two years as president. We're not even up to the second year."

The president craned his neck slightly upward, in the direction of the door. "Could you give me the list, please?" he asked, raising his voice so his secretary could hear. "I've gotta give you the list. Nobody has come close to doing what we've done in less than two years as president. Whether it's regulations or tax cuts or so many other things." Within seconds, the secretary walked into the room holding two sheets of paper. "Give that to Olivia," the president said. "These are just some of the things that were done since taking office."

The pages were stamped with fifty-eight bullet points in a large font. At the top, underlined, bold, and all caps, it read, "TRUMP ADMINISTRA-TION ACCOMPLISHMENTS." On the first page, the points related mostly to jobs numbers or executive orders or promises from the tax-reform bill. On the second page, there were more puzzling accomplishments, such as, "Republicans want STRONG BORDERS and NO CRIME. Democrats want OPEN BORDERS which equals MASSIVE CRIME."

"So," the president went on, "it would be great to have an accurately written story, because we do have—when you walk in here, I think you see, if you read something, it's totally different than the fact."

In this brief pause in his monologue, I asked a question. How was the White House different with this chief of staff around? "He's a four-star marine. He is a man who likes to see order and discipline, which I like. We came in and it was more free-rolling. We did a lot, we did a lot during the entire period, but I think there is great order now," the president said.

I asked about the effects of the supposed order. There were reports that the president had bristled at efforts to impose order on his own disorderly style. "No, I like it. I like order. I like it both ways. Honestly,

I've had it both ways. I've had it both ways in my life and in my business, and sometimes freewheeling is a very good thing. You know, it's not a bad thing. We did a lot. If you look at the first six months, we did a lot," he said.

"Like what?" I asked. "Well . . ." he said. Unhappily, he squinted his eyes in the direction of the papers I was holding. "You can take a look at some of the things on the list. Some of that was done early. Look at the pipelines. That was done early. A lot of great job-producing events. A lot of regulation cutting, we did tremendous regulation cuts. That was all done pretty early. So what I'm saying—and this is not even updated. We have achieved a lot in the last month and a half, two months, since that's been done. But we've done a really great job and it's so reported by those that are, by those that want it to be accurately reported. And I think, at least, I should be able—because I know you're gonna go in and write something—at least I should be able to tell you, out of respect, that the relationships in the White House have been very good, especially over the last six months, seven months. It's been very, very smooth. It's been a very smooth-running White House."

As we talked, the president turned his head to the door. "General!" he said. "Come here for a moment!" The chief of staff walked in the room. "This is Olivia. She's going to say very, very wonderful things about you. This is [the general]," the president said.

His head turned again to the door. He bellowed a greeting. "Come in!" he said. Close behind the chief of staff was the secretary of state. "Olivia can write badly about you," the president told him. The men laughed uneasily at his joke. "Stay there for a second. I just wanted to see Olivia for two seconds," he said. "Look, look who comes in, and we actually have lunch today." He took suspicious care to emphasize what he said was the serendipitousness of this confab.

"Look who you have here," he said. He glanced toward the door again. "Look who you have here. We had a meeting scheduled!" It was the vice president. "This is Olivia. She's a disruptive writer but that's okay," the president told him. The vice president said hello to me and looked around the room. Confusion spread across his face. There were no more chairs available by the time he arrived at what was beginning to feel like an intervention, and so he stood to my left, over my chair, his arms dangling awkwardly at his sides.

The president asked if I could "name anyone who speaks badly about me on the record." The question was rhetorical and he did not wait for a reply. "People that are off the record—I think it doesn't even exist. I think writers make it up," he said. "Generally, generally. Not in all cases, but generally."

"Well, you've cited anonymous sources before," I said. "Were they made up?" He did not respond to the question. Instead, he said, "I say this: We have a really great White House. We have a really successful White House. We have—I call it a well-oiled machine. It's ruled with tremendous people. And if you remember, you heard my story, when I got elected—I haven't been to Washington my whole life, very rarely, probably never slept over. All of a sudden, I'm president of the United States. I didn't know a lot of people in Washington. Now I know everybody that I want to know, a lot of people. And I bring changes, and those changes have been great changes. One of them over there." He nodded in the direction of the secretary of state, who was sitting behind me on the couch.

"How are you measuring that, exactly?" I asked. His eyes narrowed. "See the list that's in your hand?" I was not taking this matter of the list seriously enough for his liking. "But are you comparing it to a similar list from previous administrations?" I asked. "No, I'm saying in the first two years of a president, and we're not even at two years, nobody has come close to it. No one. Take a look. I mean, you take a look, and nobody has come close. So, I heard you're gonna do a nasty story . . ."

I laughed. "Well, but it was," the president said. His tone was suddenly sharp. "Your narrative is wrong." He stopped himself. He seemed to recall the point of this spectacle. His aim had been to flatter me into writing a flattering story. As if by magic, his face softened and his pitch raised to a brighter major key. "It's just amazing," he said. "We're all having lunch and it's so great that you're all here. This was not set up."

"It seems very spontaneous," I said dryly. "I respect you," the president said. "I just wanted you to get the real picture. The timing was incredible. This was like, it was like . . ."

"We had a lunch plan," the vice president said. I had forgotten that he was looming directly over me. I looked up at him, as confused as he was when he first walked into the room. The president smiled. "Is that a correct statement? This was just, like, perfect timing."

As I turned to leave the Oval Office, a voice called out. "Hey, Olivia!" I turned to see one of the members of the ensemble, who was said to be warring with the chief of staff and angling for his job. He was bear-hugging the chief of staff. The two of them smiled theatrically. "This is my friend!" the chief of staff said. "Yes, and he's mine," his rival said. "And I told her that. She knows that."

The chief of staff was fired three months later.

———

MAGGIE HABERMAN: Whether it is because of convenience or because he actually believes it, he is open to almost anything being real because he will verbalize almost anything. Many times he quickly believes that someone is out to get him because that sounds right, and so person X tells him that person Y did something to him, he will believe that even if it is not true. It goes to some state of emotional arousal for him. He gets excited.

OLIVIA NUZZI: Because he loves chaos?

MAGGIE HABERMAN: And because he is deeply paranoid.

OLIVIA NUZZI: You said something in 2017 that I still think about.

MAGGIE HABERMAN: Oh no.

OLIVIA NUZZI: No, it was good. You compared Trump to *Harold and the Purple Crayon*.

MAGGIE HABERMAN: Yes. Everything with him is about creating his own reality for himself and for other people. I often think of *Harold and the Purple Crayon*, which is a children's book.

OLIVIA NUZZI: Great book.

MAGGIE HABERMAN: Great book. A boy named Harold draws an entire city overnight with his purple crayon. But Harold is drawing, like, dreams and exciting things, and Trump is drawing, like, a gulag and an apocalyptic vision of the US, and there is a malevolence to Trump's purple crayon. I do think that fundamentally holds: He thinks that everything can be moved around. He told me the question he gets asked most often is whether he would do it all again. I said, "What's the answer?" And he said he thinks yes because the way he looks at it, he has so many rich friends, and nobody knows who they are. He had just told me this whole story about how he used to know people who could not get a table at a restaurant. It is a version of a story he has been telling for thirty-five years.

>Office Memorandum
United States Government

DATE: June 2, 1950
TO: Director, FBI
FROM: SAC, New Haven
SUBJECT: DAVID JOHNSON LEISK, alias Crockett Johnson, SECURITY
        MATTER - C

For the information of the Bureau, by letter dated May 8, 1950, the New York Division advised that on April 21, 1950, [REDACTED] reported that CROCKETT JOHNSON is one of "400 concealed Communists."

Subject JOHNSON is a cartoonist who is presently residing with his wife at 74 Rowayton Avenue, Rowayton, Connecticut. The Darien and Norwalk, Connecticut, voting records indicate that subject's correct name is DAVID JOHNSON LEISK: Subject's wife, RUTH KRAUSS LEISK, reportedly writes children's books under the name RUTH KRAUSS.

The New Haven indices contain numerous references to subject under his pen name relating to subject's association with the ICCASP in Connecticut. Subject reportedly is a former editor of the "New Masses" and is the creator of a cartoon strip entitled "Barnaby" which is now written by JACK MORLEY.

The New York Division is requested to furnish the New Haven office in report form any information contained in the New York files relating to the subject.

SYNOPSIS OF FACTS: Subject affiliated with the following organizations: American Committee to Win the Peace; American Committee for Spanish Freedom; Cultural and Scientific Conference for World Peace; Action Committee to Free Spain Now. Subject signed a letter to the 81st Congress, demanding that the HUA be dropped. Subject made a statement through NCASE, urging the President to accept STALIN'S offer to meet in Moscow (2/17/49). Subject was sponsor of dinner under auspices of JAFRO, 12/4/44. In October, 1930, subject was listed as an editor of "New Masses."

DETAILS: Confidential Informant [REDACTED] of known reliability, advised on October 16, 1943, that the subject was considered by the Organizing Committee of the Jefferson School of Social Science as a possible guest lecturer and forum participant. The Jefferson School of Social Science has been listed by the Attorney General as falling within the purview of Executive Order 9835 - Confidential Informant

of known reliability advised that the subject, an artist,
was a member of the American Committee to Win the Peace.

RECORDED - 105

INDEXED - 105

The FBI closed their investigation into David Johnson Leisk in 1955.
He was not a communist. Four months later, he published *Harold and
the Purple Crayon* under what they called his "alias," his pen name,
Crockett Johnson.

"*One evening, after thinking it over for some time, Harold decided to go
for a walk in the moonlight.*"

But he lacked either a walkway or a moon, so with his purple
crayon, Harold drew a fat crescent moon and a path. He worried that he
could get lost, and so he first made the path straight. Then he worried
that he was not getting anywhere, and so he made the path less straight.
He drew a field and a small forest and an apple tree. He drew a dragon
to guard the fruit. He drew the dragon too well, in fact, and frightened
himself.

"*He backed away. His hand holding the purple crayon shook.*"

His shaking drew a jagged line of purple crayon-sea. Before he realized what was happening, Harold was caught in the surf.

"*He came up thinking fast. And in no time he was climbing aboard a
trim little boat. He quickly set sail. And the moon sailed along with him.*"

"Him acknowledging that he was bullshitting made it all the more sincere," a longtime adviser to the president told me. "It's always the lack of self-awareness with zealots: They are so steadfast in their beliefs that there's no understanding of how they are perceived, or there's zero flexibility in any of their positions, and there's no ability to persuade them to see another perspective. What makes him great at what he does is that he is not tethered to anything in such an intense, immovable way. Everyone's always saying, *He's such a liar!* I get it, he doesn't always tell the truth, but there's a difference between *a liar*, as in someone who's lying to be malicious or to create an outcome that is nefarious in some way, versus a *bullshitter*. He's a salesperson, a con man. He wants to sell you the fantasy."

He was open about this, the adviser said. He referred to bullshitting as *rat-a-tat*, as in, he or she "has a great rat-a-tat." This meant an ability to "keep up a schtick," to hold a mark "on the line." He applied a hybrid of theatrical methods on instinct. There was the Meisner technique, named after the actor and teacher Sanford Meisner, which among its tenets instructs the use of repetition to achieve honesty within a performance, and there was *Yes, and . . .*, the central principle of improvisation, which calls for accepting and building on ideas with additional ideas in order to keep a scene alive. Inherent to the maxim that the show must go on is the directive to the showman who must urge it along by whatever means he can. A great bullshitter knows this. The president knew this better than anyone.

As an example, the adviser cited an episode in the Oval Office, when the president summoned one of his generals, an administration official who had served in a high rank in the military, for a dressing-down following an appearance on television about which he was unhappy.

The president huffed and puffed at the general. He screamed, "You motherfucker!" Then he picked up a newspaper, tore off a page of his bad press coverage, crumpled it into a ball, and threw it at the general. Afterward, he stood up and walked out of the room. He slammed the door behind him.

A few moments later, the president's secretary arrived to hand the adviser a note. It was a handwritten request from the president for the adviser to come to the dining room to where he had stormed off. The adviser arrived to find him there buzzing, a smile on his face. "Do you think it worked?" he asked. "Did we scare him?" The president was proud of his performance and proud in particular of his inspired impulse to utilize the prop he had launched at the general. "Didn't you love that?" he asked the adviser. "It just came to me in the moment!"

The adviser laughed at the memory. "He's an actor. I think he probably would have been a real actor in another life, if he was better-looking, he would have liked to have been one of the Cary Grants of the world."

He had wanted to be in the movie business. It is important to never forget this about him. He watches *Sunset Boulevard*, "one of the greatest of all time," again and again and again. A silent-picture star sidelined by the talkies, driven to madness, in denial over her faded celebrity. When he was a businessman, he showed it to guests aboard his 727. As president, he held screenings of it for White House staff at Camp David. He once showed it to a press secretary who later described how "the president, who could never sit still for anything without talking on the phone, sending a tweet, or flipping through TV channels, sat enthralled." And he once showed it to a biographer, Tim O'Brien, who wrote that when Norma Desmond cried, "Those idiot producers. Those imbeciles! Haven't they got any eyes? Have they forgotten what a star looks like? I'll show them. I'll be up there again, so help me!" Trump leaned over his shoulder and whispered, "Is this an incredible scene or what? Just incredible."

DONALD TRUMP: The word *rosebud* is maybe the most significant word in film. The wealth, the sorrow, the unhappiness, the happiness, just struck lots of different notes. *Citizen Kane* was really about accumulation, and at the end of the accumulation, you see what happens, and it's not necessarily all positive. Not positive. I think you learn, in *Kane*, that maybe wealth isn't everything, because he had the wealth, but he didn't have the happiness. The table getting larger and larger and larger, with he and his wife getting further and further apart as he got wealthier and wealthier, perhaps I can understand that. The relationship that he had was not a good one for him, and probably not a great one for her, although there were benefits for her, but in the end she was certainly not a happy camper. In real life I believe that wealth does, in fact, isolate you from other people. It's a protective mechanism, you have your guard up much more so than you would if you didn't have wealth. There was a great rise in *Citizen Kane* and there was a modest fall. The fall wasn't a financial fall, the fall was a personal fall, but it was a fall nevertheless. So, you had the highs and you had the lows. A lot of people don't really understand the significance of it. I'm not sure if anybody understands the significance of it. But I think the significance is bringing a lonely, rather sad figure back into his childhood. The word *rosebud* for whatever reason has captivated moviegoers and movie watchers for so many years and to this day is perhaps the single word, and perhaps if they came up with another word that meant the same thing, it wouldn't have worked, but *rosebud* works. For whatever reason.

———————

St. John's is an Episcopal church across the street from Lafayette Square, the park that separates the White House from downtown Washington. It is a simple, yellow Greek Revival structure built in 1816, designed by Benjamin Henry Latrobe, the father of American architecture, who designed, too, the Capitol itself. On this occasion, the church happened to be on fire.

Outside of Washington, the fact of the fire was in doubt. A television personality in New York said that reports of the fire could not be considered verified since the only footage available was from a right-wing television network. I looked over to my own right. Where I was standing on the sidewalk, it was hot, and there was smoke, and I saw fire. I sent the television personality a message. I could verify reports of a fire at the church, I said, because I was looking at it.

At the church the next day, the president held the Bible in the air. Images circulated that showed the Bible upside down, a perfect depiction of what the president's critics said was his incompetence and evil. The images went viral and, in an instant, became legend. According to fact-checkers, the images were not real.

I could not verify the direction of the Bible myself because at the time that the president arrived on the sidewalk, I was running away from the church. As sirens blared and flash-bangs rang out, my nose and throat burned. My eyes watered. Tear gas had been sprayed and rubber bullets shot into the crowd at the president's direction to clear a path for his photo-op.

"Is that your Bible?" a reporter asked the president. "It's *a* Bible," he said.

"He did not pray," the bishop of St. John's told the press. "He did not mention George Floyd, he did not mention the agony of people who have been subjected to this kind of horrific expression of racism and white supremacy for hundreds of years. We need a president who can unify and heal. He has done the opposite of that, and we are left to pick up the pieces."

Following the scene of violence and disorder, the United States Park Police issued the following statement:

> On Monday, June 1, the USPP worked with the United States Secret Service to have temporary fencing installed inside Lafayette Park. At approximately 6:33 pm, violent protestors on H Street NW began throwing projectiles including bricks, frozen water bottles and caustic liquids. The protestors also climbed onto a historic building at the north end of Lafayette Park that was destroyed by arson days prior. Intelligence had revealed calls for violence against the police, and officers found caches of glass bottles, baseball bats and metal poles hidden along the street.
>
> To curtail the violence that was underway, the USPP, following established policy, issued three warnings over a loudspeaker to alert demonstrators on H Street to evacuate the area. Horse mounted patrol, Civil Disturbance Units and additional personnel were used to clear the area. As many of the protestors became more combative, continued to throw projectiles, and attempted to grab officers' weapons, officers then employed the use of smoke canisters and pepper

balls. USPP officers and other assisting law enforcement partners did not use tear gas or OC Skat Shells to close the area at Lafayette Park. Subsequently, the fence was installed.

Throughout the demonstrations, the USPP has not made any arrests. The USPP will always support peaceful assembly but cannot tolerate violence to citizens or officers or damage to our nation's resources that we are entrusted to protect.

The president interpreted the statement as a victory. His campaign issued a statement, too: "We now know through the U.S. Park Police that neither they, nor any of their law enforcement partners, used tear gas to quell rising violence. Every news organization which reported the tear gas lie should immediately correct or retract its erroneous reporting."

My throat still burned as I read those words. It would burn for days. Weeks later, a major in the Washington National Guard testified before Congress. "I could feel irritation in my eyes and nose, and based on my previous exposure to tear gas in my training at West Point and later in my army training, I recognized that irritation as effects consistent with CS or 'tear gas,'" he said. "And later that evening, I found spent tear gas canisters on the street nearby."

Palm Beach zoning ordinances stipulate that flags as big as four by six feet may fly on poles no taller than forty-two feet high. In October 2006, without a permit and without notice to the city landmarks board, Donald Trump raised on the lawn of Mar-a-Lago an American flag, twenty-five by fifty feet, on a pole eighty feet tall. Complaints were filed. Requests were made. A public relations and negotiation opportunity presented itself. Trump refused to take the flag down and replace it with one that abided by code. "The day you need a permit to put up the American flag, that will be a sad day for this country," he said. "The town council of Palm Beach should be ashamed of itself." For each day of his disobedience, beginning in the New Year on January 6, the city fined him $250. About this, he was thrilled. He booked himself on television. "This is a dream to have someone sue me to take down the flag," he said, although no one had sued him for such a reason. He filed suit against the city of Palm Beach in federal court. He sought $25 million on the grounds that the demands to take down his flag and the penalties levied when he would not comply amounted to a violation of his freedom of speech and equal protection rights. "A smaller flag and pole on Mar-a-Lago's property would be lost given its massive size, look silly instead of make a statement, and most importantly, would fail to appropriately express the magnitude of Donald J. Trump's and the Club's members' patriotism," the filing said. He vowed to award damages to veterans of the war in Iraq. By April, Trump and the city were in mediation. The agreement reached waived the fines and permitted the plaintiff to wave his flag—on a pole ten feet shorter, moved 140 feet west and 60 feet south on the lawn away from the ocean. In return, he agreed to pay $100,000—a $20,000 discount on the unpaid fines incurred—to charities "dealing with Iraq War Veterans, American Flag or the local VA hospital." On September 11, he made the donation, not out of his own pocket but from the Donald J. Trump Foundation, a misuse of nonprofit funds to settle a legal dispute involving a for-profit business.

Peter Francis Stager held the American flag by its thin rod and turned it upside down. Verifiable. A sign of distress, impending, delivered by his hands.

As a Capitol police officer was dragged down the steps by the rioters, Stager lurched forward to beat him with the object, the flag waving in the force of every blow. "Every single one of those Capitol law enforcement officers, death is the remedy, that is the only remedy they get," he said in footage from that day.

In court, he said something else: He was under the impression that the officer was a member of antifa. Yet he told the judge, "I take full responsibility for my actions. I messed up."

He was sentenced to four years for the assault. He was pardoned by the president after two.

———————

On that afternoon, as the riot raged, a senior White House official wanted me to know that she had resigned but she did not want me to tell the public. "Not today. A woman died," she told me. "I'll ensure people know when it happened—I have time stamps—but today feels cheap." I said I thought she was mistaken, and I made my case for why she should let me, or someone else, break the news. "For whatever my opinion is worth," I said, "there's a tendency among staff to think that their actions could only matter in terms of how it looks for them on a cynical, personal level." I told her that I was not trying to lecture. "But I hope you think over the fact that, if any senior staff leaves today, and it is known, it truly will have ripple effects for the next fourteen days. It might compel someone else to do the right thing. It might compel someone else to be tougher on him privately. Who knows."

Two days after the attack on the Capitol, an administration official called me while he was on his way to the department where he had worked for much of the president's term in office.

"This is confirmation of so much that everyone has said for years now, things that a lot of us thought were hyperbolic. We'd say, 'Trump's not a fascist,' or 'He's not a wannabe dictator.' Now it's like, well . . ." He trailed off. "What do you even say in response to that now?" he said.

"This is like a plot straight out of the later, sucky seasons of *House of Cards* where they just go full evil and say, 'Let's spark mass protests and start wars and whatever.' I went through *Access Hollywood*, Charlottesville, all of these insane things. There's some degree of growing accustomed to the craziness. It's not like my heart is racing, like, *Oh God, how am I supposed to react to this?* It's just more that I'm depressed. For people who devoted years of their lives to dealing with the insanity in an attempt to advance a policy agenda that you believe in, all of that has been wiped out. The legacy of the Trump administration is going to be that the president sparked an insurrection and people died because he tried his best to not abide by the Constitution and the tradition of a peaceful transition of power that's been the norm since our founding. Nothing else is even going to be a side note.

"There's not a single person I have talked to at any level, from twenty-three-year-old assistants to members of the cabinet, who are not disgusted and ashamed with what has happened," he said. Conversations among remaining officials were about how to handle the last twelve days of the administration and whether to continue to be a part of the transition of power at all. "It's different for everybody. If you're a regular domestic-policy staffer in the West Wing or the EEOB, the implications of you quitting are different than if you're a senior national security official, or you're tasked with contributing to the continuity of government. We are in a terrible spot. You can't just say 'Well, this is outrageous and I quit' in this situation.

"The only way it gets to this point are a thousand really bad small decisions," he added. "He's sort of turning on everybody. The president is so visceral, he just can't hear people unless he can respect them, and he thinks everybody's a traitor, even the people who got him through impeachment. It's just nuts."

Within two years, he would return to the president's inner circle, and upon the president's return to power, he would return, too, to the designation *administration official.*

OLIVIA NUZZI: Can you explain to me what it means for chickens to come home to roost?

SENIOR WHITE HOUSE OFFICIAL: Every night, the flock heads to the same place to roost, or sleep, for the night. So for example, my chickens have been running around the backyard all day and now the sun is going down. I'm looking at them and three of the five are already up on their spot where they're about to sleep and two are kind of straggling. But they sleep in the exact same spot every night.

WrestleMania 23, 2007. Onstage, Trump was playing the camp sadist, vamping for the cameras, a razor in his hand. "How you doin', man, how you doin'?" he asked his victim, strapped down in a chair. He lifted the razor and sprayed the victim's head with shaving cream. The crowd cheered.

His victim was World Wrestling Entertainment's owner, a long-time friend and Republican donor who would support his campaign and be repaid when, as president, Trump put his wife and business partner in charge of what he promised would be the dismantling of the Department of Education. Ringside later in the program, Trump was interviewed by a wrestler turned politician who had been elected governor of Minnesota on the Reform ticket, the party founded in 1995 by a populist businessman who ran as a third-party presidential candidate; it was with the Reform Party that Trump had once threatened his own third-party presidential campaign. He never declared, but he won some precincts in state primaries anyhow. The people, as Trump would be the first to tell you, loved Trump.

"What does WrestleMania mean to a man like you?" the wrestler turned politician asked him. "Well, it means a lot," Trump said. The wrestler turned politician wanted to know if Trump would support him if he ran for office again. "One hundred percent," Trump said. "You know that, one hundred percent." The wrestler turned politician turned to the crowd. He was thinking bigger than the governor's mansion now. "You know what," he said, "I think that we may need a wrestler in the White House in 2008!"

Before he sought to be inducted into the White House, Trump had been inducted into the WWE Hall of Fame. Which as credentials go was not nothing. I wanted to see it. I figured it would be interesting at least and maybe even educational. I had concluded by now that few efforts to understand better the American public that made Trump a celebrity and might soon make him even more powerful were a waste of time. Every little thing seemed to matter. There was always something new to consider, or something to consider in a new way. In that spirit, I called WWE headquarters.

"Sorry, not possible," the receptionist said.

"Not *possible*?" I asked.

"Visiting would be impossible," she said.

My eyes narrowed. I looked out the window of my newsroom, in the Frank Gehry building on the Hudson River that looked like a big block of glacier ice. I did not like to be trapped anyplace, even somewhere I considered architecturally defensible, and I had wanted to escape today. Had been counting on this opportunity to escape. The news of the *impossibility* of a visit to the Hall of Fame depressed me.

"It's . . . private?" I asked.

"There's no place to visit," the receptionist said.

"No place?" I asked.

"Right," she said.

"It moved?" I asked.

"No, it's, you know, an idea," she said.

"An idea, the Hall of—"

She cut in.

"No *hall*. There's no hall," she said.

"Then . . . what is it?" I asked.

"It's an idea," she said.

An idea. She had mentioned that already.

"It doesn't exist?" I asked.

"Well, it exists," she said.

"Where?" I asked.

"As an idea," she said.

It was a place only in imagination.

A lone Secret Service agent, in a gray polo shirt and sunglasses, an assault rifle across his chest like a pageant sash, requested identification then nodded down the driveway.

I joined the president in the living room, stitched through with ivory brocade and festooned with ornate fixtures, sedan-sized crystal chandeliers, and what he claims to be $7 million of gold leaf. Members of the Mar-a-Lago Club, who pay $200,000 initiation fees and annual fees of $14,000, may use the space, at an additional cost, for "important occasions that inspire, enchant, and exceed every expectation."

At the galas and bat mitzvahs and weekend weddings, the president often wanders in. How could he resist a room like this? He smiles and waves. He joins groomsmen for photos. He steps onto the dance floor with the bride. Dark suit jacket, no tie, shirt unbuttoned, red MAKE AMERICA GREAT AGAIN hat on his head. He tilts his face to the strobe lights and pumps his fists in the air. Sometimes he grabs a microphone and gives a speech. He knows what the people who show up here want. It was the country outside of properties branded with his name where he was finding trouble. It was the majority of the country outside that had not wanted him in power.

In this quiet place on a winding road between the waterway and the sea, the president looked smaller than he ever had in Manhattan or Washington. Dwarfed by the gilded expanse, a lilliputian creature curled on the chair, sipping Diet Coke from a miniature glass bottle perfect for his hand at the scale rendered through satire in the American imagination.

Imagination was the occasion for this visit. The president was concerned as always with shape, with size, with story. Things had not ended so well in the White House, and though he would still argue insistently against the prevailing narrative, argue with less conviction on the particulars, he could not argue with the conclusion that led him to where he was seated across from me now. We were not in the Oval Office.

He always valued the people he called *fighters*, those who volunteered themselves to defend his honor, to spin on his behalf with special force, even at the expense—always at the expense—of their credibility, as they landed ideas such as *alternative facts* that compelled observers to mock or condemn them but compelled him, the supreme observer, the single member of the Audience of One at whom their performances were directed, to a kind of low-grade admiration. Which was as good as it would get, in all likelihood. He deserved such defense, in his view, and so it would never be repaid with anything comparable. Loyalty with the president was not a pact; it was a vow that went in one direction. That was good enough, was as good as great, by the standards of the sorts of people inclined to be *fighters*. Few of them were around now. When the king is run out of the castle, he must fight for himself.

"People have said to me, 'How do you do it?' Everybody was after me—and *still*. 'How do you do this? It is so unfair,'" he said. "I was telling somebody, they were saying 'Did you enjoy this?' Yeah, I enjoyed it, but I had two jobs. Number one was survival. Number two was running the country. I had to survive. Because that whole thing, the witch hunt, started the day I came down the escalator. That was, from day one, there was a witch hunt, and it turned to be legit."

Still he was doing just fine now, here in the quiet, he said. "I'm enjoying it," he told me. "I don't need deals." Then, just as quickly as he volunteered the idea of evolved detachment, he came to his own defense and obliterated it. "I make great deals. You'll see that." Everyone would see. He believed that. He *believed*.

Few people shared now in his belief that redemption would come, but he believed anyhow, even if he was not quite believable when he said that he believed it. It is in periods of doubt, shunned by the fair-weather phonies, in terms of exile, when belief itself performs the work toward redemption. When the king is dead, he must resurrect himself, project the self that he wishes the world to see, and he must see it so clear that through his insistent clarity he conjures the vision for others until it is not a vision at all but the truth of his existence and the truth of yours. You believe and then you see and then they will all see. He would show them. He had done it before.

First, he would show me. He needed me to appreciate this, that he had done it before, that his entire life was about making something where nothing had been, about building his world and mine, too, around an idea, around his idea. People loved to count him out, as he saw it, took immense pride in any catastrophe of which he was part or architect. Those people, the Haters and Losers, could never be great themselves, could never make anything great again, because they did not believe in magic, in his magic. When he succeeded, as he was sure he would, they would have no choice.

"Things I own are phenomenal. I own great assets. I don't think I've ever been given proper credit. I think the people believe it, but I haven't gotten proper credit. I made great deals. No matter what I do, they try and demean me. Like this piece of property," he said.

He looked up to the ceiling and then nodded his head as he looked around the grand space. And it is grand, much grander than he had ever found the White House. Alva Johnston once described the Mizner-style estates of Palm Beach as "Bastard-Spanish-Moorish-Romanesque-Gothic-Renaissance-Bull-Market-Damn-the-Expense." That was about right for Trump. He bought Mar-a-Lago in 1985 during a creditor-funded acquisition spree that included a new hotel, a new casino, a hospital, and the abandoned freight yard between West Fifty-Ninth and Seventy-Second Streets, where he threatened to build his own Hollywood above the Hudson River on a seventy-six-acre expanse that in surface area amounted to 0.5 percent of the island of Manhattan.

When he and Ivana Trump divorced, she was blamed for her attention to the fussy business of high society, something that had never been of much interest to her husband. "Palm Beach had been Ivana Trump's idea," Marie Brenner wrote in *Vanity Fair*, because it was she who aspired for the Trumps to become the new Vanderbilts. Trump did not give a shit about "Palm Beach phonies," he said. But the settlement with Ivana, who fell to her death down the staircase of her Upper East Side town house and is buried on the first hole of her ex-husband's New Jersey golf course, told a different story. He had given her the $30 million mansion in Greenwich. He kept Mar-a-Lago for himself.

The truth was that the symbolic value of the historic Mar-a-Lago estate, built by General Foods owner and socialite Marjorie Merriweather Post, was impossible to quantify. If Trump Tower was a monument to the awesome scale of Donald Trump's ambitions, Mar-a-Lago was a venue for the mythmaking required to support their expanding scope. It was not the Villages, referring to the famous Central Florida retirement community, and it was not Sunset Boulevard. Not to Donald Trump. Really, the sun does not just set on Mar-a-Lago. In fact, on

South Ocean Boulevard, the two-lane road that zigzags along the barrier island terrain on the Atlantic coast, the sun also rises.

"I bought it for very little, and it's worth a lot," he said. All values
being relative, he had scored, thanks to a stroke of genius that only spite
could have inspired. When his first offer of $15 million was rejected,
he snapped up the property next door and said he planned to build a
structure that would have blocked Mar-a-Lago's ocean view. "I grabbed
the beach," he said. *When you're a star, they let you do it.* The stunt
drove the price down and, in the end, he nabbed it for $7 million—plus
the $2 million he spent on the mad plot of the neighboring plot.

He lived in other words within this proof of his own abilities. I was
seated with him now in the realm of this proof. Here, he believed, had
all around him every reason to believe, and he believed others would
believe again. That was where I fit in. If recent history was being written, he would need me to see that he believed, so that he might stand
a chance that I would believe, too, and that way his belief would be
committed to a public record and in that way fulfilled. Belief, he knew,
was a contagion. "I'm not looking to do deals or anything. I'm really
not looking to do that because I have stuff that is great. I might even
sell some things because I like politics. I actually like politics. Business doesn't necessarily mix with politics other than it's good to have
a businessman involved in the country," he said. "I enjoy politics and
it's not that I enjoy politics, I enjoy helping people." His influence
remained great. It was important to him that I got this. "I run my business, with my family I run my business, and I run politics." *I run politics.* By this he meant that politics still ran through him. "The public
likes me," he said.

Still, he had to admit that his life was now much smaller than it had
been. "When you're president, it's very hard to go back into business,

because everything is smaller by comparison," he said. "You know, it's not very exciting to buy a jet." I asked if he was bored. "I'll explain that in a second. It's very interesting. When you see numbers that are in the trillions all the time—a trillion here, a trillion there—and with business you could run the biggest company in the world and it's like a peanut compared to the United States of America. No, I'm not bored. I'll tell you. Ohio is calling, Oklahoma is calling, Florida is calling. Everybody running for office is calling. Everybody running for office is calling wanting an endorsement."

Interest in his endorsement was an important metric: If the exiled king was still perceived as the kingmaker of the Republican Party, then widespread buy-in on his more total belief in himself was within grasp. He thought critically about his endorsements, always in terms of loyalty. This was not pure ego but ego as a kind of strategy. To compel the country to his belief, to impose again his reality, he would need Fighters in power to force that reality into existence with their belief in it, their belief in him.

"Sometimes I get somebody that's a Trumper. They call them 'only Trumper' or 'always Trumper' and those ones are easy. But sometimes I'll get one that voted for me in all cases. For instance, I have numerous people who have voted two times against impeachment of me—in other words, they voted for me in a positive way on impeachment—but then they said some bad things about something I may have done. And they're popular in their state but I could beat them. In the primary, if somebody ran against them that was on my side, we have numerous cases, a Trump person, almost every one of these people would lose. But the big vote is the impeachment vote. That's different than voting on a tax cut, regulation something, having to do with the whatever—this is very personal. Impeachment is very personal. They want to throw me out of government, that's a very big deal. How do you endorse a person like that? It's terrible what they're doing. And some of them are very deceptive. I have people who have voted for me one hundred percent and impeachment—because anybody who voted for me on impeachment, I'll never ever be with them."

He wanted to look ahead, but the past was still so near that it seemed to him still flexible, and so near that he found it intruded anyhow, with reminders of all the ways he had been let down, which was how he saw it, or how he wanted others to see that he saw it. As always, any belief aside from belief in his own mind was in considerable doubt. He enraged himself with the memory of the former Senate majority leader. "This guy with no personality stands up and he starts talking like he's this great guy. He wouldn't have even been standing there if it wasn't for me," he said. "It's too bad I endorsed him. I wish I hadn't endorsed him. He got up and he was vicious, and I say, 'Here's the schmuck I got into office . . .'" And he enraged himself with the memory of the Supreme Court, whose justices he blamed, among so many others, for his election loss. His eyes narrowed as he raised the subject of the justice on whose confirmation he had spent the most time and political capital. He had been so generous and faithful to the justice, as he saw it, and still he was betrayed. "Nobody else would have stuck with him. Most of the senators wanted me to cut him loose. I felt it on a human basis. That wasn't for politics. I felt badly for him. It wasn't a Republican or Democrat thing. I thought he was a very outstanding person. But he's a different person today. I believe he's changed a lot. I think he's afraid of the Left, I think he's definitely afraid of the radical Left. I think he's a different person than he was when I said I'm going to go with you. I'm disappointed in him and in the Supreme Court."

And now that he was thinking about all of it, it was as though he could not stop. He spiraled. He continued on: "Forgetting about all of the corruption, all of the fraud, forgetting about that poll watchers had to be taken out physically—in other words, you have to have poll watchers, Philadelphia, Detroit, and other places were unable to watch the corruption that was taking place—forgetting about all of that, forgetting about the illegal immigrants who were voting, the people who didn't live in the state who were voting, the dead people who were voting, forgetting about all of that, these states made major electoral changes, major voting changes, and in some cases just prior to the election, without the approval of their legislators. Five of the states were Republican-controlled legislatures. The Democrats went to the legislatures and the legislatures said no and they made the changes anyway. In the Constitution of the United States, you have to get legislative approval. The Supreme Court was unwilling to take the case. And frankly, judges up and down the line were unwilling to follow the law. Four judges in Wisconsin were willing to follow the law, but the judges were unwilling to follow the law. With [the justice whose confirmation was in doubt], I saved his life. I saved his career. I saved everything. I want nothing for nothing. One thing has nothing to do with the other. But that he could be voting the way he is voting is a disgrace. It's so sad to see. And now some of those senators who said to cut him loose, they've said 'I told you, sir.' They voted against me on things they never should have voted against me on . . . I haven't talked to him. I liked [the first justice he appointed, in 2017]. I liked [the final justice he appointed, in 2020]. Again, I didn't say 'I'm going to make you a judge, but you have to do this or that.' But it's almost like they go out of their way to vote against me. It's an amazing thing."

On the subject of January 6, he wanted to get some things straight:

"First of all, the crowd was massive. Far bigger than the press wants to admit," he said. On second thought, he would be all right to just straighten out the *First of all.* This most comfortable subject, the size of his crowds, was one he returned to as reflex, a safe rhetorical place to land anytime conversation veered into dicier terrain, such as what the massive crowd had done after his speech. Now that he was within the preferable general topic of crowds, he sought to move further away from that winter. He bridged the divide of the entire four years of his presidency, from inauguration to what he insisted was not, as a technical and legal matter, an insurrection, in one breath, through a single conjunction, as though compelled by no conscious thought process. "And I've always said this, and I can show it in pictures, when we had the inauguration, my crowd was massive, and with television and everything else," he said. What his press secretary claimed at the time, that the crowd was of historic size, "was true," he said, though it was not, "and to show you how dishonest much of the media is, they took pictures of the field long before people were there that day." He went on like this, talking about the event he preferred to talk about rather than the one he was asked about, and then he went on talking more generally about his large crowds and about how the dishonest media never wanted to admit just how large they were.

But what of the crowd on that day, January 6? "This crowd was the biggest crowd I've ever spoken to, and I think I spoke very moderately. I hated to see what happened. They were there because of the election and that they felt that the election was a fraud. They felt that the election was stolen. That's why they were there, in my opinion, more than anything else. I believe that very strongly. I think, personally, that there is massive evidence of it. I think [the vice president] made a terrible, tragic mistake," he said, referring to his decision to abide by the Constitution when, as president of the Senate, he presided over the certification of the votes. "I liked him a lot. I liked his family. I got along with him very well. I was very surprised he wasn't willing—what Thomas Jefferson was willing to do—a much lesser version. Thomas Jefferson kept the votes, you understand that? He didn't send them back for adjudication. He said, 'We will keep the votes of the great state of Georgia' . . . I think judges didn't have the courage to overturn an election that should have been overturned."

He returned again and again to the crowds. Crowds were the most important metric of all. It was the crowds that set him apart from every other candidate for office. It was the crowds that illustrated the phenomenon of his rise to dominance. It was the crowds that had been ignored by the political and media establishments in the 2016 election. And it was the crowds that proved to him now that the 2020 election had been stolen. He needed this to be understood. "When you have a rally in Butler, Pennsylvania, and fifty-two thousand people show up, that's the ultimate poll. Fifty-two thousand. This in Butler, the middle of Pennsylvania. There's ten thousand people in the town. Fifty-two thousand people showed up. When you have a rally of seventy-one thousand in the airport at Miami a week before—and I won Florida by a lot," he said. "I think I won in a landslide. I think it wasn't even close. A lot of people come up to me and say, 'Sir, you won that election in a landslide.' It was a rigged election, and they stole it."

———

Here and there, glimmers of clarity. At times it seemed possible to categorize the corruption of reality within the field of the president's distortion. He succeeded by making even those who said they loathed him behave sometimes quite like him. His lawlessness inspired lawlessness. His rejection of norms called norms into question. Yet on occasion it seemed that notions of ideological direction, a political Right and Left, still held. The Right distorted reality with the untrue things they were willing to say; the Left distorted reality with the true things they were unwilling to say.

Was that fair to say? Such assessments fell apart upon sustained review. The president had lost the election. He would not say so. He had encouraged a crowd of his supporters to go to the Capitol, where they became a mob that carried out a riot and assaulted police officers. First he would not admit that the crowd and the mob were formed of many of the same people, then he began to question the events themselves, then he denied them outright. The subsequent president was too old to serve. He said he was perfectly fine, said that he was and would remain the Democratic candidate, and when he did not remain so, the fabricated enthusiasm for the new nominee was accepted and promoted as legitimate by a population concerned that skepticism would be interpreted as socially intolerable dissent. That we build our own reality is an idea supported at different degrees by different sciences; in reaction to the president, the construction of new realities flourished through a kind of consciousness anti-raising, collective agreement to disagreement, commitment to recognize that which appealed to existing biases through positive and negative affirmation and to shut out all else.

As the government itself remained locked in a state of terminal polarization, Right and Left crisscrossed; any pretense of philosophical allegiance was replaced by cold tribalism. The angel and the devil on my shoulders now sounded alike. It became impossible to say who believed what, whose beliefs were real, whether such a thing as realness could be verified and whether it even mattered. Verified by whom? There existed no agreed-upon neutral arbiter of facts. Value could not be quantified. Standards could not be determined, formed as they are through consensus about that which we value. Who was *we*? Did such a thing as a collective ethic, an American public with a shared understanding of *value*, have any basis in our present reality? Did we share at all? Less and less, the verdict came down.

The distortion outbreak. Elsewhere, everywhere, reality and perception were open questions sprawling wider to encircle the whole of us. Thin notions of reason, of certainty, stretched thinner, pulled apart and apart and apart and apart.

The closer you get to a black hole, the more you fall apart. The what and the when of you. Past and present and future stretch and overlap into scenes on a single stage. The world folds, over and over, layer upon layer. Time becomes space and space becomes time; this is physics.

The beginning of the end of the world would be beautiful, if it ended like this. On ascent, bathed by the colors of the aurora borealis as the northern lights shoot off also south and east and west to encircle the whole of us. This glorious prelude to ruin a kind of mercy.

Then ruin would come, with the air and seas departing first from the atmosphere, a great whirl of wind and water, followed by the shell of the planet cracking up and its guts of magma launching skyward in a global volcanic eruption.

Looked at from some other rock, this, too, would be beautiful, just as through the eye of a telescope the apocalypse of a supernova is a dazzling pyrotechnic flash.

> *Like easy belief, thinking the stars are pure light, not firestorms raging.*
>
> —Betsy Sholl

From the outside, time slows as matter nears the event horizon. For the matter, time ticks by the same as it ever has.

Spaghettification is the term astrophysicists use to describe what happens to all matter as it enters the border of this realm. It is a silly word for a gruesome process. "There was this medieval torture with horses, drawing and quartering," a Harvard scientist told me. The murder mechanism saw one half of a person tied to one horse and their other half tied to another horse; the horses were then compelled to run in opposite directions, at which point the person was torn to pieces. That is the best way to visualize spaghettification, the scientist said: pulling apart and apart and apart and apart, reduced to ever smaller and smaller parts, dissolved right down to our very atom parts and then beyond them, beyond any concept of us, beyond any trace of our existence.

But energy never dies, and as Stephen Hawking theorized, what enters black holes may find its way out. How else to explain the ring of light around their darkness? They are setting free what does not belong to them. Even black holes must learn this lesson: Nothing is yours to keep.

The size of the black hole would determine the shape and speed of its distortion and destruction. Black holes exist at the center of most observable galaxies. At the heart of ours there is a very large one, called Sagittarius A*, and its plasma sphere would zap any living thing to death in an instant upon contact. "The radiation will fry the earth in half an hour," the scientist said. If somehow a surviving organism slipped through, the process of spaghettification would spell immediate death: "It would all be over in seconds and probably even less than a second."

Cosmologists claim that they would know if we were approaching one. There would be signs. But how early would the signs begin? And how to trust such assurances? It is an article of faith that the tiniest movement, a flicker of energy anywhere in the cosmos, may have untold ripple effects untold light-years away. Everything matters that much. Every little thing. Might there be then a cosmological equivalent to the faint sound of distant footsteps?

Space-time moves in one direction: not ahead or back but down. At the heart of the heart, at the very bottom of a black hole, Albert Einstein thought we would locate the end of time, what he termed the *singularity*. A final frame. The last gasp. I will meet you there.

———

A friend called from Washington, a city to which he had vowed never to return. Such is the power of this president, bending all to his will. He was going a mile a minute about the hideousness of the Washington perma-class, rendered in much sharper relief now on his second tour of duty.

He said, "It's so strange that you're not here with me but you know what I was thinking?"—and he was talking about his thoughts during a particular event, some gala or other, one of those dubiously funded confabs that Sally Quinn would call "a ratfuck," which she insists is the correct usage of the term, although my understanding of *ratfuck* had always been as a verb, in the manner of the president's Trickster, but certainly I am not going to question Sally Quinn and her authority as it relates to the correct terminology for Washington events. What he was thinking, he said, was, "I can't believe that you were ever here. It makes no sense that you were ever here at all."

When I was even there at all.

Housekeeping left a note on the pillow: "The best preparation for tomorrow is doing your best today." It was printed in type made to look like handwriting, rather than what it was, which was impersonal. It was attributed to H. Jackson Brown Jr. I had never heard of him. "Think ahead," read the words printed below, and then there was the next day's weather report: "Sunny, with a high of seventy-nine and a low of sixty-seven."

I dreaded my return from the road to the stillness of Washington. I had convinced myself the problem was the rain and the heat, the qualities that make Washington in summertime even more unbearable than Washington the rest of the time, if you can believe that. The rain and the heat had for months suffocated me, a creature who must walk in circles and call *sources familiar* and people *with knowledge of* this or that, and people *close to the president*, and my mother. A creature who once did nothing but walk through Central Park, or along the West Side Highway, or down Ninth Avenue and back up again through Hell's Kitchen to the Upper West Side or from the West to East Village and into Chinatown and the sliver of the borough that we still call Little Italy. Listening to Lou Reed and texting.

I used to joke that I would die on the sidewalk in a twelve-millennial texting pileup. Instead I am alive in Washington, a place where you cannot live, really. Where you cannot look both ways to cross the street without seeing someone you wish to not know. A place where you cannot hide, where you will step outside to be alone only to run into John Kerry or Newt Gingrich, where you will realize that those two are not even close to the worst people whose lives are devoted in one way or another to ensuring that they never have to leave Washington, can always get a table from Franco at Cafe Milano, where for some reason we all pretend that the waiters are not rather obviously spies, where we do not apply our allegedly foundational and resolute skepticism to curiosities such as,

Why is there another Cafe Milano in the UAE and no place else?

I talk about the people I know here like the problem is the people I know here—and here I am talking about other reporters, though I do not think of myself as a reporter, really—as if what repulses me about them is not what I see of myself in them, as with almost anything else on earth, and as if they do not at least know when the president will be walking along the driveway and up to the sticks to talk to the right-wing television network and everyone else, rather than learning of this only after the fact, having slept through an alarm, or several alarms, and then having woken up only briefly and having read a text or two and then having fallen back to sleep until sometime after ten and then having forgotten to answer any of the texts and then having forgotten to show up to the White House altogether.

I am never sure who I have met before in Washington and it is as though the social contract here includes a conspiracy clause that ensures that is so. Here, the standard greeting is *Nice to see you*. I had long considered it a coward's salutation, an attempt to avoid embarrassment, deny fallibility, present oneself as connected and knowledgeable and all of the invisible qualities that people tend to value here more than they do in other places. That is nice for them. For me, I am always a little confused, making my way through a cocktail hour or enduring the buzzless start to a dinner party or a book event or a strange gala at the residence of the ambassador to I-never-know-what. Do I simply not recall having met the senator or the lobbyist or the flack or the socialite or the talking head? Could I have met and forgotten so many people? "I feel like I know you!" these people often say. I do not feel that I know me. There is the consumable me, a character who appears on television, and then there is the distant source material of my interior on which she is vaguely based. It was after maybe the fortieth time that I said "Nice to meet you" and somebody, offended, said "We've met before" that I succumbed to the environment and started saying "Nice to see you," though I cannot say it without wishing to be struck down in that moment by a merciful God whose existence seems less and less assured with each passing day in Washington.

The executive invited members of the media to his home, near enough to the home of a former president that Secret Service lingered at the path to the door. The occasion of the dinner party was officially no occasion at all and unofficially an announcement that the executive was dating a movie star. She waltzed along the terrace holding a cicada in one hand and a vape in the other. I liked her instantly. "It's okay to smoke," she said as she nodded at my cigarette, "just never smoke the filter." It had not occurred to me that one might endeavor to smoke the filter of a cigarette, although I did once light such a filter on fire while driving through unfamiliar terrain in rural Alabama, where I was due inside a barn in the woods to witness an accused pedophile, who had been endorsed and defended by the president, refuse to concede that he lost his campaign for the United States Senate. I put the fire out as I turned onto a dirt road.

That was in 2017; as of 2025, he still had not conceded. The executive draped his arm over my shoulder. He wore the distinct smile of a man dumbfounded to be dating a movie star and the distinct confidence that accompanies such luck. "You're so fun," he told me. The movie star was by now holding the cicada aloft and marveling at how it glowed in the moonlight. "Do you like to have fun?" the executive asked. I did not think that I would like to have fun in the manner of subtext his tone suggested and so I laughed the kind of laugh that means no but registers no sound of rejection: *ah-ha-ha.* Later in the kitchen, I stood with Maureen Dowd, which is the safest place to stand in America unless you are a fraud, in which case it is the most perilous. The movie star, not a fraud at all, in fact a shock of honesty in this weird little town, approached and grabbed my face. "Olivia, the secret to life is to be rapeable," she told me. "You are rapeable."

In the West Wing, I sat in an office a few feet from the Oval with a senior aide to the president. A sepulchral space with no windows, decorated by an American flag and a vase of pink roses and an abstract painting that resembled the inside of a cyclone. The sound of the president's voice vibrated from down the hall. Another senior aide poked his head through the door. "You have no idea what I prevent from happening every day just by being here," he told me. He nodded in the direction of the Oval. "Just by physically positioning myself right here, you have no idea who I prevent from getting in there."

A birthday party for an elderly heiress at the Museum of Natural History. I had just a limited understanding of who she was. Democratic megadonor. I went to her house once for dinner on the Fourth of July and she had live musicians who were very good, a girl with green hair especially. She was a vocalist. I cannot remember what she sang but I remember how it made me feel. The house was a cold and hideous marble monument to her wealth and then she sold the place to get an even bigger place to make room, she joked, for the orchestra.

On this occasion she was turning eighty-two years old. She seemed much older than that, if you were judging all eighty-two-year-old women against Sally Quinn, which I was, since she was the first eighty-two-year-old woman I had ever known. Sally seems thirty-five, and she is still beautiful and hot, palpably and electrically sexual in her eighties, which I love. Sally hates this woman, and I cannot remember why, not that it matters, but it might be amusing. Inside the museum there was no Sally, needless to say, which was the first problem. It was one of those old crowds of the Regulars, the people who will never leave Washington, all in some sort of debt, social or otherwise, to a very wealthy person, with no obvious other connective tissue. Surrounded by literal fossils.

In the theater, the conductor welcomed onstage a succession of Tony winners, and Tony Fauci sat to my right. He goes out a lot, I notice, which I guess means that I go out a lot, and I guess my general awareness of Tony Fauci was a function of the pandemic to begin with, and his retirement coincided with the resumption of "normal life" and big parties and all of that. Who cares.

Later in the evening I was a bit stoned and I was talking to a cabinet secretary and his wife, and she remarked with pride that they had been married for over twenty years, and I asked if they had any advice. They addressed the question so earnestly, it was very sweet. She said you have to find time every day to connect with each other even if it is really minor-seeming. He picks up the phone no matter what, for instance, but usually during the day he answers and he says, "HiICant-TalkRightNowIllCallYouLaterILoveYouBye." On Saturday mornings, they drink coffee and play a word game together and they look forward to it all week and they try to come up with fun and interesting words.

At the end of the evening, I got stuck talking to the secretary again, and surely he felt as though he was stuck talking to me, too, and his wife was turned to face someone else, and he joked that the real secret to marriage is everybody cheats.

These exchanges happened in the shadow of an enormous elephant replica. People kept looking up while meandering around the room with their cocktails and plates of oysters to say, *Oh my God, there's an elephant here! I didn't notice! Why didn't anyone tell me! Look, it's an elephant!* An elephant in the room, yes.

On a weeknight at an arena, the president delivered remarks for an hour and eighteen minutes. He talked about all the things he has been talking about since 2015, when he began his campaign for the Republican presidential nomination, and all the things he has added to the list of things he talks about since then. The arena was in America, which he says is a great place now, but could become a bad place very quickly were voters to make the wrong choice in the next presidential election. Members of Congress and the First Family were inside. Members of the Proud Boys were outside. We were all in Orlando, but we could have been anywhere.

The glowing banners in the Amway Center said KEEP AMERICA GREAT, the slogan the president has been halfheartedly referencing since he was elected. Smaller banners said MAGA, the acronym for the old one. The president sounded uncertain about the alteration. As if talking to himself onstage, he asked, *Who would change the most successful political slogan of all time?* If he lost, he added, people would attribute the loss to his decision to adopt a new slogan. He riffed on this point for a few moments until he seemed finally to soothe himself out of his anxiety. He concluded that the campaign had picked a new slogan that worked. He is preoccupied with whether or not things *work*. He is less concerned with why they work or whether they should work or whether they are working in service to any kind of good. He is also superstitious by nature, and believes, more than anything else—in fact it may be the only thing he really believes—in his powers of manifestation. At his request, the crowd chanted the new phrase attached to his movement, the one he was sure would not cast a spell for failure: "Keep America Great!"

Standing next to me in the press pen, a congressman was watching but not chanting. In Florida, the congressman represented the First District, but in Washington, he often represented the president. He was a loyal supporter and frequent television surrogate for the administration. He was in the press pen, in fact, because he was looking for a television camera. I asked the congressman why he was not chanting. "I'm chanting on the inside," he said. Then he added, "If he loses, people will definitely point to this moment as the turning point, not Charlottesville," referring to the demonstration in Virginia in which white nationalists had chanted racist and antisemitic slogans and killed a counter-protester. The president had said there were "very fine people on both sides" of the event. I said that I could not tell if the congressman was bullshitting me. With a smirk, he said, "Yes, you can."

Against my skin, the brush of a manta ray. It was night in the Pacific, and the creatures were swimming up to the surface of the water to eat plankton. They are huge and majestic and their fins wave with grace, floating flashes of white in the dark blues; they call them *angels of the sea*. The manta ray opens its mouth as it moves to the plankton. The swallowed sea enters a system of honeycomb filters that sift debris as tiny as some microplastics out and direct plankton in, pumping oxygen into its blood while the sea exits through its gills. The complex feeding process unfurls effortless, an underwater ballet.

Humans have no similar filtration system and we absorb small fragments of plastic through the air, through our skin, and through our stomachs. The Olmecs used the sap of Mesoamerican gum trees to form rubber around 1600 BC, and acids transformed the waxy matter of evergreen and timber trees into hard plastic in the mid-nineteenth century. *Plastic* is now a broad categorization for materials made of spindly chains of flexible chemical compounds derived most often from crude oil. Plastic is now lodged inside our brains, lungs, hearts. I considered this as I dipped my head back into the water to watch the manta rays. Who was supposed to be the more intelligent form of life here?

The president was at his private club and residence in Bedminster, New Jersey, and he was still spinning. I asked if he was embarrassed by what had been carried out on his behalf on January 6. "They did it on their own behalf. I said 'peacefully' and 'patriotically,'" he said. I referred to the huge number of hats sported by members of the crowd that day branded with the president's name and political slogans. "And *other hats*," he said.

He mentioned again the size of the crowd, which still impressed him, and he emphasized that he had asked them to demonstrate peacefully. I countered with the fact of how not peaceful the demonstration turned out to be. "If you look at what happened in the Capitol, I don't believe they found one weapon in the Capitol. If they did have weapons that would have been a whole different story. I don't think they found one weapon. Is that a correct statement?" The president directed this question to an aide, who quickly affirmed that the president was correct, although he was not correct. He continued on without acknowledging the aide: "They didn't find any weapons, not one person had weapons out of all of those people—which was a tiny group, relative to the people listening to the speech—but I don't think they said one weapon, I don't think one person in the Capitol had a weapon, not one weapon."

The president was by now in a world of legal trouble, entangled in investigations into allegations of fraud and other misdeeds by a battery of government agencies: federal prosecutors (over the events at the Capitol, the handling of classified documents, and election interference) and the District of Columbia attorney general (over the presidential inaugural committee finances) and the Manhattan district attorney (over the Trump Organization finances) and the New York State attorney general (also over the Trump Organization finances) and the Westchester County district attorney (also over the Trump Organization finances) and the Fulton County, Georgia, district attorney (over election interference in Georgia) and the Securities and Exchange Commission (over plans to take his social-media company public through a SPAC) and the House Select Committee on January 6 (whose hearings were the runaway TV-ratings hit of the summer).

He blamed this, for the most part, on corruption and disloyalty.

"I've never been overly trusting of a lot of people. That's the way it is. That happens to a lot of presidents," he told me. "People are very good and then somebody offers them a couple of bucks for a book, and they say, 'Wow, I've never seen that kind of money before.' And then they have a book that doesn't sell. Those books haven't done particularly well. The positive books have." In fact the books advertised as tell-alls against the president sold considerably more than the books that amounted to hagiography and propaganda. "The *unselect committee* is an example. I watch it with people I hardly know, and they make up stories and pretend. I call it *the pretend witnesses*," he said. "I have a great company, an unbelievable company. The numbers are fantastic. I just have a racist attorney general in New York who campaigned on the fact that she was going to get Trump without even knowing me." *Racist?* I asked. *Did he think he was being investigated in New York because he was white?* "I think she's a racist, yeah. She's a racist and she's a corrupt politician. You don't run for office as a prosecutor because you're going to get somebody."

Target on his back aside, it was a beautiful day and it had been a beautiful weekend, one that affirmed the choice he had made about his own future, the future of the Republican Party, and the future of the American experiment. At a rally in Alaska on Saturday, he told me by phone, his fans were adoring. "More love," in his words, "than I've ever had before." His voice was humming with excitement. He was still in awe. After all this time, after so many rallies, so many crowds, so many winding speeches and chants of "Lock her up" and "USA" and "Build the wall" and the familiar sounds of "Tiny Dancer" and "Memory" (from *Cats*) and "You Can't Always Get What You Want" and "YMCA" and that goofy little dance and the delusion and the fervor so great that it built up to an attack on the democratic process at the center of the Republic itself, the novelty of this had not faded.

As a technical matter, the Anchorage event was on behalf of Trump-endorsed congressional candidates, but like all such endeavors, it was for its star a means of discerning through an energetic test of the zeitgeist as it materialized in his crowds what traditional polls could not so reliably or completely tell him. What it told him this time, he said, was that his voters wanted to and would bring him back to power.

"Do I go before or after? That will be my big decision," he said. He was referring to the timing of an official announcement for his third presidential campaign and whether he ought to wait until the midterm elections. He was thinking aloud now. "I just think that there are certain assets to before," he said. "Let people know. I think a lot of people would not even run if I did that because, if you look at the polls, they don't even register. Most of these people. And I think that you would actually have a backlash against them if they ran. People want me to run."

A former adviser to the president explained the legal logic: "A lot of people are saying, 'You've got to announce so you're protected. It's a witch hunt, they're trying to do this to you again. You've got to do it before the grand jury meets.'" The president dismissed this idea. Shielding himself from prosecution was not among his reasons for running for president because he was not at any risk of being prosecuted, he said. "Well, I did nothing wrong, so I don't see that," he said, "I did absolutely nothing wrong." This was about the country, he said, not about him. "I'm not bored. I'm very busy with everything actually. Amazingly busy." But, he admitted, "nothing compares to getting things done that you can't do from any other position other than president. I made America great again, and I may have to do it again."

The three middle-aged women wore neon construction vests and solemn expressions. They sat on metal chairs at cheap folding tables made of aluminum and linoleum. Although they were plotted across the cold space at a great distance from one another, they moved as though synchronized, with all six eyes focused intently on the materials fanned out before them: swaths of nylon and polyester, spools of thread, and big plastic bags full of brass rings.

The first woman scrutinized the work of an autonomous device, a JUKI sewing machine imported from Japan, which had connected a ribbon of white fabric to a ribbon of red.

The second woman fished a rectangle of blue from a pile of blue rectangles. These swatches were woven each with fifty white stars, an intricate task performed by a large machine designed for this particular celestial embroidery and custom built in China. The machine was stamped with warnings written in English and Chinese: MIND YOUR HANDS. NO STEPPING ON SURFACE. She manually fed what she termed the "star field" into a device, another JUKI, to connect it to a ribbon of white.

The third woman lifted a patchwork into the air and shook it. She pulled it close to her face and adjusted her eyeglasses. She squinted, inspected its seams, poked at the brass grommets that punctured its canvas border, and nodded. Satisfied, she folded the patchwork and placed it at the top of a stack of identical folded patchworks.

In the vale of the San Gabriel and San Bernardino Mountains, in a twenty-thousand-square-foot warehouse, as many as one thousand American flags may be manufactured in this manner by as many as seven workers per eight-hour shift.

The company that owns the warehouse and makes the flags was

founded in 2020 by an immigrant from China who says he arrived in the United States in 2010, served in the navy, and studied computer science at a community college in Southern California.

I found myself there on a Wednesday morning watching the flags get sewn together while semitrucks backed noisily into loading docks at nearby warehouses, where they were stocked with inventory that ranged from packaged food-like substances to luggage to construction materials to tech products from major corporations and independent ventures alike before they wheeled off to disperse the goods throughout the vast country.

The expanded space of the new factory meant there were expanded opportunities to profit. Besides flags, the warehouse is also a drop-shipping center and a distributor of whimsical modern excesses such as a birdhouse equipped with a video camera for recreational bird surveillance and plastic vats of bird feed guaranteed to lure the creatures to their closeups. But all of that is just side hustle. The central business is American flags, mostly sold in bulk to retailers at wholesale, though the company also produces flags to commemorate veterans, folded into triangles and stored in triangle display cases, and in much smaller quantities different types of flags altogether, including the California and the Gadsden, which seen side by side raises the question of who would win a fight, the grizzly bear or the rattlesnake?

Warehouse operations are managed by a young woman dressed in a sweatshirt and blue jeans. She is from the same small province in mainland China as the company's founder, and like him she also studied computer science upon entry to the United States in 2012. She laughed as she told me this. She gestured at the expansive factory around us. She was really putting her degree to good use here, she said dryly.

She would be lying if she claimed to have deep attachment to the American flag, she said. Flags were not really flown by citizens in China the way that they are here, at least not that she could recall, since the Chinese flag is not woven into the fabric of Chinese culture the way that the American flag is woven into American culture. She allowed that when she arrived in this country she understood the American flag held extraordinary sentimental value. "I thought, maybe . . ." She paused for a moment to search for the right words. "American dream?" She shrugged. She was practical by nature and not caught up in sentimentalities of any sort. She did not fly a flag herself, she said, because she lived in an apartment. Where would she put it? Hanging off her window?

The company literature bears a seal of olive branches that reads, "Service Disabled Veteran Owned Small Business." The product literature reads, "This Flag Has Been Proudly Made By Our California Workers Using 100% U.S. Material."

I eyed the dozens of cardboard boxes scattered along the rows of sewing machines that teemed with spools of thread and reams of fabric. They were stamped each with Chinese shipping labels. At first I broached the subject delicately, and at first the manager insisted that all the flags were made with entirely domestic materials. I tried another tactic. I raised my eyebrows, focused my gaze, and smiled. *Come on*, I said. *I do not believe you.* The manager laughed. *Okay*, she said. Not all the flags sold by the company were made of entirely domestic materials. Some flags were polyester, a thinner and shinier fabric more prone to wear, and those were made partly from materials imported from China. Polyester flags were cheaper, she said, and less popular.

Looked at one way, the scene was the achievement of three decades of globalization.

An American flag made of raw materials possibly from China, stitched together with sewing machines definitely from Japan, in a factory where the workers are immigrants from Mexico and China, who work for an immigrant from China who served in the US Navy, sold to retailers at an average wholesale price of seventeen cents per three-foot-by-five-foot flag, the most popular size.

Those retailers, which include the multinational everything-chain known for its "supercenters" and a multinational home improvement chain, sell the flags for between $14.99 and $29.98 apiece, and advertise them with the following qualities: "Made of durable nylon." "Sewn stripes, embroidered stars." "Quadruple stitch on the fly end, double tack down on corners for durability." "Canvas header with brass grommets will last a long time." "3 ft. x 5 ft. size can be seen from a distance."

Most important of all is this promise: "Made in the USA."

The president called. Twenty-eight days earlier, impeached and voted out of office and impeached again, amid multiple state and federal investigations, under threat of indictment and arrest, on the verge of a congressional-committee verdict that would recommend four criminal charges to the Feds over the attack on the Capitol, he had announced his third presidential campaign. Since that time, he had not left the state of Florida. For twenty-eight days, in fact, he had barely set foot outside the perimeter of Mar-a-Lago.

He was sensitive about this. He did not like what it suggested. So he did not accept the premise. "Sometimes I don't even stay at Mar-a-Lago," he told me. *What do you mean you do not stay there?* I asked.

Where do you stay? "I *stay* here," he said, "but I am outside of Mar-a-Lago quite a bit. I'm always largely outside of Mar-a-Lago at meetings and various other things and events. I'm down in Miami. I go to Miami, I go to different places in Florida."

What he meant when he said "Miami" was that his SUV rolled down the driveway, past the pristine lawn set for croquet, and through the Secret Service checkpoint at the gate, for the two-hour trip to another piece of his branded real estate, the Trump National in Doral, about eight miles from the airport in Miami-Dade County. There, he met regularly with an impressive, ideologically diverse range of policy wonks, diplomats, and political theorists for conversations about the global economy and military conflicts and constitutional law and I'm kidding. He went there to play golf. "He just goes, plays golf, comes back, and fucks off. He has retreated to the golf course and to Mar-a-Lago," one adviser said. "His world has gotten much smaller. His world is so, so small."

He was sensitive about smallness. His entire life, he had rejected smallness. Tall buildings, long ties, big head, big mouth, big swings, big league. "When he was in New York in 2016, the whole world was coming to him. Now we've got the Villages, and it shows," the adviser said. Trump did not like the way that sounded for Trump. He still talked that way, in the third person. "I think I've always been relevant. Like, I've been relevant from a very young age. I've been in the mix, to be honest," he told me. "This was the same thing in 2016. They said first, 'Oh, Trump is just doing it for fun,' and then they learned that wasn't true," he told me. "And then they said, 'Well, he won't win.' And they learned that wasn't true."

When we had last talked in the summer, I asked whether his lawyers had advised him it was worth a shot to run as soon as he could, as fast as he could, in the direction of the White House, with or against the political winds, on the thinking that prosecutors, worried already about accusations of political persecution, might be spooked by an active presidential campaign. That was before the FBI raid on Mar-a-Lago. Before we knew about the classified material stashed in the basement. The appearance of legal pressure only mounted in the month before he began the new campaign. In the span of twenty-four hours, the January 6 committee announced referrals for criminal charges (obstruction of an official proceeding; conspiracy to defraud the United States; conspiracy to make a false statement and to "incite," "assist," or "aid or comfort" an insurrection), and the House Ways and Means Committee announced it would release six years of his tax returns, information he had fought bitterly to keep private throughout his earlier campaigns and presidency.

"That didn't play into it," the president told me now. He did not like this, either. He would not like most of my areas of inquiry on this phone call. "I did nothing wrong," he said. "I don't know how you get indicted if you've done nothing wrong. I've done nothing wrong." He repeated that phrase, "I've done nothing wrong," nine times in thirty minutes. *I've done nothing wrong. I've done nothing wrong. I've done nothing wrong. I've done nothing wrong. I've done nothing wrong. I've done nothing wrong. I've done nothing wrong. I've done nothing wrong. I've done nothing wrong.*

———

At a studio in Sun Valley, Marissa Ysagurre builds interior and exterior lives at doll and miniature scale using a wide range of materials that represent the waste and excess of the modern world: pulverized egg cartons, delivery boxes from the digital everything-company, bones of birdhouses discarded on the side of the road, and little gold bricks and micro-weapons from foreign marketplaces. She makes intricate glass and manicured grass and scenes of war and murder. There is a drug ring behind a day care front, a botanica with an apothecary downstairs and human skulls on an altar upstairs, and a perfect suburban idyll that warehouses enough firearms to wage an anarchic rebellion.

Ysagurre waved me inside an installation. "You can come on in and look," she said. It was a treehouse on the outside, a war room on the inside, and in totality a theater in which a tale of obsession unfolded. Where fear intersects with technology, madness may flourish. Ysagurre constructed the treetop surveillance headquarters for a character named Remi, who tracks the movements of her target through footage recorded on spy cameras and projected onto monitors rigged at her command center. The walls inside the treehouse are a mosaic of eighty individual square mirrors, which means the footage of her target is iterated in eighty individual reflected frames that span floor to ceiling. That's eighty individual opportunities for Remi to form new theories or judgments, to clock new details or turn old ones over until they appear new again. Ysagurre took inspiration from Elvis Presley, cooped up inside his gilded Memphis estate. "At Graceland, he had probably three or four security screens," she said, "but because the walls were mirrored, it looked like he had a ton of them."

Remi paces inside this disco ball cage for hours and hours, absorbed in the task of knowing more and better. She finds that the task of knowing more and better becomes a kind of compulsion. She finds, too, that through her gaze she achieves a sense of ownership over her target; in the eye of the beholder. It is right there in that word, *beholder*, this idea that what comes into our field of vision comes also into our possession.

Genesis

When God returns to Eden and demands to know if Adam has eaten the forbidden fruit, Adam does not hesitate: He sells Eve out. "The woman whom thou gavest to be with me, she gave me of the tree, and I did eat."

Adam was a rat.

An antelope can become a lion—but only by being devoured.

—Bishop Robert Barron

From the start, it had been about trust. Of most matters between most people, this much is true, but rarely is the pact made so explicit as our circumstances demanded. "You'll need to be brave," he told me. Here, I did not yet think of him as the Politician. Here, my allegedly foundational and resolute skepticism was, suddenly and resolutely, suspended. Clichés were offered and accepted. "I would die before I hurt you," he said.

Now in daylight, in motion, it is all right. In darkness, in stillness, I am in trouble. As the coyote, my heart makes itself heard. As the coyote, it cries. For days, I do not sleep. When I sleep, I do not dream. I never know what day it is, what time it is. I listen to the sea. To the coyotes. To the owl. I wonder about his eyes. They might be orange if he hunts at dusk or dawn. Brown like mine if he hunts at night. The darker an owl's eyes, the greater his capacity to absorb light. I wish upon this data point.

The sun rises. It is always doing that.

The arrival of a new day startles me to awe the infinite grace of a Creator who sends up the sun to provide a chance for us to see the truth, to speak its name, and when it sets on our failures, He does not call the whole thing off but forgives us time to restore ourselves and then calls for another take.

On set, David Lynch holds a bullhorn. When he speaks, he is cheerful and clear.

"Okay, let's try that again," he says. "This time, good."

From the grass I look east, where two mourning doves sit on the fence past the lemons near the pomegranate trees. One piece of fruit, low on a branch, cut open by a single bite, guts of seeds spilling onto the earth where a new tree will sprout, where old desires will grow, where the sinner will feast in starlight and flee by daybreak, belly a sack of jewels, teeth daggers of stained glass, mouth an open wound bloodied by hunger.

East and back, I consider the pomegranate that wrought curse in Eden. The unoriginal story, in which seduction is a means to subduct and no gift not given by God is without cost for its recipient. An early arrival on the Eastern Mediterranean and to myth, the idiosyncratic fruit from which a dose of six seeds bound Persephone to Hades in the underworld long before Egyptians planted apple orchards along the Nile Delta or Romans brought apple seeds to the British Isles.

I have never liked pomegranates and so I wrote of apples. It was a silly poem, as most poems are, and though I felt tempted to perfect it, to make of it something impressive, I left it alone. There was a purity in its elementary expression that I liked. It was in some sense a greater striptease than any I had performed, leaving me much more naked than I had ever been before him or anyone.

For a long time, I did not show him. Not until he shared his poem, in the same language of innocence. Nothing really to be perfected.

I was at the Bowery some months later, and it was very late, and he was eating this big green apple. Deeper into the night, when he threaded floss between his teeth, he excavated a shard of fruit.

From the moment the Politician began his pursuit of office it had been a collision of conspiracy and error that made it so that he could not win, could not come even close. He knew that for a long while. In an easy, sweet manner he acknowledged it.

I liked the way his resignation did not veer into bitterness or defeat. I liked the way he was able to laugh about what was going wrong at any given moment, and at the fact that at any given moment, something was going wrong. I liked the way he carried on with his task anyhow, even as he wished that it was already over. He counted down the days, in a literal sense, reminding me specifically how much time we had left until he was free, but he did not discount outright the days that remained. I thought this was honorable.

Late in the summer, the Politician spent many of those remaining days in court, where he was fighting efforts to exclude him from state ballots, and when he emerged it was often to new bad news, and he would absorb and analyze this as he retreated to a drab hotel room, updating me as he got undressed.

He exited court one afternoon to find that his own vice presidential nominee had gone rogue, announcing in an interview that the campaign was weighing whether to cease operations so that the Politician could endorse the president. The Politician laughed as he told me about this. His feud with the woman funding the campaign and with whom he shared a ticket had become a more frequent drama. On a recent call she had berated him, he said, "screaming like a banshee." She was "a piece of work," he added, shaking his head. He said he had been warned about her by the South African tech billionaire with whom she had reportedly had a drug-fueled sexual encounter while she was married to a different tech billionaire, but by the time he received the call that informed him she was "crazy," it was too late. The deal was already done. Now her antics had the effect of forcing his hand, compelling him to make a public decision about whether to remain a candidate when he was not yet prepared to do so even privately.

There was pressure from every direction, from everyone in his life. He asked me what he should do. I did not think it my place to offer prescriptive advice as it related to most things, nor did I think that I knew for sure what he ought to do anyway. I did know about the president, though, and I did know what it was to engage with him, had seen over the years over many episodes what it looked like when someone was able to bend his peculiar ways to their will, or what it looked like when someone tried to do that and failed, and I did know what the outcomes of any deal with this devil were likely to be.

I approached his dilemma Socratically. Mostly that is what I do, ask questions and listen. Mostly that is what I am good at. "How do you feel when you visualize standing onstage and endorsing the Democrat?" I asked. "Nauseous," he said. "How do you feel when you visualize standing onstage and endorsing the Republican?" I asked. "Nauseous," he said. He laughed, but he wore a pained expression. I had not before now observed him like this, so unsure of himself and so worried. He was exhausted, and he threw himself onto the bed, his pink shirt unbuttoned, revealing my favorite parts of his chest, and his blue tie still tied loose around his neck.

As he saw it, if he stayed in the race, he might forfeit his only chance to address through policy what he had sought for many years to address through activism. The value of his endorsement was high only when it meant he would abdicate his place at the head of a political movement, neutralize himself as an electoral threat, and encourage his disciples to follow him to the camp of another candidate. He could not see the campaign through and hope to negotiate for influence with the victor. The time to negotiate was now.

Still, he wondered if it would be a mistake to walk away from the contest. It was just anecdotal, he said, and there existed not one statistic that suggested it was more than that, but if he were to judge enthusiasm on the number of people who approached him in any given airport, he would have to conclude that he was a contender. I laughed. When he called from airports, it was true, our conversation was reliably interrupted by his fans. It was just anecdotal, I said, but I did see literal signs of support for him all over the country, in numbers that seemed to match or exceed the displays of enthusiasm that I saw for the other candidates. We both shrugged. It was impossible to know what value to assign to such phenomena.

He knew that he could not make a proper assessment on the basis of anecdote. Just as he knew that if he endorsed the Democrat, the Democrats still would not accept or entertain him. They had no interest in his ideas and saw no value in appealing to his followers. They would not even meet with him. He knew, too, that if he endorsed the Republican, there would be political and social consequences, and more than that, there would be personal consequences. He did not have support privately, he said, and he worried about hurting those he loved through his political choices. Yet he understood that this option seemed the surest way to maximize his influence.

I laid out the various ways it might go, based on my observations of the ways it tended to go. The president might not keep his word, might go back on any deal that was struck; a version of this had already happened the last time the Politician had attempted to work with the president. Or the president might condemn him to a purgatory in which he served essentially as a figurehead. Or the president might axe him the second something seemed to go wrong, or axe him in order to deflect from something unrelated that had gone wrong; this kind of humiliation had been the standard fate of many officials in the first administration. Then of course there was the scenario, and it was always likely, in which things really did go wrong, in which the Politician was consumed in any of the possible calamities that might erupt, as calamities always seemed to erupt in Donald Trump's Washington. You could prepare only so much for this variety of known unknown. Those were the downside risks to factor in.

Still, the same uncertain environment, the same spirit of chaos, also presented an opportunity: Those who could abide the ridicule inherent to associating with the president would have the chance to benefit from his uncommon openness and suggestibility. I cited the example of Kim Kardashian. In the first administration, she had managed to lobby the president successfully to commute the sentence of a woman serving a lifelong prison term for a nonviolent drug offense and to sign into law criminal justice reform legislation called the First Step Act. For her willingness to appear foolish standing alongside the president, a kind of courage, she had wrought genuine good for others.

There were political considerations, too, and we talked these through. The Politician was not delusional about the realities of his political present or political future. His experience in the current campaign had confirmed for him that the American system would not allow for a presidential candidate to succeed with a third party. Of 2028, he said, "I'd have to do it as a Republican." He was also clear-eyed about the president himself. "I always thought of him as a novel: hundreds of lies that amount to one big truth," he told me. As someone whose job was to bear witness to the president and explain what I had seen to others, and who had devoted many thousands of words over many years to doing so, this concise description struck me as about perfect. As a writer I was almost jealous—and I loved that.

The Politician felt that no matter what he did, it would be in some way wrong. He was preoccupied with what he was sure would be personal fallout from his decision. He did not want to be a source of unhappiness for anyone. This factor tormented him and made it so he could not think clearly about his dilemma. I asked him to turn his focus outward, to think about what it meant for people to support him, to donate their money or time or faith. What they were communicating was their belief that they could trust him, more than any other candidate, to make decisions that would affect them, and implicit in that communication was the belief that he was committed to acting selflessly, that he would put their interests before any other factor.

It was his responsibility to try his best to live up to their belief, to treat his every decision as a candidate, even if the decision was to end his candidacy, as a presidential decision, made in the manner of a public servant, with all personal concerns—about backlash in Hollywood and related friction in his private life—pushed aside in favor of the central concern of what would be best for the country. I was sure he could do that, I said, because I trusted him that much. He started to cry. "I wish I could just be with you," he said.

Now they were my tears.

Late in the day on a Friday in September, I was in a conference room in Lower Manhattan with the man for whom I worked. I had been published by the magazine since I was twenty years old and since 2017 I had served as the first Washington correspondent in its fifty-year history. It was an off week for the publication, which meant there was no magazine going to print, which meant the office, a soulless place in a bad location with bad light to begin with, contained virtually no souls at all. Just me and the man for whom I worked. That afternoon, I had run into a friend, another writer from the magazine, in the lobby of the Standard on Washington Street. I mentioned the meeting. "The office?" the writer said, puzzled. "At five o'clock on a Friday?" Nothing about this seemed amiss to me.

The man for whom I worked had seen me pass through earlier in the week on my way to film promotional materials for a story about the president that I had written for the cover of the latest issue of the magazine, out that week on what few newsstands still existed. This was a rare occurrence, my presence in the office. I was most often on the road or in Washington and when I was back in New York I seldom showed up there. It was quiet and siloed, more like a sterile tech startup than a newsroom, and my walk-on guest-star status made it so that my time there was consumed distracting and being distracted by colleagues. I did not find the office conducive to the solitary tasks of reporting or writing.

In retrospect I came to think the man for whom I worked had looked at me in a strange way when he saw me and waved from down the hall, but then he had a strange way about him, a hard-to-read quality that I quite liked, actually, and so I did not read into it. "How long are you in town?" he had asked me. It made sense that he would suggest we find a time to catch up, and it made sense that the time available was at the end of a workday. I did not read into this, either. He was busy and I was busy. I thought nothing of it.

Then, around the conference table in the empty office that Friday, the man for whom I worked meandered unsteadily from small talk to the subject of what he called *the rumors*.

I never feared bosses because I never had cause to fear them. I was often late on deadline and I filed provocative expense reports, but no one complained. I was an improbable success in the straight world, named to all the silly lists that connote mainstream status and valorize youthful achievement, celebrated for work that brought accolades and attention to the organization; I was, on balance, good for business. If anything, bosses seemed to fear me, feared that I would leave, always asked if there was anything they could do to make me happier. I saw the indifference or disrespect with which other writers were regarded; to say I received special treatment would be an understatement. It had not once occurred to me that this meeting might be some sort of trap. It had not occurred that the man for whom I worked might know anything about my relationship with the Politician. It did not occur even when he first raised this subject of rumors unspecified.

"Rumors?" I asked.

My best guess as to what he meant by *rumors* were my recent disagreements with the creative director about which she had berated me and a collaborator days prior. As the man for whom I worked stammered, I began to formulate a response in my mind. I believed I was right on the substance of the disagreements and I knew I was right as it related to my conduct; I was calm in the face of outbursts from the creative director. I had never even made a disrespectful remark as she snapped at me. The task I saw before me in the conference room would be tricky to navigate: How to defend myself to the man for whom I worked without smearing her?

I loved working with the creative director. I thought she was a genius. On a personal level, I could take her temper. In a way I was just happy that there were still people in this dying trade who cared enough about the work to erupt in rage over it. But it was not acceptable, in my view, for her to behave that way toward contracted artists and others with no confidence that they could stand up for themselves without professional repercussions, and I had told her so in as diplomatic a manner as possible. How else was I supposed to navigate a woman shouting about chains of command and agents in Paris and various perceived threats to her successful dictatorship?

As I thought this over in silence and with some degree of anxiety, the man for whom I worked arrived at the words he had been searching for. He began to explain *the rumors*. The creative director did not factor in at all. That was the first surprise.

The second surprise was what he said next: "Rumors—" and said this now, *rumors*, with extra vowels, beyond the British spelling, like he was set to slo-mo, like he did not want to reach the end of the word. I did not register his hesitation as dread over the words that would come next. All I remember is that I squinted at him in utter confusion as he continued on: "—about you and [the Politician]."

He had received the information from a woman who had mentored me, who had been a mother to me when my mother died, whose baby I had sung to sleep. I would only learn that later. How she received the information would become clear to me later, too.

His face was red. As he spoke, he appeared to brace for each syllable to hit him with an electric shock. His eyes were fixed on my face. I wondered if it was red, too. He did not appear to blink. He did not appear to breathe. As though he might miss some crucial tell in my expression were he to engage in the processes of being and staying alive.

As he went on, I had the thought that I had never before lied to him, had never before lied in a professional context, and I did not quite know how to do so. I had the thought, too, that insistence on truth is what I found so attractive about the profession to start with. My childhood was an exercise in the daily management of fiction, in the upkeep of lies for survival, in the introduction of new lies to prop up existing lies or paper over lies that could no longer be maintained. I found there was a kind of paradise within the privacy of a lie. I found the paradise was at turns a prison. The work I did was an escape from these dynamics; it was the one place where I could never lie and where I could never abide someone lying to me. Even when the work was complicated, this was always clear.

In the conference room, the threshold of this pristine territory was breached. I breached it. Reflexively and repeatedly, I denied the allegation. Yet I could see on his red face that the man for whom I worked did not believe me. Still, I lied. He offered details that suggested he had reviewed some of my communications with the Politician. I kept lying. Then he presented an ultimatum: Tell the truth and we could "find a way forward" in which the fact of the relationship could be contained. Continue to lie and corporate leadership would decide how to proceed and there was no telling what they would do or how they might do it.

The nascent ethics and optics crises were intertwined; because the Politician was now associated with the president this meant that by the laws of communications I was feared associated with the president. My critical reporting on the incumbent president, who had been the Democratic candidate until he was swapped in the summer for his younger vice president, "made things more difficult," as it was articulated to me around a different downtown conference table a few days later, in a meeting attended by a small group of senior officials from the magazine and the in-house public relations executive, because already I was deemed adversarial to the liberal establishment of which the liberal media institution for whom I worked was part.

In 2019, I had documented "concerns, explicit or implicit, about his ability to stay agile and alive for four more years." I observed then that watching him on the campaign trail "can feel like being at the rodeo. You are there because on some level you know you might see someone get killed." More recently, in the period just before he was replaced as the candidate, I had written about the conspiracy of silence among his supporters on the subject of those old worries, which persisted with new urgency as he sought reelection. I reported that he was cocooned within layers of bureaucracy and disengaged from his responsibilities as the chief executive of the country. And I reported what I had been told by high-level actors within the Democratic Party about his apparent memory loss and more general waning cognizance.

In January, I began hearing similar stories from Democratic officials, activists, and donors. All people who supported the president and were working to help reelect him to a second term in office. Following encounters with the president, they had arrived at the same concern: Could he really do this for another four years? Could he even make it to Election Day?

Uniformly, these people were of a similar social strata. They lived and socialized in Washington, New York, and Los Angeles. They did not wish to come forward with their stories. They did not want to blow a whistle. They wished that they could whistle past what they knew and emerge in November victorious and relieved, having helped avoid another four years of Trump. What would happen after that? They couldn't think that far ahead. Their worries were more immediate.

When they discussed what they knew, what they had seen, what they had heard, they literally whispered. They were scared and horrified. But they were also burdened. They needed to talk about it (though not on the record). They needed to know that they were not alone and not crazy. Things were bad, and they knew things were bad, and they knew others must also know things were bad, and yet they would need to pretend, outwardly, that things were fine. The president was fine. The election would be fine. They would be fine. To admit otherwise would mean jeopardizing the future of the country and, well, nobody wanted to be responsible personally or socially for that. Their disclosures often followed innocent questions: *Have you seen the president lately? How does he seem?* Often, they would answer with only silence, their eyes widening cartoonishly, their heads shaking back and forth. Or with disapproving sounds: "Phhhh-wwwaahhh." "Uggghhhhhhhh." "Bbbwwhhheeuuw." Or with a simple "*Not* good! *Not* good!" Or with an accusatory question of their own: "Have *you* seen him?!"

Never mind that what I had reported was accurate, and never mind that I had been adversarial to the president, too, that I had warred with his White House and had been subject to his personal insults for my critical coverage of his campaigns and administration. "The Fake & Corrupt News is only getting worse!" he said in one statement. "The reporter was a shaky & unattractive wack job, known as 'tough' but dumb as a rock, who actually wrote a decent story about me a long time ago. Her name, Olivia Nuzzi. Anyway, the story was Fake News, her 'anonymous sources' don't exist (true with many writers), and I'm happily fighting hard for our GREAT USA!"

I was on a flight to Eleuthera when he issued the remark. I remember how I stared at the words and absorbed his distinct oddball and sort of brilliant-in-its-way syntax. And I remember how I turned from my screen to peer out the window, and how I felt the way I felt when officials in his White House would drag me into their displays of dishonorable behavior, how it was an embarrassment to be involved in such dishonor even when you were just its target or audience, like how being groped is an embarrassment even when you know on an intellectual level that the only party with cause for embarrassment is the one who has committed the offense. And I remember that I thought how strange it was, that a bitchy little insult such as this should be entered into the official record, that for the rest of our documented history it would be the case that the president of the United States had at one time called me "dumb as a rock" and "shaky & unattractive." And I remember I had the thought that it was stranger, still, that the president of the United States had called me both beautiful and unattractive.

I was met with shrugs when I pointed this out. I was met with narrow stares when I insisted that the Politician and I were not sleeping together. We had been careful, I said, words that rose to the level of satire given the context in which they were spoken. "It doesn't make a difference," the man for whom I worked said. We were not dealing with the world as it was but the world as it appeared. Media is a business and I had jeopardized this one. I could not fault anyone else. No amount of goodwill or history of good work or technicalities that made some sort of minor plea of innocence within the big verdict of guilt or context about the circumstances by which the information, *the rumor*, was now stalking me like a drone about to strike could change the fact that the facts were bad and they looked even worse.

Containment lasted about three business days. Once the calls from the press regarding an "anonymous tip" about the Washington correspondent and the Politician began, the pretense of intertwined fates and collaboration between corporation and employee collapsed.

The man for whom I worked was by then in Milan for Fashion Week. He managed his organizational, reputational, and literal mistresses over spotty service at the Fendi show. He called and told me that the man I did not marry had asked to speak with him and that he planned to do so. I protested. Even before I had been confronted over *the rumors* in that Friday meeting, the legal department and my direct supervisor had been informed of my belief that the man I did not marry had intruded on my digital privacy and that the security breach had bled harassment into my work. I asked the man for whom I worked to reconsider his decision to speak to the man I did not marry. I did not have the words to articulate the depth of this violation. In my mind I saw myself pressed against a door I had managed to swing shut in the nick of time. I saw, too, the man for whom I worked as he ambled over to the side entrance and invited my attacker in. I was trying to escape him, I thought I had escaped him, and now he was in everything. About this, the man for whom I worked was defiant. "Olivia, I'm a journalist," he said.

"That has been the hardest thing for me in my job," he later told *Interview* magazine. "Every day in Milan and for most of that week, the story hadn't yet broken, and navigating that was so stressful . . . Once I knew that she had had that relationship, it was clear that we would have to disclose it to our readers, and how we did that was an incredibly difficult process to get through. But I knew where we had to land."

It was determined that there was only one way for me to survive such a public relations crisis: *Tell all*. Spare no detail, spare my job and my life as it was. That was the offer on the table: "You could write your way out of it," the man for whom I worked told me. I did not consider this.

When your privacy is violated, there emerges the expectation that you must respond by further violating it. I thought of that phrase, *Tell all*, often over the months that followed. Tell what, exactly? Tell why, exactly?

What occurred in private was supposed to be private, and it had not been my choice that it ceased to remain so, nor that a corporate media outfit with a political reputation to uphold had been spooked into participating in what I considered a siege of hyper-domestic terror, and through their actions would help to transform that terror into a public harassment campaign.

The Politician had been, briefly, my subject. We had argued about the story I wrote on the topic of his campaign; he hated it. Then, well, we had stopped arguing. He had not been my source. He was not, for the most part, plugged into the kind of information that I required access to for my work. Had he been, would I have relied on him for intelligence? Maybe I would have; there is no way for me to know now. As it was, I considered the circumstances a misfortune. In his dramatic style, he called the circumstances "heartbreaking." On the level of what seemed within control, it had not required much effort to avoid his presence interfering with my work once we "crossed the line," as he referred to it, since his campaign was not of considerable mainstream interest in the election until its very end.

When it emerged that our summer visits to meet the president at Mar-a-Lago might overlap, I proceeded with caution. I knew the president liked to stack his meetings and introduce his guests on their way in and out of his presence; this allowed him to demonstrate his importance and, just as important as his established importance, provided for him the components crucial to continuously affirm that importance: new cast members with whom to perform and a new audience for whom to perform. He was always producing the show. The risk of being dragged into such a production alongside the Politician was high. The risk within that risk was even higher.

"We cannot be there at the same time," I told the Politician. He laughed. He did not see the big deal. "I think it would be fun," he said. I shut my eyes tightly, as if it might un-reveal the revelation that he did not appreciate how sophisticated an animal he was dealing with. The president was more adept at reading people and dynamics than was possible to understand at a distance. He conducted and processed all human energy around him; the man who appeared among earth's least sensitive was hypersensitive to the primal *Homo sapien* frequency imperceptible to those tuned only to the modern social din. What he determined to do with the information he downloaded left the impression that his was a variety of egocentrism unconcerned with others; he was, in fact, very concerned with others, needed others more than he needed anything, could not perform the work he performed, which was the work of performing, without access to others. I had seen it, had studied it, was sure that his powers ought not be underestimated. My concern was educated. With one scan, he might clock our energy with total precision. This was not the sort of information I wanted the president to have. It was not the sort of information the Politician should have wanted the president to have.

He might at least clock enough data to wonder, and when the president wondered, he wondered aloud. This was not the sort of question that I wanted the president to raise with the sorts of whoever-is-near people to whom he might raise questions, which would catapult the question to the status of rumor. This was not the sort of question the Politician should have wanted the president to raise with the sorts of whoever-is-near people to whom he might raise questions. "I need to make sure we're not there at the same time," I told the Politician. "I'm serious." *Did he take me seriously?* I had little cause to consider the question before now. The meetings, for my story and his endorsement, were scheduled one day apart, a stroke of dumb luck, emphasis on the former, and a resource dwindling scarcer by the second. The Politician maneuvered to keep his presence at the estate quiet. A few miles away, I met our mutual friend for lunch, and when the friend asked if I had heard anything that might confirm what a source had related, that the Politician was in town to resume his negotiations with the president, I lied for him. It would not be the last time.

I had planned to go to Arizona with the president for his rally there. Around the same time, the Politician planned to end his campaign in California. Then logistics scrambled. The Politician planned instead to go to Arizona with the president, too, and offer his endorsement there. It was lonely, the choice he made. I assessed it at a critical remove, not to form judgment but to find reason. I could see how he had come to see it, that the chance for any good was worth guilt by association with what was bad. I did not assess how his associations could complicate mine. An event in which the Politician featured in a serious way, in which it would not be possible for me to omit him at serious scale from coverage, was a new and serious problem.

"Baby, it's okay," the Politician said. Plans had shifted fast and details remained unsorted. He could offer assurance that it would be fine but no absolutes about what aspects of set and setting would form what I might interpret as solace. Yet his own anxiety was so easily activated that I found his calm registered with special authority. When he was not worried, even about developments that seemed an occasion for both of us to worry, I was not worried. "You should come," he said.

I had wanted to be there for my work and I wanted now to be there for him. I could not convince myself that what I wanted now was consonant with what I wanted beyond there, beyond the confines of an auditorium in Phoenix. We had survived to the end of his campaign without trouble, but it was not yet over, and my presence in the final hour would increase risk for both of us.

Distracted writing his speech on the eve of the event, he asked, "You'll be there?" More than I wanted to be there, for him, I wanted to be there for him, and to be there for him, I concluded, meant I should not be there. I did not want to interrupt his focus on something so big with something so small. "I still haven't decided," I said.

The Politician exited the stage. I told him I was proud of him—and I was. I was not proud of him because I agreed with his decision; I did not think about it that way, in terms of agreement or disagreement. I was proud of him because I believed he believed the decision was the best means to be of service to others, and I was proud of him for doing what he believed was right even though it had been hard. "Where are you?" he asked. I was still in New York, I said. We could just see each other there.

The Politician endured dinner with his skeleton campaign staff and then slipped away to his hotel room, validated by something he had not quite expected from the experience of the rally. "That was, like, electrifying," he told me. He was awed by the sight of the crowd, by their energy, by the way he absorbed their energy. "There were so many people," he said. "It was . . ." He paused, shook his head, and smiled. "Wow," he said. He looked practically lit from within. After all that time in the wilderness, he had found warmth. He did not want to be cold again.

This presented a complication, but one I believed I could manage. In the end it managed me. Still, I never did think of him, not until much later, and then for reasons that came as a shock, as a politician. I have known in my life many candidates for office; he was not that, even as he was, literally, that.

Tell all. There is what people tell you and there is what they want you to understand about what they cannot tell you. I could tell you the facts. I could tell you the truth. I could tell you that where facts end truth begins. I could tell you, probably, nothing that you would like. I could tell you, almost certainly, nothing that would redeem me. I could tell you that the year flew in birds. And I could tell you that the year flew in bullets.

———

When I was little, I had a parrot who bit everyone but me. He loved me because I dared tickle him under his wings. Everyone said, "How can you love that awful parrot?" I thought, "He's adorable, but I don't want others to know." It was my secret.

—Jane Birkin

———

The Politician was working on a raven. "How do you work on a raven?" I asked. Every morning, he said, he would step outside and throw a treat into the air, and every week, the raven would fly less skeptical. "The raven gets closer as she gains more trust in me and confidence in our relationship," he told me. It worked this way, according to his plan. "I want to get her to eat from my hand. I want to hear her croak. I want to see her cock her head and hold her gaze and admire her glistening feathers at close range," he said. "I can't tell her my intentions."

He always named ravens for Edgar Allan Poe, and so we named her Lenore and we named her mate Charley. Soon they had babies, and one of the babies had a deformity on his beak. "In my mind I call him Pinocchio," he said. He called me his baby bird, babydoll, babylove. He was boyish beneath his gruff exterior just as I was girlish beneath my icy exterior. Seldom did I permit anyone to see that, but he had over time earned my total trust, as he intended.

In New Hampshire in the spring, I arrived at the radio station to find a bank swallow, head tucked gracefully, wings outstretched, dead on the doorstep in the shape of a crucifix. I was there to film an interview with the governor. I waved the crew over to look. I could think of nothing else. This soft little life in the freeze of death. The governor stepped to the door and I pointed to the bird at his feet. He shrugged. I disliked him instantly.

A few moments later, the bird was gone. The governor flashed a grim smile. "What bird?" he said, his tone mock-conspiratorial. "We had someone take care of it." I was reminded that I hate politicians.

There was a time when this particular sort of bit, in which the politician plays politician, would have landed with me as a clever meta commentary on the whole enterprise, would have made me think the politician in question, smart enough to assume a wry posture, was an improvement on the less self-aware or more earnest types. Here was a politician who at least could appeal on the level of cynicism.

I thought back to Iowa, a few years earlier. In the town of Clear

Lake, where Buddy Holly crashed and the music died, I sat with Taffy Brodesser-Akner near the stage at an event called Wing Ding. It was the summer before the caucuses, and candidates were arriving as livestock to barns and halls across the state to speak as the professional voters, which the active voting populations in early voting states seemed to be, eyed them critically over dinners of pork and corn and other local fare upon which industry and the politicians who require the support of industry depend.

Here is what Taffy wrote in *The New York Times Magazine*:

At the Wing Ding, I heard all the candidates talking about their Democratic ideals, about being "the party of the working class," of not being "afraid of equal rights" and overcoming "darkness with our light" and about how no matter who you are in America, "you ought to have a chance to build a secure future."

It was easy to get carried away. I clapped along with the voters of Iowa, all of them sitting and willing to listen to anyone who might have a good idea. A political reporter sitting next to me said, "Taffy," and put her hands over mine to stop my applause. But when she looked at me to scold me, she saw that I was crying. "Dear God," she said. I knew it was untenable for everyone to get to see this up close, to understand that there is something strong that is still intact in our democracy—that devotion to these ideals is a kind of love.

I was the "political reporter" who leapt on the grenade of her clapping hands. Since then I had tired of cynicism. I had tired of the glorification of emptiness. I no longer thought it useful, no longer felt that I needed to fabricate a barrier between human events I witnessed and human feelings about those events.

I was moved by the sight of the swallow, by how dignified her final pose had been, and because I figured whoever had taken care of the optics problem posed by her body had not taken care in her burial, the governor repelled me.

From Concord I drove back to New York, where I was meeting with witnesses for the president's ongoing criminal trial. Mostly I was trying to keep the year straight. A lot falls away as power installs. In new context, people take on new shape, new meaning. It is hard to explain what it was at the start, where you came from, who you were.

In the Hudson River, the body of a turkey bobbed near the dock. All walnut feathers and candy-red neck. I thought of his journey for the rest of the day. Later, a central witness, the president's former fixer, would err himself viral when he became enraged that his head was stuck in the image of a turkey on his screen.

In Kona, I fed hemp seeds to the yellow-billed cardinals. I envied them of their weightless flight. I was there on the Big Island in the sunshine when the president survived, when he was clipped on the ear by that which could not kill him, when the blood ran down his face. At that moment I thought of many things, many of them serious, but one thought of dubious relevance that I could not keep from intruding was the way he talked about birds.

For years, the president claimed that wind turbines were a primary predator of avian creatures. They are not, but he was insistent. Somewhere between 140,000 and 328,000 birds die each year from collisions with wind turbines, while an estimated 2.4 billion are killed by cats and hundreds of millions by collisions with man-made structures such as skyscrapers.

"Wind turbines threaten the migration of birds," the president said once. "The Chinese are illegally dumping bird-killing wind turbines on our shores." In response, the American Wind Energy Association told me, "We have no idea what he's talking about with China dumping turbines. He is likely confusing them with solar panels."

His hatred for turbines seemed really to be about his love of valuable oceanfront real estate; his property in Scotland had faced existential-aesthetic threat when it was proposed that a grove of turbines, termed a wind farm, be planted within view of his golf course. The president called the devices "wing bangers," which he said was, "the name given to wind turbines by bird lovers for the thousands of birds they kill in the U.S." The spokesman for National Wind Watch, an anti–wind turbine activist group, told me, "That's the first time I've seen the term." The term offended the spokesman's sensibilities. "It's awfully clunky," he said. The name activists do use, "bird Cuisinarts" or "Cuisinarts of the sky," has the effect of being less clunky and more precise.

Back on the mainland, I needed to be alone, to drive through the desert alone. I never thought much about Marilyn Monroe, but I often thought of something she said: "I restore myself when I'm alone." I needed to be alone because I needed to think about the shooting in Butler, Pennsylvania, to figure out how I thought about it, and I needed to think about that in the context in which I felt most myself and most American, which is alone in a car winding through our highways. And I needed to be alone because I needed to leave.

For more than a year, I knew this, but I do not make big changes fast or without deliberation. My mother told me that I never crawled, that I watched the movements of other people, my head turning to track legs and feet as they plotted across the ground, and then one day, after it seemed I had thought about it enough, I just walked. I resented the drain of psychic energy that this step through my life required. I

140

resented the space it demanded in my mind when I had so much else I wanted to think about, so much that seemed, because it was, more important. I resented that I had devoted so much to making a relationship work, yet I had not stopped to wonder if it should work, if it was working in service to any kind of good, if something that requires so much to work could really be considered something *that works*.

It worked for a while to drive away from the problem. I like to drive through the country. Ten years earlier, on assignment in Las Vegas with a presidential candidate, I looked out the window of my suite at the Wynn to the Sierra Nevadas and realized that I could not breathe. I was late already for an event at the Peppermill, and I was not ordinarily given to panic, but I could not breathe. I could always see the water. I had never before been landlocked. On the floor of the suite I looked up through the window where across the strip a big golden tower sprouted from the dry earth. There was a name scrawled across the top floors: TRUMP. Curled in a ball beneath this expression of the president, I resolved to get it together, to become a citizen of my country, which is when I began driving everywhere.

I found that much was lost dipping in and out of airports while covering an election. Traveling that way, I missed a lot, would not know for instance where gas was expensive and where it was cheaper, would not see the truck driver buying the lotto tickets, or the waitress stacking tips at the end of the night and, upon placing the last bill at the top of the pile, exclaiming that she now had enough, factoring in tax, to get her daughter a computer, would not hear the shouting over the chess game in the park, or the bell as it tolled, would not get sick from the smell of the oil fields, would not notice just how many lawn signs from the last election were cut up or spray-painted or otherwise marred to remove the name of the former vice president whom the president's supporters now considered Judas, and would miss just how few signs were staked in the dirt anyplace to express support for the Democratic candidates.

It was summer and I set out around midnight from Los Angeles. I made it to Vegas by 4 a.m. I caught the sunrise in Virgin River Canyon. In Utah, a bird of prey circled overhead, the only other creature in the whole expanse. The Politician, on his way to the Republican National Convention to attempt to broker a deal with the president, said he thought it was a golden hawk, though he could not quite tell.

In Nebraska, a bird fell out of the sky and smacked my windshield, terrifying me and the artist Isabelle Brourman, whom I had picked up in Colorado for the drive through the heartland. We screamed. We were on our way to the Republican National Convention to broker a deal with the campaign: We proposed that Isabelle would paint the president's portrait while I conducted an interview. We figured he would go for it for obvious reasons related to ego and attention and novelty and his twentieth-century attachment to analog media that we also shared. The bird on the windshield was an unusual purplish color. A symptom of bird flu, we later learned. When she collided with the glass, she thumped in such a way that she seemed already dead. She did not bleed. We named her Kali. We said a prayer.

There were more live birds than dead ones, that much was verifiable, but I did note just how many dead ones were showing up. I had not asked God for any signs. A few miles north of the Mason-Dixon Line on Highway 15, the sign read, CHRISTIANS AND POLITICS: WHAT DOES JESUS SAY? CALL 83-FOR-TRUTH.

Due to fear, and in that way, really, due to cowardice, I had stayed too long someplace that was not meant for me, and more and more, I thought of the story of the Maine hermit, the man who walked into the mountains sometime around the explosion at Chernobyl and built for himself a life in the woods, speaking to no one, seeing no one, until some decades later when he was finally caught stealing candy from a camp in the dead of night.

"Do you want to know how you make me feel?" the Politician asked.

When he was a very small boy, he said, maybe four years old, he was in Virginia, at his family estate, a place called Hickory Hill. He was on the back of a horse when the horse suddenly took off running. He remembered how he held on tightly, and how, for an eternity of a few moments, they charged through the woods, him and this horse, until his little neck was caught on something. His body lifted off the horse and he was flung into the air. When he smacked into the earth he broke a bunch of bones. He spent weeks recovering in a hospital, he said, but he could not recover the world in which he did not know what it was to fly so fast. Even now, all this time later, he could think himself onto that horse, could return to those woods, could feel the air as he cut right through it.

He closed his eyes. They are a startling kind of blue. Not blue as the seas but blue as the flame. When he opened them again, he was crying. It was the most free he had ever felt, he said, and he searched for that feeling, for that freedom, for his whole life. He felt that freedom, he said, with me. "That's how," he said. "That's what you feel like."

I told him about my dream of solitude in the woods. Shirtless, as he often was, he showed me Charley and Lenore over his shoulder. "Can I bring them?" he asked. I smiled. He knew by solitude I meant with him.

Into this furnace I ask you now to venture,
You whom I cannot betray.

—Leonard Cohen

People ask me now about anger. About my lack of it. *How? How could I not be enraged?* I think this over. I scan the terrain of my body. My chest, my spine, behind my belly button. I look for pale pulses of idle fury, waiting for the alarm to sound at the trip wire of my veins. There is nothing there. There is nothing there because I loaded a gun. I loaded a gun and set it on my nightstand.

You cannot live in America without thinking about guns, without thinking that one day you might not live anymore in America, and the reason will be a gun. 46,728 lives ended in America in 2023 because of a gun. 27,300 suicides. 17,927 homicides. 604 police shootings. 463 accidents. 434 undetermined. On the 405, a billboard announces that gun injuries are the number one cause of death for American children. You think: *A gun will protect me from guns.* Then you recall the statistic, that a gun in your home doubles your chances of dying by homicide. Still I loaded a gun. I loaded a gun and set it on my nightstand.

I could blame all who reached for it, who fired in my direction, who dove as it fell to the floor, who fought to wrest control of it, who rose to stand over me, who emptied the barrel into the parts of me that seemed still alive. But the violence began with the act that preceded the shots and the struggle. It began when I loaded a gun and set it on my nightstand. I loaded a gun.

"I would take a bullet for you," the Politician said. He always said that. "Please don't say that," I said. I always said that. From his mouth the bullet theoretical launched the bullet possible. I did not like to think about it. About the armed man at his speech. Or the armed man who broke into his home. Or the armed men he paid to guard him from armed men who sought to harm him while the federal government denied his pleas for protection from the security agency whose modern protocols were carved by the same bullets that cut boughs from his family tree and cut the track of the American experiment.

I did not like to think about it just as later I would not like to think about the worm in his brain that other people found so funny. I loved his brain. I hated the idea of an intruder therein. Others thought he was a madman; he was not quite mad the way they thought, but I loved the private ways that he was mad. I loved that he was insatiable in all ways, as if he would swallow up the whole world just to know it better if he could. He made me laugh, but I winced when he joked about the worm. "Baby, don't worry," he said. "It's not a worm." A doctor he trusted had reviewed the scans of his brain obtained by *The New York Times*, he said, and concluded that the shadowy figure was likely not a parasite at all. He sighed. It was too late to interfere with what had already vaulted from the sphere of meme to the sphere of screwy legend, but at least I did not have to worry about the worm that was not a worm in his brain.

In Volcanoes National Park, no cell reception, except just over there, at the top of the slope of rock, for a few seconds. Long enough for the veil of paradise to be pierced by the bullet literal that had flown in Butler right at the president's head.

The Politician left the Midwest for the East Coast. The deal with the president had fallen through. The moon was big and gold and we marveled at this. "I do pay attention to the moon," he told me once. We had been born under the same kind of moon, the January waxing gibbous in Capricorn, 97 percent illumination, thirty-nine years apart. "Do you think this means we're compatible?" he asked me. "I don't know," I said. "Maybe."

Our similarities seemed to excite him. "We have identical tastes and curiosities," he said. I had to agree. Lone wolves, each of us. We were alike in strange ways. We shared common language, common skepticisms, common ideas about what was beautiful, common beliefs about what was valuable. Like me, he loved rock and blues, surrealism and naturalism. Like me, he moved through the world with amused detachment and deep sensitivity, contradictions that worked somehow in concert. He was the only other person I had ever met who could be moved to tears by the sight of something so trivial as a rose. I felt that I understood him and his particular complications and particular darkness. His darkness did not scare me anymore; I saw in his darkness softness. I felt that he understood me the same. At the time I did not interpret this as a manifestation of narcissism, his or mine. I thought it was sweet.

Now he was looking out at the Atlantic and he told me that he was wounded. Something about a boat and his siblings and their contempt for his willingness to entertain the president. It was always something about a boat. Betrayal seemed to manifest through the politics of boats. "I'm not complaining," he said. He was the abandoned boy, abandoned again. He expressed something more like disbelief. I judged his family for their lack of loyalty. Everywhere he was a pariah, everywhere people concerned with themselves told him what to do next and what he had just done wrong and what he was presently doing wrong, and for his willingness to endure suffering to pursue what he believed was right I admired him.

Much later, when I would wonder if it had all been a kind of fraud, I would think of how for most of his life there had been little reward for his independence, and that whatever it yielded was tiny compared to what he could sow if he had instead been agreeable to the establishment with which his name was associated. If his aim was just power or profit or status, there were easier ways. He was so often so honest in such a way that seemed so excessive not just for a candidate for any office but for any person that I assumed that was how he was; I did not think him the kind of man who said things he did not mean. I believed in him and believed him. I took him seriously.

He told me he loved me. The first few times he said this I did not say it back although I knew that I did love him. This occurred as a flash of a thought, suppressed fast. I had been falling asleep, and we were still talking, and the notion intruded, that I could hear the smile in my own voice, that the sound of him made me smile, that the sight of him made me smile, that just the thought of him made me smile, and when he asked if I was tired and I said I was and he said, "Sweet dreams," as he always did, the notion intruded, that l liked very much to fall asleep hearing this, hearing him. This rang an alarm of implication. I sat upright and silenced it. Sometime later, upon learning something that made me laugh, my first thought was that I should tell him, that it would make him laugh, and when it did, I was terrified, terrified first that I was right, and next by what this suggested, a force and depth of affection that felt just below the surface uncontrollable, even if I would not yet admit it to myself; the Politician characterized what he felt as "powerful waves knocking me down," and that description made sense to me. When he read my work or saw me quoted in the press or referenced in a book and told me that he was proud of me, I was concerned that I cared, that it meant anything to me at all, that it was important to me that to him I was not just the way I looked, though we were, both of us, vain, and our shared reverence for physical beauty was, in part, what bonded us. "Did I fall first in love with her mind or her body?" he asked in a poem he wrote me. "Or was it her language or her boldness?"

Then one night I was back at the Bowery and he showed me a photograph of himself as a young man. He was always showing me photographs of himself as a young man, a reminder for himself as much as for me that he had once been young, as well as an expression that he did not appreciate that I liked him just as he was right now, as I knew him, not as he registered as an idea. Here, mounted on the back of a bull, his hair long, his chest bare, a cigarette dangling from his lips. At this sight of him I was overcome with a terrible sadness. I could acknowledge that he was beautiful, but I did not want him. What I wanted was to mother him. To protect him from himself, from the world. What I wanted was to mother him even as mothering him would keep me from ever knowing the man forged from that boy's pain. At the idea of this loss, a ripple from my chest through my fingertips. Pain, great and physical. Pain, like something had been torn right out of me. I would accept this pain, I thought, to spare him pain. I wished that I could do that. A wave of nausea struck and then the flash of the thought again. I could not suppress it this time. *I love him*, I thought. *Oh no. I love him so much.*

Still I did not say it, because in the same way I knew I loved him, I also knew that he was inclined, as I was inclined, to stand on the ledge over the abyss, to go as far as he could and still balance, and then just when it seemed he might fall, to run back over the hill, heart racing, to stable ground. I did not say it back when he said it first in passing or as part of goodbye. I said it back only after he said it very intently, as an announcement, as the whole point. "My beautiful girl," he said, "I love you. I really do. I love you." And when he told me he loved me, when he said it easily, when he said it often, or when he began to say it and stopped himself and cried instead, I believed that, too. I took that seriously.

What I did not know to take seriously as it related to me was the language of intoxication and compulsion.

The Politician was hyper-interested in whether I did drugs or took pharmaceuticals or drank alcohol. He loved to discuss drugs, psychedelic trips, all manner of related mind-altered esoterica. He said he was sober now and told me stories about when he was still using, a period that had lasted for more than fifteen years.

I did not really drink, I said, but I liked uppers. I told him that I took Adderall. "My kids take that," he said, "I can't." He lived for a summer with John Phillips and Keith Richards above a pharmacy where they were all strung out on amphetamines, he said. Phillips had purchased the pharmacy in a stroke of junkie entrepreneurial genius.

I credited psilocybin with saving my life after my mother died. I had not intended to utilize the psychedelic compound for therapeutic reasons; it just happened that way, that the grief I had been running from approached while I was on a moderate dose and I found that in such a state I could sit with it. He told me one of his sons processed grief with the assistance of ayahuasca.

The Politician still did some psychedelics for fun, he said. He described how he waited until his wife was not home to go outside and smoke DMT, just as he waited until she was not home to call, or else he would call while locked in the bathroom. "Is that the one with the toad?" I asked. He laughed. "No," he said. DMT, or N,N-dimethyltryptamine, considered among the most potent hallucinogenic drugs, sends users into the stratosphere of ego death and back to earth in fifteen minutes. Psychedelic toad venom was something else. The DMT was laced in cigarettes a friend had given him. "What's it like?" I asked. He thought for a moment and flashed a mischievous smile. With a shrug, he said, "It's your classic psychedelic experience."

The bag of toiletries he traveled with was full of so many prescription pill bottles it seemed to barely zip closed, and the sight of it worried me, though I never asked—or because of that I never asked—what they were all for. I had heard he used another drug and there were rumors it sometimes interfered with his ability to perform the work of campaigning for office. When I raised the subject, he denied it. If he was willing to tell me about the drugs he did consume, like DMT, it did not make sense that he would lie to me about others. His sobriety was a central part of his self-mythologization; because of that, I did not question his definition of *sober*.

When a friend, a young guy he helped through recovery, died in the summer soon after his wedding, the Politician was devastated. I was devastated for him. It was the middle of the night, Father's Day, and he had just landed in Los Angeles. He told me about his friend and about his day campaigning. I was writing when he called and had just calculated, for the purposes of my work, how much longer it was until Election Day. The number was still present in my mind when the Politician volunteered his more precise calculation. "You know what I'm thinking," he said. I felt that I sometimes did.

We tried to be careful when we spoke in writing. "I'm communicating what I really want to say telepathically. Did it work?" I asked once. "Yes. I know what you are thinking. We are aligned," he said. Most of the time it seemed we were. "I love you, Livvy," he wrote. "I love you, [the Politician]," I wrote back. He erased his message. I erased my message. "My heart is bursting," he said.

Among common experiences, we had each lived with the uncommon horror of borderline personalities who self-medicated with alcohol. We knew a volatile state of fear, of fear of fear. That is, at least, what he told me. In the same period, about a hundred miles away from each other, we dodged knives wielded by dark-haired women whose eyes flickered with certain mania, with chemical imbalance and chemical manipulation, with a slippery hold on consensus reality. He told me about how he held a door shut and moved his hands out of the way as the tip of the blade stabbed through the wood. I told him about the high shelf where I would climb to stash the knives out of reach. The diamond at his iris. He had a scar in his eye. The nail through my skin. I had a scar on my arm. "I think it would be so much harder to be the kid in that situation," he said. "I think it would be so much harder to be the father," I said. What I did not say was that he and my father shared a story; I did not want him to think that I saw him as similar to my father, and I believed that I did not, aside from the fact of his hands, which felt rough and honest in a way I recognized and respected, and the less likely fact that with his hands he had shielded his children just as my father shielded his, shielded me, from the same kind of violence. The Politician survived. My father did not.

Before we met, I had heard about the dark-haired woman he later described. In New York, people talked, talked the same way, said the same things when they talked. In New York, everyone seemed to know some piece of the story. The people who talked, who knew pieces, advised me to be careful on assignment. There was, they said, real darkness there. I shrugged. I was in the business of darkness. I walked into darkness. I emerged in light every time. Besides, there existed a campfire economy based on legend related to the Politician's family. Half-truths at best seemed to form the basis for much of it. I was not interested in the genre and did not take anything I heard too seriously.

Real darkness there. I was reminded of the words of caution when

I looked up at him for the first time in the fall of 2023. I found him to be an imposing presence. Tall and broad. He did not cast a shadow; he seemed to be one. We did not make eye contact. He did not say much. He directed me over to his van. I got in.

The nature of the work is that you get in. You get in and you go wherever the subject takes you. In my life, I would not descend the steps to an unfamiliar basement to retrieve a document. I would not follow a man through a corridor to speak confidentially. I would not be alone with a man I did not know, or even most heterosexual men I do know, anywhere; I am a realist about the animal kingdom. In my work, though, I get in and I go, and often the scale of the risk I have assumed does not occur until it would be, if things were to veer dicey, too late. Night fallen, service lost, desolate area accessed. It occurred to me in Mandeville Canyon after the Politician made a jagged turn off his property onto the road. The van smelled of death. There were no seat belts. The mirrors were smashed to pieces. In the back, his dogs went flying. When they barked, the Politician barked back.

He scared me. I liked that. It interested me. To be scared is to be affected. I liked to be affected. I was always in search of that which might affect me. He had my attention. I liked to stare straight at the source of my fear, to convince myself that it had been conquered through my understanding, that fear was a monster and a monster was just a man who could be comprehended to death. This appealed, too, to my ego. Anyone could spar with monsters. Fighting is easy. Who could tame the monster? Who could be open enough to find within the monster something to relate to, to empathize with, to love? I could. I took perverse pride in this. I did not consider its cost to my integrity. I did not consider, in any conscious way, risk.

We talked as we made our way along the trail in the canyon. He thawed. At the summit, I removed my sunglasses and met his stare. It started in that moment, with a change in his eyes. He smiled a deep, soft smile. He was soft with me from then on. I came to believe the darkness was a bruise around this softness. I wanted to believe that.

I knew alcoholics. I had been raised by alcoholics. I did not know other types of addicts in the same way. The Politician told me once, talking about someone else, that all addicts were pathological liars. He was rarely as judgmental as he was about other addicts. I did not think to apply his assessment to him or to our relationship. I did not think to apply it even when he referred to me as an intoxicant.

Like all men but more so, he was a hunter. In a literal sense, he used not a bullet but a bird. It was not about a chase but about a puzzle of logic and skill that amounted to a test of his self-mastery. He was the mouse and the architect of his maze. The giver of his own pleasure and torment. He desired. He desired desiring. He desired being desired. He desired desire itself. I understood this just as I came to understand the range of his kinks and complexes and how they fit within what I thought I understood of his soul.

"My heartache," he told me once. "You give me a deep-seated yearning, gnawing hunger." He wanted, fundamentally. He was restless, anxious, running out the clock that ticked on his ability to control his impulses, in a state of constant interior debate over the nature of imprisonment and liberation. When he held himself captive, he longed to be freed; when he set himself free, he was captive to desire.

"I need everything from you, Livvy," he said. He always said that. Mostly it seemed sweet, earnest. "Everything is yours," I said. I always said that. He told me that he wanted me to have his baby. This seemed earnest, too. We stared at each other and picked out our favorite features. My mouth, my cheekbones. His eyes, the little dimple in his chin. There was no question about his nose, which was assured, the same nose carved into every face in his family. In his fantasies of creation, I wondered if he sought destruction, too. Mine and his. A spark of life, an ember of death. A man rejected by his mother may never transcend the wound, but he can make a girl whom he controls into a mother, and through this confirmation of his power, triumph over the uncontrollable power of her void. A man cannot deny his mortality but he can forge a new beginning to better ignore the end.

He liked to feel as though he had been led to the ledge. He found adrenaline and ecstasy there. He found, also, shame. I attributed much to our shared Catholicism, another common set of ideas and sensibilities. I did not want to be a source of his shame and so I was careful to allow him to lead. When he would set for himself a boundary, I observed it. When he would trample right over the boundary he set, he seemed still in control, a player in a game he invented and in which he wrote and rewrote the rules. He did not come across as vulnerable; he was not merely an adult but a seventy-year-old man who was, even if he seemed on occasion to forget, running for president of the United States.

Ulysses was the subject of one of my favorite Cream songs. Before I knew the Politician, that was all Ulysses was. But the Politician saw himself in legend, heard his own name in the call of sirens, and recognized his fatal curiosity and longing, his self-loathing, in rituals of suffering. In his home in Los Angeles he hung a print of a painting, by John William Waterhouse, in which the sirens surround Ulysses, who is tied to the mast of his ship. According to myth, he wanted to hear their song, and so he instructed his crew to cover their ears and bind him to the mast so he could listen without fear that he would steer them all to ruin. It was the Politician's ten-year wedding anniversary, and as he showed me the painting, I noticed on the table below a photograph of him and his wife, dressed each in suits, backs turned. He noticed it, too. He flipped it over, out of sight.

I would sometimes bristle in silence at what felt like a minor flattening of my being into novelty—into substance, into effect. The very qualities that led him to melodramatic worship led him to blame me for his weakness, transforming me divine and then unholy and then divine again. Both extremes came at the expense of my humanity. I did not like being made to feel as though I was some great temptation that enthralled or terrified him or enthralled him by terrifying him, depending on his mood.

In proclamation or poem, when he said he was *unhinged*, or *going through withdrawals* from me, or *counting how many days* he could go before he cracked and professed again his love, it did not occur for a long while that any of it was meant to be wholly literal, and I did not appreciate for a long while the distinction: He did not tell me he felt unhinged. He told me, "You have made me unhinged." His expression of what he felt was an accusation. He was unhinged and for that I was responsible. "I'm sorry," he said once when I answered the phone. "Sorry?" I asked. He did not, as far as I was aware, have anything to apologize for. "I'm sorry," he said again, "I had to do that for my sanity." I did not understand. "Do what?" I asked. He was frantic as he launched into an explanation for a trivial absence. I cut him off. "You don't have anything to apologize for and you don't need to explain anything," I said. He paused. "Oh," he said. He sounded shocked. I had the thought that women were probably mad at him a lot. Then, as though he could not stop himself, or could not accept that I was not mad at him, he continued on with his explanation. "I want to talk to you more than I want to do anything else, more than I want to do the things I'm supposed to do," he said. "You push me over the edge." *You push me.* He was beyond the edge and for that I was responsible.

When he spoke he would sometimes turn away from me, fix his gaze right or left, and then shake his head toward his shoulder as if he had just emerged from surf with water in his ears. I loved his ears. In certain light I thought they made him look like a big rabbit. At first the head shakes seemed a bit of physical comedy, a goofy dance. I laughed. He did not laugh. It was not a joke. It was a serious effort to shake out the intrusive thoughts inspired by my presence. *Carving deep blue ripples in the tissues of your mind.* The summits and valleys of his patterns first confused me but with time became familiar, predictable, and though I found them compelling, I would not recognize them for what they were until it was too late, until I was already hurt.

My brother is a mountain of a man. Six foot two, football player turned triathlete. Late in the summer he stood in his driveway, American flag billowing behind him, arms crossed. As I began to explain the situation, in which a blade now loomed over my neck, he stopped me. "Wait, wait," he said. He lifted me off the ground and moved me to the grass. He gestured to the security camera above the garage. "I don't know who's listening," he said. I nodded. His attention to OPSEC was better than mine. "Okay, continue," he said. I rushed through the ordeal. He listened, expressionless. Then he stared off for a moment, his face contorting in confusion. He turned slowly back to me. "The guy with the fucked-up voice?" he said. "I like his voice," I said. He turned away and thought for another moment. He turned back to me again. "You don't have any interest in, I dunno, a nice thirty-two-year-old in private equity? I know a lot," he said dryly. He was staring at the sky now, as if he might find some answers there. "It's not daddy issues, right?" he asked. I did not think so. "Yeah, so, I don't know what the problem is," he said. I waved my hands to halt his psychological assessment, not that I could disagree with the imperative. We could deal with that another time, I said. The point of this visit was to brief him on the security crisis that was on the verge of becoming a more general crisis. We had shared a phone plan since we were kids and I did not yet know how exactly my privacy had been breached, whether it was a hard problem or a soft one, whether a device or account had been compromised or if the network had been infiltrated.

Shots rang out. The story of the relationship had broken, the bullet metaphorical. My phone rang again. "I need you to take a bullet for me," the Politician said. "Please."

My mind flashed to where I had been, across town overlooking the Hudson, when he had first vowed to take a bullet for me. "I feel very protective of you," he had said then. Now he said, "If it's just sex, I can survive it." If it was anything more, he could not. The deal he made with the president wrought personal complication; already, his wife had told him she would not be seen with him until after the election. Now she was in Milan reading the news, hysterical, he said. It was fragile, the alliance with the president. Nothing was certain.

Any new problems could upend the whole thing. The Politician had been through divorces before. He knew how fast they could get ugly, how little could be controlled. The election was less than two months away. If the president won, decisions about the new government would follow soon after, and if what had been promised was delivered, congressional hearings would follow after that. Personal drama might spell political peril. He needed to avoid that. He would need my cooperation.

My feelings about such a request aside, I did not think it fair that he would be harmed in what increasingly appeared to be a mad plot to harm me devised by the man I did not marry. I did not want the Politician to be harmed, too. At that moment my feelings were aside. I am good in a crisis. I had trained my entire life in a battlefield of crisis, the peace broker of my childhood home. The settings that enabled me to survive there switched on, and as the twister whirred faster around me, I slowed down, impervious to its force.

The Politician read me a message he sent to the man I did not marry. It was a response, he said, to a threat he had received. In the message the Politician accused the man of violating our privacy and stalking me. He told him if it continued, he would go to the FBI. He then referred to *me* as a stalker. He interrupted the reading of the message to interject a comment. "I'm sorry, I had to say that to exculpate myself," he told me. I had not heard that derivative of the word *exculpatory* before. He was a lawyer by trade. He was supporting what would become his case with written evidence.

I was still pacing around the Upper East Side. I stopped in my tracks. I have never cared for the energies of the East River.

There had been no question in my mind: I knew that I would not interfere with the Politician's efforts to save what he determined he needed to save. I did not protest. I did not see the use. I would do whatever he needed me to do, I told him, but we could not lie publicly, and he should not attempt to assassinate my character; besides being wrong, it was also an unwise communications strategy.

I was learning that the Politician was not good in a crisis. He did not handle stress well. He alternated between his usual gentleness and a frantic and accusatory posture. He was furious, for instance, that when confronted with evidence of our relationship, I had not said that it was a "deepfake." I was learning, too, and at just about the worst possible moment to learn such a thing, that the Politician, despite being a subject of media interest for his entire life, did not know much about how the media worked.

I did my best to explain: Any separation between his story and mine amounted to empty space, and in a developing news event, especially one generated in bad faith, especially one with political implications in the throes of an election, empty space would be seized and projected onto by opportunists. This meant that if there was a suggestion of a *he said/she said*, it would not matter if there was a *she said*; if I did not provide my side of the story, it would be written for me.

Even more concerning, the threat the Politician had received included the claim, he said, that the threat maker in question had a trove of intimate materials he was prepared to distribute to the press. If the Politician lied, the bar for publishing those materials, which was likely legally permissible, would fall to the floor; as an official associated with the president, there would be a public interest in disproving any false assertions he made, and a lie like "deepfake" would make it all much worse.

I urged him to be rational. "Think of a story as a fire," I said. "To stop the progress of the fire, you starve the story of its oxygen: new information." He mumbled the communications lesson back to me. "A fire," he said. We both needed the story to die, he agreed, but he had more immediate needs, and to secure his desired outcome, he would first feed the flame with a sacrifice staged for an audience of one. Within a few hours, his lifelong psychological war with desire and control would be externalized and doused on our tabloid melodrama, provoking a hard-to-contain blaze that would spread fast and burn hot; the man on his third marriage, engaged in another of his innumerable affairs, would become in his narrative the unwitting victim of a woman redrawn as a two-dimensional sex-crazed cartoon. If it was just sex, he could survive it.

The Politician did not tell me about his plans now. By 2:30 a.m., he was much calmer. More like his usual self. What he told me was that he wanted me to try to sleep. Before we hung up, we would need to do one more thing: "Let's pray for each other," he said. I prayed for him as I always did and continue to, even now. I have to assume that he prayed only for himself.

In my mind a shrill symphony: the coos of the birds and the smack of the bullets, and the Politician, his voice, the subject of so much derision; it was to me a fire crackling, a sound that made me warm. I could still hear him. "Sweet dreams, my love," he said, "my little baby bird." Now I had seen the earth torn apart by fires that crackled. Now I thought of birds that push their babies from their nests. I closed my eyes and walked back into a spring morning, at the house where I lived in Georgetown, Twenty-Eighth Street between P and Q, when I stepped onto the patio and looked down at the stone to find a blue eggshell, shattered into jagged pieces, and I scanned the maze of bricks and stretched onto my toes to peek at the nest, but there was no baby bird that I could see, and I froze my body and stopped my breath so I could listen, but there was no baby bird that I could hear, and I knew already, when I was trying to see and trying to hear I knew, that she had been swallowed up by some kind of monster, that in her first and final act, she had made the monster stronger.

Was she not then made monstrous, too?

She fed the monster, sustained him, was transformed in surrender to become part of him. She might tell you, if she could, that having seen him from the inside out, she knows the monster as only the antelope knows the lion, as only Jonah knows the whale, as Ulysses could never know the sirens. She might tell you that until you are devoured by him, you cannot know who the monster is. She might be right about all of that, but I no longer think it matters.

New York closed in. City and magazine. New York I fled. I drove west. I did not feel alone now. Not yet.

What I felt was that the country had snaked its hand up my skirt. What I felt was that I had been lanced by the teeth of a trap set by a man who could not let me go; that as I tried to free myself, the man for whom I worked had run off with the key to the padlock; that the contradiction in terms, the man I trusted most, the Politician, had walked by the scene whistling, and when he saw me there, a mob on the horizon moving closer, he reached out to me, not to lift me to my feet but to pin me down, to drive the teeth of the trap deeper into my flesh, to hike my skirt higher, to wave the mob over to look, to invite the country to lay its hands on me.

It does not matter how it felt. I knew this then and know it now. After all, I was asking for it.

The highways were dark and I was not thinking consciously or clearly. I was not really there. I was only moving.

A friend told me the man I did not marry had reached out. "He said, 'If she wants to come back, I would still take her back.' It was like *Cape Fear*."

MARSELLUS WALLACE: The night of the fight, you may feel a slight sting. That's pride fucking with you. Fuck pride. Pride only hurts. It never helps.

—*Pulp Fiction*, 1994

A newspaper reporter was in pursuit of a comment. The *she said* was being written, though I was not saying anything, just as I knew it would be. The reporter cited a *source familiar*.

I asked her to list all the claims she wanted me to respond to. I waited until she was finished. "Off the record," I said, "this is such bullshit." Which was bullshit. Some of the claims were true. We could not lie publicly, I had told the Politician. Implicit in that directive was the acknowledgment that, privately, we would both continue to lie. The spin agreed upon was this: *It had been a flirtation. Nothing more.*

"There are two parties here who could confirm or deny whether or not these allegations are true, and I am telling you that these things are not true and I am certain that the other party involved in this would tell you that these things are not true, because they're not true," I said. "And I don't know what a *source familiar* is, but there are only two people who could be familiar with this, and one of them is saying it's not true, and I'm sure that the other one would say it's not true."

Already, I suspected, the identity of the *source familiar* might pose a problem with standards at this newspaper. The tabloids were lawless, the mainstream press less so. With my off-the-record lie, I had trapped the reporter. It was now the word of an anonymous secondary *source familiar* against an off-the-record primary source who refuted the word of the *source familiar*. She sounded green, and I knew she would not know that it was a rookie mistake to allow someone to respond to a spate of claims off the record and all at once. Taken as a whole, I could tell her it was all bullshit. Taken one by one, my response would be more complicated. Speaking off the record, I could say whatever. Speaking on the record, I would say nothing at all.

"I hope that you never write anything about this and I hope that this story dies," I said. "I hear you," the reporter said. "I just wanna—and I understand, like, exactly what you're saying—" I cut her off. "Sorry, I have to take another call. Let me know if for some reason you decide to keep pursuing this, but I hope that my denial matters to you, and I assume the other party would deny this as well and I would hope that would matter. That's all from me. Thank you for calling." I hung up to answer the fictional other call.

Thirty minutes later, a real call, from the Representative, with word of an inquiry from the newspaper reporter. "I already handled it," I said. "No," the Representative said. In response to my denial, it seemed the reporter had conferred with the *source familiar*, who provided what sounded like some of the intimate and no-longer-private materials the Politician told me he had been threatened with. Materials that countered my lies. The reporter had related some of the materials to the Representative.

The leak landed as a two-bird precision stone strike, designed to fuck me professionally, as my workplace contracted a law firm to "investigate" me, and to fuck the Politician personally, interfering with his efforts to convince those he needed to convince to buy the story of his smear campaign, which might fuck him professionally, too.

Among communications related to the Representative from me was an exchange in which I had told the Politician, "I know you'll make the best decision for the country. I love you." When he sought or I volunteered my opinion, what I offered most often was advice about how to think through a decision, not about which decision to make; it was not my place or interest to tell him what to do, but to be helpful and supportive while he weighed his options. My contribution was to encourage him to tune out those who sought to influence him from motives that were, as he described them, shallow and selfish, and to listen to himself instead. That nuance would not translate, I knew, in how such details would be reported or interpreted in the public discourse or by the lawyers hired to interrogate me. On the occasions when I did volunteer prescriptive advice, he almost never took it, and when he did take it, it was almost never how I meant.

I told the Politician about a strange story I had heard about a dead bear cub found in Central Park a decade earlier. Its carcass had been staged by the Politician, and once discovered, his connection to the scene had been covered up with the help of his friends in positions of power in the New York government. I thought it was among the zanier efforts to kill a campaign I had heard to that point in the election. I figured it was nonsense. *Opposition research* is a fact of our politics, the practice by which organizations working for or on behalf of a candidate dig through every aspect of their lives in search of negative data to weaponize against them. Sometimes the mined *oppo* leads to fair and legitimate public scrutiny, but sometimes it comes up short, meaning the researchers identify an attractive rumor but do not produce the corroboration required to transform the rumor into a publishable news story. In the elections I had covered, I had encountered lots of information that fell into that category. There was a presidential candidate who was alleged to have pelted a staffer with a shoe, another who was alleged to be a swinger, several who were alleged to be closeted homosexuals, and one who, in what I optimistically interpreted as a sign of social progress, was alleged to be a closeted heterosexual. When I told the Politician about the matter of the alleged dead bear cover-up, he was silent for a while. I found this curious. To observe him talk in public left the impression that he did not plan much how he talked. He was seldom silent, and by then I knew that when he was silent, it was because he had not yet told himself the story he would tell others. I knew that he loved great stories, and he wanted to be the hero of great stories, and he held great appreciation for the powers of the form because it was through stories he devised about his own existence that his existence charged forward. It was, I thought then, the way he most resembled a politician, and maybe the only way he resembled a politician at all. After the silence, he had some follow-up questions. "They said I killed the bear?" he asked. "No," I said, "that you moved it—think of the bear as Vince Foster." He laughed. He asked to call me back that night. Hours later, he told me a winding saga about how he had been out falconing with a woman he was seeing, and he found a dead bear cub and put it in his trunk, and then forgot it was there, and when he remembered it, he decided it would be a good gag to prop up its body in the park beneath a bicycle as if it had been hit. He described the events in great detail, his delivery labored and even more deadpan than usual. "Are you fucking with me?" I asked. He sighed. "No," he said. His face was bright red, and he shut his eyes tight like he was in pain. "Baby, you have to understand, I used to do something funny every week," he said. I thought that was one of the funniest things I had ever heard. I burst out laughing.

How to handle such an unprecedented communications strait? My advice seemed sound to me. "I guess, if I were you, I would get ahead of the story," I said. *Getting ahead of a story* is media jargon for nullifying negative facts by introducing them yourself in the most positive light possible. The Politician liked that idea. "It'll help me with rednecks and hurt me with liberals," he said. By *get ahead of the story* I did not mean to suggest that he should appear on camera to introduce the facts through a more entertaining story than his enemies could ever dream of planting in the press to a shocked and horrified-looking Roseanne Barr.

Among communications related to the Representative from the Politician, there were refrains from explicit poems he wrote me—"I am a river. You are my canyon. I mean to flow through you. I mean to subdue and tame you. My Love"—and a passage in which he described, along with other feralities, his plans for my "womb." This contradicted in color the black-and-white narrative he had spun in private and in the press. The Representative could barely choke the details out. I cut in to spare us both. I had heard enough to recall the content in its beautifully depraved entirety. I had heard enough to be terrified.

What other materials did the *source familiar* have? Which other news outlets had the materials been handed to? The present task was to prevent the publication of these materials in this publication, but that might not prevent the *source familiar* from making them public through some other means. And what else was the *source familiar* capable of? I had not anticipated any of his actions to date. I was used to his efforts to control me, but I did not think him inclined to risk his own reputation through reckless behaviors that would involve uncontrollable outsiders and variables. I was not at all confident in my abilities to anticipate what he might do going forward.

When he first told me of the threat he received, the Politician said, "This guy's a coward. His voice was shaking." He let out a prideful laugh. Still, he took the threat seriously. It had been bold and specific. It had not come across as an outburst, but something considered. "I just hope he doesn't do it before the election," the Politician said. "I just need until the election." After Election Day, if the president won, his political value would be confirmed, and he would be less vulnerable. He asked me to find a way to "de-escalate" the situation. I tried. I failed.

Now it was dark, and I looked in my mirrors, looked over my shoulder. Before I set out from New York, a friend helped me search the car for GPS trackers. What if we had missed something? My knuckles were white on the steering wheel. The roads were empty. I did not know where I was, but that did not mean no one knew where I was.

The reporter told the Representative that she would not allow me to see the materials on the grounds that it would compromise the identity, as if there was a chance it was not already known to me, of her *source familiar*. She wanted instead to read them to me over the phone. If I agreed, I knew she would be able to say she had provided, in media parlance, an *opportunity to respond*, which would make it more likely

that she would be able to publish the materials. Everywhere, new traps.
I refused.

———

My brother called to check in. When I explained the immediate crisis
within the big one, he thought for a moment. "Did we know he was
this smart?" he asked, referring to the *source familiar*. "No," I said, "we
did not." He thought for another moment. "I can't kill him?" he asked.
"No," I said, "you cannot."

———

A lawyer told me that he had, "well, not a conflict, exactly, but a complication," that he figured "you might see as an optics problem." My
tolerance for lawyers was somewhere in the realm of *Henry VI* to begin
with. My patience was thin. "What is it?" I asked. He responded to my
question with a question. "Are you familiar with Sirhan Sirhan?" he
asked. My eyes narrowed. "I am familiar with the events of the twentieth
century, yes," I said. "Well, I sort of represent [the Politician's] whole
family in trying to keep him incarcerated, and as you may know, [the
Politician] is on the other side of that issue," he said.

———

A request for comment from a tabloid: Had the Politician grabbed
my ass on the hiking trail? No, he had not. The following day, another request for comment from the same tabloid: Had the Politician
grabbed my arm on the hiking trail? No, he had not. The day after that,

a magazine reported that the Politician had held my hand on the hiking trail. In an expression of the absurdism inherent to the news cycle, the magazine cited multiple sources to support this claim about two hands. In a competitive huff, the tabloid reached out again with a request: In the future, when denying an incorrect allegation, could I volunteer correct information so that the tabloid would not get "scooped" on news such as this? It was as though the media was holding up a doll of me and gesturing at random to different parts in search of kindling to feed the fire of the story. *Show us on the doll where the Politician touched you.*

––––––––––

"W*hy won't Olivia play ball?*" The tabloid scribe was confused. Speaking to the Representative, the scribe expressed that he could not understand what, exactly, the client did not understand about the ways of the tabloid world. It was a simple transaction: *Play ball* meant *work with* them, and *work with* meant provide information. The tabloid did not want to be so hard on the client, the tabloid scribe told the Representative, and in fact the tabloid scribe worried tabloid readers were sick of the tabloid being so hard on the client. It was getting boring. It was getting to feel like the same story day after day. Consistency is the thief of content. But since the client refused to *play ball*, and the tabloid could only work with what the tabloid had to work with, the tabloid would have to publish more dubious claims that were hard on the client. Not publishing more stories did not occur as an option. Consideration is the thief of content. Conscience is the thief of content, too. Since content was assured, the client should just surrender, the tabloid scribe said. *Play ball* like everybody else. Give the tabloid new claims that shifted focus or vilified somebody else in the story. It did not matter if the client told the tabloid what they had published or what they were about to publish was false. The only thing the client could tell the tabloid that would prevent a false or unfair story from being published was that the client would give the tabloid something better or at least something new. That the client would *play ball.*

I would not *play ball.*

The Politician had orchestrated a narrative in which I was not just reduced to my sexuality but into a hyper-sexualized honeypot. He did this by engineering stories that relied on anonymous allegations from himself—"this is from *a source close to [the Politician]*," he told one writer—and from people who worshipped him and were eager to comply with his requests and others he had just met through his new association with the president who were eager to assist him in his efforts.

One was a longtime adviser to the president whom I had known since 2015, though not especially well. He had asked me to write about him during the Russia investigation, and I had agreed to do it because it was a good story and he was a good character. I had found the process to be a nightmare. My bar for what I would classify as inappropriate behavior from men is much higher than modern standards, which I consider absurdly low, and the adviser did not meet it. But he was one of those subjects, not uncommon, who lacked boundaries. He required endless attention, hours spent listening to him yap on the phone or over dinner as he basked in what Janet Malcolm termed the *narcissist's holiday* of the reporting period.

He would often call on his way to or from a Russian bathhouse, an experience about which he would wax poetic, a minor abuse of the dynamic in which a reporter must assume the role of willing audience whenever the subject feels like having one. On a personal level, I was not especially comfortable with this, but I was not listening to him on a personal level, and for my purposes as a writer interested in the natural comedy of life, I was pleased to have a character involved in the Russia investigations inform me with great enthusiasm and incredible detail that he recreated at Russian bathhouses.

The adviser was highly emotional and prone to breaking down, and often this was justified, since the ordeal of his role in what he called *lawfare* had been an enormous stress on him and his family. But just as often, his hysteria related to matters that fell far outside the scope of my concern, such as Jerry Garcia's death. I endured the tragic saga of the fact that he did not get to see Garcia in his final performance at least half a dozen times over the course of the reporting period, such that I came to anticipate the junctures in the story when the adviser would begin to breathe in a labored manner before he burst into tears. The adviser was just another Deadhead, like many conservatives I knew, and he had not known Garcia. The Politician had known Garcia and I figured that contributed to the adviser's sudden sycophancy.

On the Politician's behalf—and therefore probably in some way on Garcia's behalf—under the pretense that what was on his behalf was now also on behalf of the president, the adviser provided blind quotes to the press in which he overstated his connection to me, inflated his importance as my longtime source, and claimed, falsely, that I had flirted with him and used my appearance as a tool for manipulation while performing my work.

Of the lies told about me, this was among the hardest to take.

The Politician was outed to me as the architect of these stories by members of the media who hoped to compel me to retaliate. The

Politician knew me well enough to know I never would. This business, sustained by participants who believe that you may fight fire with fire, that it is better to scorch everyone in a bigger blaze than endure a burning at the stake alone. I guess I just disagreed.

––––––

"Look, honestly? I wish I wasn't doing this story," one reporter told me, "but I could really use the money."

––––––

In between calls from reporters I did not wish to speak to and lawyers I did not wish to know and people I wished I had not disappointed, it was just the Stones, the only sound that could triumph over the static. *Strange, strange skies.*

––––––

I hesitated on approach at a coffee shop, where two women had just started their shifts. I did not know how long I had been driving or what time zone I was in. The sun had not yet risen but the night was through. It had been dark for what felt like several nights.

"What state are we in?" I asked.

They answered at the same time.

WOMAN 1: "Florida."

WOMAN 2: "Missouri."

The gas station was lit up by a neon sign: ON THE RUN. I had to laugh.

Now Texas, I was pretty sure. The FBI on the phone. A straight, long road of flat, endless country. The type of terrain on which you cannot feel 110 miles per hour. I was filing a report. The alleged stolen materials, the apparent distribution of such materials to at least one major newspaper, this kaleidoscopic caper, this inverted reality in which what was harmless now harmed, in which what was beautiful morphed hideous, in which I received the signal to run but was not told who from. I did not know what else to do.

On the line with the FBI, I spoke with special precision. I had seen over the years the trouble encountered by those accused of lying to the FBI, though they always insisted they had not, or that they had innocently misspoken, or that they had been coerced or had their words contorted by the FBI. I referred, only when necessary, to "the other party involved in this matter." I understood that a report would be written by the Special Agent, that my words would be circulated inside the department, that there was no way to control what others might do, that there was no way to know what agenda I might serve, that law enforcement leaks, that governments scheme, that where power may be concerned no such thing as *good guys* can be assured.

The Special Agent was nice. He referred to me as a "victim." I asked him not to call me that. "You are the victim of a crime," he said. He explained that I could be the victim of a crime and not be *a victim.*

At the end of the conversation I asked him to remind me of his name, which I had forgotten as soon as he introduced himself. His voice became softer. "Olivia," he said, and he said my name in a distinctly familiar way. Then he explained why. "It's [the Special Agent]," he said.

He was someone I knew socially. He apologized. He thought I had been aware all the while of his identity. I had not been aware.

The impression developed that I was trapped within a bad script, as though artificial intelligence had been prompted to write a Lifetime movie in the style of the Coen brothers. Tawdry and farcical and circular.

The tale suffered, too, from a variety of ensemble claustrophobia for which there is Hollywood jargon: *tiny town.* Before I knew the term, I tried my best to diagnose the affliction as it cropped up again and again in my coverage of the president. When the television host who was one of his closest friends, and who used his platform as a means of generating propaganda for his administration, was named in court as part of the prosecution of his former fixer, I described the psychic effect of the news this way:

> Its obviousness was almost too much to take without something snapping. It was ridiculous, in the way that *Law & Order* is ridiculous if you do not suspend your critical faculties: The same few detectives are present and central at every pivotal moment of each case, as though there are no other cops in all of New York.

As it happens, this already-phantasmagorical episode of my life would become inspiration for an episode of *Law & Order*, in which the fictional version of me kills the fictional politician, which itself would contribute to the now self-fulfilling impression of phantasmagory. Even on a theatrical plane, I was disturbed by the suggestion of violence, by anger imposed on a concept of me when I did not feel any, by such energies compelled into the ether. More than ever, I was convinced of the power of thought, convinced that any word could land a prayer, convinced that wherever focus may be directed, reality may take shape. I thought of how many hours I spent watching the program as a small child and what effect that may have had on my psychic development. The way things were going at the moment, it could not have been a positive one. The pulling apart and apart and apart and apart. The time-lines stretching and overlapping. Executive producer Dick Wolf. The scenes superimposed, layer upon layer, on the single stage. *These are their stories.* The moment now, again, when the tail met the jaw.

Even the image that prevailed to accompany the narratives, me in a leopard-and-red-silk gown that may as well have been a vixen costume, implied a kind of satire. Ordinarily I wear all black. *For the poor and the beaten down, for the prisoner who has long paid for his crime,* and to simplify my life. My brother joked that I am like a video game character, dressed more or less the same each day in one of a dozen identical black shirts, black pants or black pencil skirt, and black boots or black stilettos. Dressed in this manner I could interview a rioter or a judge, I could stand in the eye of the demonstration or inside the Senate chamber, I could disappear through the emergency exit or I could appear on television, float between contexts, travel by whatever means to whatever place I needed to be.

I had been on mushrooms when I purchased the gown and then forgot about it, and I had agreed to pose for photos only at the insistence of the public relations department of a television network I was writing for and whose executives I had brought as guests to the White House Correspondents' dinner. I hate red carpets, what they call *step-and-repeats*, because the photographers yell at you. *Over here! To your left! Olivia! Down! Up!* I do not like yelling. I like being yelled at even less.

A friend observed with me the strangeness of this image, in which I looked so unlike myself but so perfect for the story in which I was cast against my will. "This is why I always put so much effort into the White House Correspondents' dinner red carpet," she said, "because I know if I ever fuck up, that's the photo they'll use."

After a while its pervasiveness and its separateness from my appearance and sense of identity made it so that the entire saga felt separate, felt like a nightmare about this leopard-clad *star reporter*, the characterization the media collectively decided on in an instant and stuck to with the sort of commitment more often reserved for ordeals that inspire a *-gate* suffix. The press, especially the tabloid press, inflates the importance of characters involved in public dramas through subliminal editorial choices that communicate to readers and viewers that the drama is worthy of their valuable attention. It is for this reason that red carpet photos from wire services are selected by editors as often as possible and it is for this reason that terms like *star* are attached to people whom most people have never heard of. The *star reporter* was a fiction. The fiction proved popular.

You could write your way out of it. I would not have written it like this.

In the little house at Zuma, I kill all the orchids. I try very hard to not kill the fig tree. I am not a killer. This I now know for sure. Just as I know how easy it is to kill her, if she is not a killer. Just as I know that who you are under pressure is who you are, that the pressure reduces you to your essential qualities, that there is no action taken under pressure that does not reveal your character.

In the bluffs I walk through the Santa Ana winds. Were it not for guilt and shame that tethers me to the dirt I think this surge of heat would send me right off the cliff. I imagine it takes me, the wind, to dance through his blitz; I imagine my body, light streaming through the wounds, blood beading down a Pollock as I am wrung out in the air. My body is red. A muleta, suddenly. The bull, too. But whose blade is that? He is victorious. I wonder now if he thinks victory is owed to his own skill, or if he understands that to hold an arrow is to hunt for any heart, but to wear horns is to guard carefully your chosen hero.

I find a scrawled reminder in a notebook:

> *I am twenty-eight years old. If I take after my father, I have thirty-two years left to live. If I take after my mother, thirty-one.*
>
> *The expert black humorist, he taught me to find cause to laugh in any gallow. For years he said that the day I got my driver's license he would drop dead. Italian Americans are always talking about dropping dead, always over routine matters. Then, in fact, the day I got my driver's license, my father dropped dead, and I had to hand it to him: As final punchlines go, it was hard to argue with.*
>
> *I cannot write about my father. I cannot find the words to describe his hands. On the left, a tattoo like an asterisk, etched into his flesh by someone unknown to me someplace I have never*

heard of under circumstances undisclosed to spare me, to spare
him; an asterisk denoting what he believed to be a complication to
fixed ideas about the heroism a daughter assumes of a father, of all
veterans of the battle to keep the world away from the tiny palace
of her innocence, even as she is aware that it is being waged and so
it is in that regard already a defeat, like Vietnam, like one we do
not—as a country, a family—acknowledge in those terms and that,
like Vietnam, could never have been won anyway, based as it was on
delusion. On the right, dry and bleeding in the winter from the icy
winds of dawn in suburbia and the commute and the nights spent on
the couch at one job or another or his sister's house or in the ghetto
of rejection within his own house; the cracks in his skin a metaphor,
inescapable, for all the ways he was not cared for, for the care he
denied himself but gave so freely to others, to me most of all.

Seven months after she died, it occurred to me that I needed to
call my mother. In a normal way, I felt this. As if she had only been
waiting for me to call all this time. I did love her. I do love her, still. I
had a dream last week where I was explaining to somebody, maybe it
was to her, that she was dead but she was not really really dead. Not
dead in the sense that she was not here. That was a different kind of
dead, a final dead, and she was not dead like that yet. I worry now,
to the extent that it is possible to worry actively about a thing like
this, that she is in some sort of restless place, a purgatory, somewhere
unsettled. I do not believe that it was her fault, any of it. I do not
believe that people ought to be accountable for their limitations. It is
so hard to be a person. It is so hard to be a person in pain. To inflict
that pain on others is more pain. She never really hurt me, even when
she hurt me. She was innocent, in a way, even as she was guilty.
Childlike. Motherless girls always say their mothers were beautiful.

She really was. I am so rarely angry but when I am, I see her face in mine. I am so seldom drunk but when I am, I see her face in mine. I could never be angry and drunk at the same time, though, and my eyes could never be bright green or blue depending on the light; she called me once to tell me that she had read on the internet that my eyes were black. She scoffed. They—and by They she meant the entire internet—should know that my eyes were the color of espresso, except in the sun, when they glowed almost amber. At the time I registered this with an uncharitable spirit, as yet another expression of her vanity. I told her not to read about me on the internet. Looking back I see that to observe me and to find on the surface qualities that she could understand, that she deemed worthy of praise, was her way of trying to connect to someone who had always been, even as a small child, distant and inaccessible to her. I had been protecting myself, protecting myself from her, and I think somewhere within her she knew that. More pain. Kneeling at the shore of my memory, I see her, tan and freckled in the sun, telling me how to survive in the ocean. Any wave could be cut through, she said, if I did not think I could get over it before it crashed. There was never a reason to panic. Any current could deliver me to shore so long as I abided its demands, did not fight against its flow. She tried so hard to be our mother. I never wondered if she loved us and I think that is an ultimate kind of success, a triumph over every other failure. I do wonder if she knew that we loved her. I worried then and worry now that she thought we counted all of it against her. I hope that she can be set free, wherever she is, and that she knows I will call her just as soon as I can.

In vignettes, I see, still, I was a daughter. Skyward, feet kicking through sunshine to the nearest branch. Leaves lit up as panes of glass at St. James on Sunday. Green and young and alive. Everything looks alive when you are young. The nature of vignettes being what it is, I see, too, the edges zoom into a cartoon circle. The circle gets smaller. I was, smaller, a daughter. The circle closes in, as if to say, That's all, folks.

That was three years ago. For the first time, I am happy that they are not here. At least they do not have to witness this. The witness, witnessed. An ugly sight.

———

I make my gums numb, my lips, my tongue. I get so cold my teeth chatter. At the Bungalows, a photographer traps me at the table and a flash goes off in my face. There is no photography in here.

———

The movie star nods from across the room. He walks over and crouches down beside me at the table where I am seated next to an actress. "What's your name?" he asks. I offer my first name. He pauses. Then he nods again as a smirk spreads across his face. "Oh, I know who you are," he says. "I know exactly who you are." It has been months since I was a daily presence in the press. His tone is satisfied. His eyes transform into eyes that suggest he has seen me naked. I feel sick.

———

UNIDENTIFIED MALE: That was the first time that I realized that being a known person was a liability or could result in a threat.

OLIVIA NUZZI: Do you remember the first time you saw a private photo of yourself posted publicly?

UNIDENTIFIED MALE: It was this site, mostly gossip, mostly shit-talking. Which I had a hard time with already because I've always cared very deeply what people say about me, for a lot of, like, stupid childhood reasons. It's the reverse of that Oscar Wilde quote, *I don't care what anybody says about me as long as it's not true.* I care very deeply if someone says untrue things. And then there was this photo, and it was a dumb fucking photo that I had taken with my face in it.

OLIVIA NUZZI: Did you recall sending it?

UNIDENTIFIED MALE: Yeah, it was someone who ultimately was a catfish.

OLIVIA NUZZI: How do you mean?

UNIDENTIFIED MALE: It was someone I was flirting with on [the gay hookup app], trying to set up a hookup, and sending material to each other. He was sending stuff to me that in retrospect was definitely stolen, nudes that were stolen, to use as lure. And then once I had sent images in response, he disappeared, and when I realized what had happened, it was like the trapdoors came down. At the time though I thought someone had just been jerking me around. It didn't occur to me, *Oh, they have these private images and they might use them in a public way.* I thought it was just a fucked-up private exchange.

OLIVIA NUZZI: How did you feel when you saw the image again, in a public context?

UNIDENTIFIED MALE: I felt stupid. Like, *Of course this had happened. Of course this was the logical result of sending identifiable photos of yourself into the world. Of course I was never going to be able to get them back. How fucking dumb am I to have not thought, until this moment, that there could be consequences?*

Rain in Los Angeles is a crisis. For me personally. It is as though the rain washes away the artifice. The rain reveals the truth, something of a surprise to me. I am not, as I have assured everyone who asks, and as I have assured myself, doing okay. The sunshine blinds me to this fact, directs my focus to the beauty around me. The mountains. Flowers. Birds. Sea. In the veil of mist, the Pacific barely perceptible, my ability to walk off unpleasant thoughts hindered, I sit still longer than I would like, long enough that everything I have been running away from seems to find me.

Everyone is doing coke again. In Bel Air, the producer explained why she would not be snorting the drug with rolled-up cash. Too many contaminants. Plastic straws were no good, either. Microplastics. The ideal instrument through which to inhale schedule II chemicals was one free of germs and unintended chemicals, like how people say you should not commit a misdemeanor while you commit a felony.

The model was not doing coke tonight by any mechanism because she liked coke too much, and so she took a little ecstasy, which was for her like drinking coffee in the afternoon, she said. A subtle buzz of energy. Sometime later, it had been raining for a while, and she had long ago drifted across the grass, and she was very wet, and she looked up and thought for a moment and then she said, in a sweet and innocent way, "Did anyone notice it's raining?"

Around 2 a.m. a few nights later in the Hollywood Hills, I could no longer bear the sight of people trying to cut lines on a ceramic plate. I transported the apparatus to the surface of a copy of *Miami* I had picked up at Mystery Pier, and a personal trainer who for reasons not explained to me goes by a single initial looked at the book when I offered him a line and asked, "Is that good?" and when I said I did not yet know, as I had just started to read it, he said, with beautiful enthusiasm, "I'm just getting into reading!"

For a while, that was Los Angeles in my mind. Everyone seems to look only inward. Nobody seems to see anybody else. I did not think this shallow. I considered it a virtue.

———

The rains brought a big snail to my window. Stuck to the glass, looking right into the bedroom, eye level as I opened my own. As I registered his presence, I noticed that without thinking I had lifted the sheets over my breasts. I do not feel safe anyplace, not even alone, not even in bed. I do not feel quite alone anyplace. I thought of that Spanish science fiction book I read a few years ago, an English translation, about the popular pet robot surveilling the human race through its eye. I thought about the girl who told me once, at a friend's wedding, that she was working on adapting her thesis project into a novel, about a girl convinced she was being followed by a drone, and the girl comes to like the drone, performs for the drone, lives her life to please the drone. I thought of my own surveillance. The way that I policed my behaviors and then, because a cloud is an extension of consciousness, I began to police my thoughts. I recalled the third grade, how my Sunday school teacher had met my gaze when she said that God knew who was guilty, and how I worried that above my head there might be a thought bubble like in comic strips, and everyone could see the movie of my mind projected there, and how this terrified me. Now it feels like a premonition.

———

At the stakeout, the Paparazzo was getting restless. "I've been here since eight a.m. and nothing's happened yet," he said. It was close to 3 p.m. now.

He never knew how long he might be parked outside someplace waiting for his subjects. "It could be thirty minutes, it could be one hour, it could be five hours," he said. Time today moved especially slow. Inside his car, with his camera and extra-big lens idle on the passenger seat, his mood grew more sour with each passing minute. "I'll give it two or three more hours," he said, "and then I'll go home."

This gamble was one the Paparazzo took about once a month. He would drive out of Manhattan to an East Coast town where he knew he might strike gold. Once there, he would wait. He could return with nothing, but if he got lucky, and often enough to maintain some baseline optimism he did, he would return with the Great Get, the kind of exclusive that he prided himself on, the kind that he believed set him apart from "the other paps," as he called them, a little acid in his voice.

If he could wish a photo into existence, it would be "Jennifer Aniston and Brad Pitt together anywhere," he said, since such an image would easily fetch what he estimated to be half a million dollars. Any paparazzo, "the other paps," would say the same. That kind of photo did not require any imagination. What he was really after was not something so practical or obvious. He was after the Great Get.

What made a Get a Great Get was not the quality of the image or the star wattage of the subject or subjects in question. A Great Get as far as he was concerned was any photo that proved him to be especially clever, especially dedicated, especially dogged, or especially well-connected or well-trusted.

The "other paps" might fight for scraps on the sidewalk outside the usual celebrity haunts on either side of the country or they might battle for supremacy behind the rope at a red carpet, and while he participated in norms of the trade such as this, what he wanted was something special, something that would inspire awe and envy among his rivals.

"The other paps, they talk. They talk shit," he said. "I get photos other paps don't get and when they see them, they say, 'How'd this fucking guy get that?'"

On this occasion, the Paparazzo's would-be subject checked two enticing boxes: One, the subject was obscure in identity while still of interest to the usual tabloid suspects. Two, the subject was located outside the general geographic radius patrolled by the other paps. "I'm looking," the Paparazzo said, "for some royals." Former royal singular, to be precise, a once-royal who had defected from a royal family. "Two months ago, I found [the subject] and I got pictures," the Paparazzo said, "and [the subject] liked the pictures." The subject had been appreciative, the Paparazzo added, about his attention to optics concerns. The Paparazzo understood that when a person is of interest to the tabloids, and involved in public dramas of any sort, whether they are smiling or scowling in a photo can be the difference between a positive or negative turn in the tenor of the news cycle. "[The subject] was cool," he said.

More recently he heard a rumor that, if true, would amount to a new twist in a public drama. Photos that confirmed the rumor would for sure sell. If he scored, the Paparazzo would hand the images over to the agency with whom he is contracted, and his reps would do their best to spark a bidding war between the likeliest buyers, TMZ and the *New York Post* and the *Daily Mail*.

"I'm like a baseball or soccer player. I sign a contract, they offer me money, they say, 'We will give you this every year, you will make certain royalties,'" the Paparazzo said. "I save my ass. I've gotta make sure that I make my money."

The Paparazzo guessed he had been working in the trade for close to three decades. As a child in another country, he recalled, he would go to the local kiosk and use his money to buy newspapers. The images printed inside were a window into a bigger world—a world he realized he could claim some piece of through his own lens. "I'm twelve years old, and I'm like, 'Oh shit! I can't believe, nice photos of Madonna. One day, I'm gonna be there and I'm gonna go and take pictures,'" he said.

Had he ever photographed Madonna?

"Oh my God, a hundred times," he said.

What was it like the first time he photographed her?

Upon this question the Paparazzo paused. By now we had been talking for twenty minutes or so and although I had been dodging him for months, and although I had never before asked him to call me, he had not yet asked why I had asked him to call now.

"Wait, are you interviewing me?" the Paparazzo asked.

Yes, I said. I was doing precisely that.

"You can ask me all you want," the Paparazzo said, "but there is a catch: We have to do the photos."

I whipped my head in the direction of the sound of branches snapping. Outside, my ears are more important than my eyes. I listen for the rattle of the snake, or the faint whoosh of the bobcat as he cuts through the air, or the heavy footsteps of the more likely predator, the adult human male, but what I listen for most of all is silence. So long as the grass rustles under the minor weight of paws or claws and the air hums with the birds' song, all is well. It is the absence of such organic chatter that signals a threat. Animals quiet themselves when they sense danger. This snapping, though, registered as peculiar. It was loud. An aberrant cadence. Not another hiker. Not an animal. Who, then? What, then?

I heard the sound again. I turned my head. I could have sworn this time I saw something, a flash of colors, orange and black and bright blue. I could have sworn I felt eyes. I emerged at the top of the trail to find that in the time I had been hiking, a children's party had formed on the grass. Dozens of tiny people raced through the field. Someone was playing music. "Somebody's Watching Me" by Rockwell. And just then, upon the hook, *I always feel like somebody's watching me, and I have no privacy . . . Tell me, is it just a dream?* I clocked him. The Paparazzo, walking backward, camera positioned in front of his face, banging into the cement facade of the public restroom and nearly losing his balance. He darted off. The bad script, the satire, the scene stretched.

When I saw the images, I thought of the Martin Scorsese film *Shutter Island*. A detective, investigating a woman's disappearance at a mental institution, turns out to be a patient institutionalized after his own conviction for murder. In the throes of psychosis, he has hallucinated himself free, a hero. Upon this realization, his face contorts into an expression of primal horror. I felt a similar connection to deep reserves of fear at the convergence of my split realities. The witness, witnessed, witnessing herself witnessed. In this record of surface, there was no detectable soul, no suggestion of any other dimension, as if I were a kind of bot, a crisis actor in the crisis of my own life. I asked the Paparazzo how much it would cost to buy the rights to the images myself before they were sent out to bidders. "But you look beautiful," he said. He did not understand that I could not judge the images that way, that the nature of the images precluded their categorization as *good* or *bad*, that to me it looked as if someone had drained my body of blood like the Black Dahlia and strung up the shell of me at the Macy's Thanksgiving Day Parade, and that in any event, this float meant yet more fodder in the procession of content about my existence that I did not want. The Paparazzo continued his protests. My cover was already blown, he said. I would never be able to exert so much control over the when and where and how in particular my privacy would be violated as I could claim right now. If I forfeited this opportunity to participate in the violation of my privacy, it could be gone for good. "You have to let me do the photos. You help me, I help you. I will always protect you, but, please, let me do the photos," he said. "We can do them some other time," I said. This was a lie. "Okay, you promise?" he asked. "I promise," I said. This was a lie, too. I wired the money as fast as I could.

In the mob, Britney Spears lost her balance. She was holding her baby on her hip, and as the photographers jostled for their shot, she fell over, and her baby fell with her, and in the photos taken next, through the window of a restaurant, she sat there, her face red and wet, her expression sad and hysterical. The photos were everywhere. They posted the photos on the national altar of television.

My mother looked at the screen. "That poor girl," she said. "That's her baby." I looked at my mother. Her face was red and wet, her expression sad and hysterical. I had seen it before.

To the center. The first thing I remember.

The gravel was black. The cherry blossoms were pink. My blood was red. My skin was ivory except for where it had transformed into a blur of colors, into blots of black and pink and red, the expressionist aftermath of the fall, and then, quickly, a bruise was born bright blue around where my open flesh painted the ivory darker and darker shades of red, Scorsese red.

My poor mother. I was her baby.

At the arraignment, I tiptoed up to the crowd. I braced for mobs. I looked for signs of the porn star's prophecy. But the scene was controlled, the fights mostly contained. "This is Indictmentchella," one young man, fratty in demeanor, remarked. "Two genders!" a woman yelled. "Two brain cells!" a man yelled back. They faced off like this for a few minutes. Bystanders laughed. Someone walked around with a sign: VIRGINS 4 TRUMP. Inside the courtroom, the president and defendant entered his plea: "Not guilty."

One year later, Max Azzarello held a sign in the air: TRUMP IS WITH BIDEN AND THEY'RE ABOUT TO FASCIST COUP US. He had traveled from St. Augustine, Florida. It was cold in New York, and as he stood in the park outside the criminal court, he kept himself warm with red gloves.

It was a Friday afternoon and jury selection had just concluded for what was termed by the media the Hush-Money Trial. This was the matter of the thirty-four-count indictment related to the $130,000 payment issued just before the 2016 presidential election to secure the silence of the porn star.

The courthouse was a zoo. The president was captive. The first president in American history to face criminal trial. I got lost inside the building and ended up on a floor with cells, with prisoners inside the cells, and a guard seated in the doorway with a big key ring on his belt. In the basement, when I went to buy water, a shackled inmate was ahead of me in line with his public defender. They only accepted cash and I did not have cash. Well, I had two euros. The woman at the checkout counter looked at me with justified disdain. "American cash," she said. She said this very slow, as if she figured I must be. A cop intervened and paid for my water with American cash.

In one of his final acts, Azzarello published a manifesto on the digital publish-everything platform:

These claims sound like fantastical conspiracy theory, but they are not. They are proof of conspiracy. If you investigate this mountain of research, you will prove them too. If you learn a great deal about Ponzi schemes, you will discover that our life is a lie. If you follow this story and the links below, you will discover the rotten truth of 'post-truth America.' You will learn the scariest and stupidest story in world history. And you will realize that we are all in a desperate state of emergency that requires your action.

To my friends and family, witnesses and first responders, I deeply apologize for inflicting this pain upon you. But I assure you it is a drop in the bucket compared to what our government intends to inflict.

Because these words are true, this is an act of revolution.

Azzarello believed cryptocurrency was an elaborate "Ponzi scheme" designed to steal all the world's wealth and that the leaders of both major political parties were actors cast in a deep state plot that ramped up in the late 1980s, with the election of the former head of the Central Intelligence Agency as president, and that anyone who stood in the way of their dominance was squished into submission with intimidation, threats, phony investigations, or blackmail.

When they present themselves in public, they are acting as characters that are against one another, practicing kayfabe as wrestlers do.

As it turns out, we have a secret kleptocracy: Both parties are run by financial criminals whose only goals are to divide, deceive, and bleed us dry. They divide the public against itself and blame the other party while everything gets worse and more expensive and a handful of people take all the money.

Since it is fully parasitic, a secret kleptocracy is an incredibly unstable form of government—left to its own devices, it can only lead to fascism or failed state.

In every part of our culture and commerce, from cartoons to canned water, he saw evidence of the plot, which required ceaseless reinforcement through propaganda to further demoralize the unwitting public into a catatonic state. Corporate news existed to traffic "apocalyptic messaging," and corporate entertainment existed to "brainwash us," and participatory corporate entertainment, or social media, was "flooded with nonsense conspiracy theories and memes reminding us that we are hopeless, helpless, anxious, depressed, ironic, scared, apathetic, escapist, lonely, misguided, and jaded, telling us we can't do anything but have a laugh at our circumstances."

When we piece it all together, we understand the truth: We are in a totalitarian doomsday cult.

This is obviously very bad news, but the biggest lie we've been told is that we are powerless. We've got one way out of hellworld, and that's for the public to realize that we've been conned completely so we can build a united movement that shatters every lie they've told us, mocks this rotten farce as loudly as it deserves, and aims at nothing short of abolishing our criminal government so we can build one that serves the public.

To understand this story is to see right through the con, to become immune to the endless sea of criminal propaganda, and to feel the great joy and power that comes with freedom.

If a small number of people quickly put on these truth-colored glasses, we are in for an unimaginably bright future. If not, we get an apocalypse.

He directed readers to documents and pamphlets and ephemeral digital content he created to support his argument. "I apologize for leaving things so scattered, but this has been an exhausting affair. So long as you understand this (true) ideology, you will be able to learn the whole story," he said. He mentioned a lawsuit he had filed and noted that he filed it to preserve the findings from his research, not as a gesture toward legitimate litigation.

I was terrified and hadn't slept in days and it shows, but it served its purpose of keeping myself alive long enough to keep learning and telling this story.

I no longer have my original research files from the crypto rabbit hole. If you want to see them, you'll have to get my laptop back from the government. Ask them how they got it—it's a very fun story.

I hope you know how powerful you are. I wish you a hell of a lot more than luck.

Max Azzarello

In the park, Max Azzarello threw pamphlets in the air. It was windy, and they fluttered around the pavement, flew through the fence, drifted into the street. Then he lit himself on fire.

Inside the courthouse, news of the fire spread like the metaphor. Courthouses are fiefdoms and everyone inside is subject to strict and often confounding rules. In the overflow room, reporters were being held for a period of time after the jury had been selected. The high-ceilinged space buzzed with anxiety. The news event was outside. How much longer would we be in here? The second we were set free, the stampede began to the elevators. It was an old Art Deco building and its bones creaked.

When you chase news as it breaks, you do not know what you are on your way to bear witness to. You do not think about it, do not have time, do not have capacity. You are not really there, you are only moving. The stampede was spit out the doors and down the steps and into the street. Here I say *the stampede* as if I was not a part of it. I was not a conscious part of it, but I was a willing part of it. Is that not the story of any stampede?

Outside, the stampede collided, we collided, with the haze of Max Azzarello. The wind sent him swirling all around and east with the pamphlets he threw. The air was thick with Max Azzarello. Burning flesh is not just a smell but a texture. The rest of his body was loaded into an ambulance. We would learn later that parts of him were still alive when he left the scene. Max Azzarello was caught in my throat. I gagged.

The stampede stopped, dispersed. Individual reporters scavenged for pages of the pamphlets before the NYPD could snap them all up. Law enforcement would soon hold a press conference about the matter. The press waited on the street corner. We were due back in court shortly. Conflicting interconnected news events. Stay out here or return inside to witness the president on trial? Then word made its way through the scrum: The digitized manifesto confirmed that Max Azzarello had staged the act at the trial not to protest the proceedings or the defendant but because of the concentration of cameras.

In the makeup room at a television network hours later, one of the reporters told me she had been standing outside for a live shot when she heard a loud commotion, and she turned to look, and she saw him there, his hands raised high, the flames raised higher. It was a good bet the press would care about Max Azzarello, whose self-immolation aired, in part, on live television. It was the wrong bet. It was not about Donald Trump and so it did not matter. In her ear, the reporter said, a producer barked at her to turn away from the blaze of his body and back to the camera. The makeup artist had seen it, too. They stared off, both of them, expressions dazed.

Max Azzarello died that night.

His final message, digital and ephemeral, said this:

I love you I love you I love you
I love you I love you I love you
I love you I love you I love you
I love you I love you I love you

Paranoia blooms. As the lupin flames and the poppy burns, paranoia blooms hot.

"He always said, 'It only takes one,'" a longtime adviser to the president said. In the very beginning, when he first began his political career from his Midtown television studio turned campaign headquarters, the only security he had were a few tough guys he trusted who had worked for his private company for years. The head of security was a big man with dark hair and mustache named Matthew Calamari, dubbed "Matty the Squid" by the writer Matt Labash. The president resisted the arrival of his Secret Service detail. He liked to make advance decisions in the moment, on emotion, on instinct, and the armed entourage added not just logistical complications but psychic weight. He had enjoyed, on a whim, directing the chauffeur of his one-car motorcade to fast food drive-throughs, and rolling down the window at red lights to surprise strangers, and throwing cash at children he passed on the street. The Secret Service cramped his style. Plus, they wanted him to wear a bulletproof vest, which was hot and bulky and heavy with weight and implication; the request invited him to contemplate the subject of his own mortality, something which, more than most men, he sought to avoid. He was not even sure that he felt safer with them around. The adviser said that, in fact, the presence of the Secret Service seemed to activate his anxiety. He would gesture with a subtle nod of his head at one of the heavily armed men in the swarm of heavily armed men whose job was to insulate him from heavily armed men. "'Just one of these guys. It only takes one,'" the adviser recalled him saying. He was not preoccupied with worry about a mentally ill kid perched on a rooftop somewhere. He was more worried about a shot fired from inside.

———

Across the driveway at the little house at Zuma, I heard a distinct buzz. There it was again, the drone, right over the bushes near the gate. It hovered, stayed there like that for a while. It was a small drone, the kind you can buy to use recreationally. I had first seen it a few weeks earlier. If it was not so loud I might mistake it for a hummingbird. There are lots of hummingbirds here and I love each one of them. They zip around deep into dusk. I thought of asking the owners of the property if they had seen the drone or knew whose it was but I did not want to make my fear more real by speaking it aloud.

———

The president was talking about dying. It was the first October of the pandemic and while his doctor had told the outside world that the president's symptoms were nothing to worry about, the president himself, cocooned in his suite at Walter Reed National Military Medical Center in Bethesda, Maryland, was telling those close to him something different. "I could be one of the diers," he said.

The person on the other end of the line could not forget that unusual word the president used: *dier*. A seldom-said dictionary standard, it was a classic Trumpism, at once sinister and childlike. If being a loser was bad, being a dier was a lot worse. Losers can become winners again. Diers are losers forever. But are we not all diers in the end? Donald Trump, the least self-reflective man in America, was contemplating his own mortality. He said it again: "I could be one of the diers."

As infections swelled nationwide, the virus had made its way inside the president himself, an epic security failure with no modern analog. It was amid a pandemic in 1919 that the twenty-eighth president got sick in Paris. His White House blamed what it called a cold and a fever on the dreary weather, though he was sick with the Spanish flu, which killed hundreds of thousands of Americans as his administration looked away. A hundred and one years later, the story of the president's "mild symptoms" became less and less true as the hours ticked by. His fever crept up. His cough and congestion grew worse. Doctors gave him oxygen and administered a high dose of an experimental antibody treatment unavailable to the ailing masses and made using fetal tissue, a practice his administration opposed. Still, he resisted going to Walter Reed. "I don't need to go," he said, according to a person who spoke to him. "I'm fine. I'm fine. We have everything we need here."

Down in the polls and high on steroids and irritated by his highly emotional chief of staff who would not leave the hospital and slept in a nearby room, he tried to distract himself from the illness that had confined him to these sterilized quarters. He plotted his escape, planned public relations stunts, watched television, and took calls from friends, members of his staff, and Republican lawmakers. He remained consumed by what the doctors told him about his chances of survival. It was not a sure thing. Still, he tried to stay positive. On the phone, he remarked, "This change of scenery has been great."

Fist. Flag. Flame.

The director leaned over the table. He was not a conspiracy theorist. He was sure about that. Conspiracy theorists were the sorts of people ruining this country, the sorts of people who would vote for a fraud like the president who would facilitate the ruination of this country. He was not one of them. He hated them. He was the kind of person who believed in facts and believed that facts mattered. He was reasonable and the observation he was about to share was reasonable, too, since as it related to the actions of the president, all doubts were within reason. Plus, he spoke from experience. He knew what he saw. He had seen it before: "It looked like prop blood," he said.

Pink. An ovular rose. Big and smooth. A complex commonplace instrument. And, as far as these things go, a rather nice one. Isolated from the head and all that roils therein, and to which it is, famously and miraculously, still attached, you have to admit, if you can: It is beautiful. In Palm Beach, sunlight streamed through the window to find its blood vessels, setting the whole device aglow. Auris Divina, Divine Ear, protector of The Donald, immaculate cartilage shield, almighty piece of flesh.

The president raised his right hand and grabbed hold of it. He bent it backward and forward. I asked if I could take a closer look. These days, high off his own survival, he came from a Place of Yes. He waved me over to where he sat, in the same low-to-the-ground chair upholstered in cream brocade in the grand living room at Mar-a-Lago where we had spoken before.

"Let's see," he said. He tapped the highest point of the helix. "It's a railroad track." He tapped it again. "They didn't need a stitch," he said. "You know, it's funny. Usually, something like that would be considered a surreal experience, where you sort of don't realize it, and yet there was no surrealism in this case. I felt immediately that I got hit by a bullet. I also knew it was my ear. It's just a little bit over here—" He used his hand to wiggle the ear. "Right next to—" He gestured at the side of his head, at his brain, and raised his eyebrows. "It's amazing." He shook his head in disbelief. "And the ear, as you know, is a big bleeder."

It did not feel surreal. The president kept mentioning that. How unexpected it was, the matter-of-fact way in which he managed to process the attack as it unfolded. But on that July afternoon, he was tethered to the earth as if by cosmic cord. He could not be pulled into the void. He was so clear about each moment of that afternoon. At Butler Memorial Hospital, he said, he asked the doctor, "Why is there so much blood?"

This was due to the vascular properties of cartilage, the doctor told him. "These are the things you learn through assassination attempts." He laughed. "Okay, can you believe it?"

He can never fully see his own ear. He can never fully see himself as others do. I inched closer and narrowed my eyes. The particular spot that he identified with his tap was pristine. I scanned carefully the rest of the terrain. It looked normal and incredible and fine. Ears do not often become famous, and when they do, it is because they have suffered some sort of misfortune. Van Gogh's self-mutilation. Mike Tyson's cannibalistic injury to Evander Holyfield. J. Paul Getty III, whose kidnappers cut the whole thing off and put it in the mail. And now this, the luckiest and most famous ear in the world. If you were the kind of person inclined to make such declarations, which the president is, you might call it the greatest ear of all time.

An ear had never before been so important, so burdened. An ear had never before represented the divide between the organic course of American history and an alternate timeline on which the democratic process was corrupted by an aberrant act of violence as it had not been in more than half a century. Yet an ear had never appeared to have gone through less. Except there, on the tiniest patch of this tiny sculpture of skin, a minor distortion that resembled not a crucifixion wound but the distant aftermath of a sunburn.

"It was like a *sssslap*. It wasn't that it hurt so much. Don't forget, I've got tens of thousands of people I'm speaking to. Whether you're a politician or not, and oftentimes you wouldn't like to even say this, but you are performing, to an extent. And you're getting hit, and you don't really know what it is, but it was a *whack*. It was, uh, it was, immediately it was a bloody mess. And for some reason, it didn't seem surreal. It seemed like I was hit. I went down. They came to my aid very quickly. I wanted to get up. I wanted to get up immediately. I heard bullets going over my head. You hear them, I didn't realize this, that you hear. You know, I was never shot at before, in all fairness. It's just a *whiz*. You know, just, *wwwhoooiiiiiishhhaaa*. It's just like a *whiz* sound! And there were a lot of them.

"The pain was from the ear, also. I didn't have pain elsewhere. Other than, I had big people—" He extended his arms out to demonstrate the size of the agents who had piled their weight on top of him. "It was a different pain. Because it was a slap. It was like getting smacked in the ear. I guess that's the best definition." As a performer, "to a certain extent," he knew how to calibrate his actions onstage to address the needs of his audience. Blood running down his face, he raised his fist and punched the air. "Fight, fight, fight!" he said.

"The amazing thing is, with all those bullets, I guess he fired eight, and the sniper, the Secret Service sniper, he fired one shot, and from a much further distance. Because the podium was here, and our person was here, and he was here, and so he went across. There were a lot of bullets flying. And you hear those things go over your head"—he laughed—"and you say 'This is not comfortable.'"

Had he ever fired a gun? "I have, over the years, but not to any great extent," he said. He mentioned that his sons were more adept with firearms. "They know so much about hunting and about weapons. I sometimes say, Where did you come from? You know, I'm not, not into it"—here he caught himself—"other than I protect it." He seemed to recall that he would need continued support from the powerful gun lobby. He went off on a tangent about how, despite his recent injury, his support for guns was unchanged. "You know, I have total endorsements from the NRA and all of that from day one," he said. "I'm very much about gun rights. I feel very strong, very strongly about it."

When I asked if he had been afraid in those moments when he heard the gunshots, when he felt the smack, when he saw the blood, he said, "I didn't think of fear. I didn't think of it." In the president's understanding, fear is not a feeling but an idea that you may choose to entertain—or not. He moved right along to an idea he preferred to think of. "You know, I got so many nice calls from people I really don't know. [The digital everything-company billionaire] called. He said, 'It is the most incredible thing I've ever watched.' And he appreciated what I did, in the sense of getting up and letting people know. I said, 'Despite the fact that you own *The Washington Post*, I appreciate it.' He couldn't have been nicer. [The digital everywhere-company billionaire] called up and said, 'I've never supported a Republican before, but there's no way I can vote for a Democrat in this election.' He's a guy that, his parents, everybody was always Democrat. He said, 'I will never vote for the people running against you after watching what you did.' So I mean, people really appreciated it. I don't—I think it was very natural what I did. I think it was natural.

"Prior to this, I believed in God, but one—" He jumped from his own thoughts to the lower-stakes thoughts of others. "This is actually an interesting situation," he said. "I've had people that didn't believe in God that said now they do because of this. No, this is divine intervention. And look, this is something." He added, "It's like the hunters were saying: If the deer bolts, you know, you're ready to shoot. And sometimes the deer bolts and they miss. In a way, I bolted. You know, I guess my sons told me that sometimes you're ready to end the deer. As you squeeze in the trigger, the deer is bolting. I sort of bolted. Yeah, it was an act of God, in my opinion."

I wanted to know how he felt about a God that would intervene to spare his life but take the life of another man and seriously wound two others. Had he thought about it? "Yeah," he said. He talked for a while about the man who died and what a big fan of his he was. And he talked about how a friend of his had given $1 million to the widow, and how they had set up a fundraiser for the families, and how they had raised $5 million or $6 million. He kept talking and talking about the money. "I already gave the wife a million dollars, and she was great. I mean, look, she couldn't believe it, but she would rather have her husband." The check, he said for the third time now, was for a million dollars. "I don't care how successful, it's a check for a million dollars," he said. "And I gave it to her. She was—she couldn't believe it."

I tried again. Had he wondered why his was spared and another life was not? "No, I haven't wondered why. I should wonder why," he said. He looked off and he seemed to really be thinking. "I've been so— I've been working very hard on the campaign, and I also run a business during the time that I'm here, you know, with my family. It's a great business. It's an incredible business. But I am involved in running that, but mostly it's the campaign because, you know, you have to do that. That's got to be the focus. And my children run the business now and do a good job. Eric runs it, and Don helps him and runs it, also different aspects of it." He was still looking off. "But no, I've never asked myself that. I've never thought of it. I don't like thinking about it too much, because it's almost like you have to get on with your life. So I don't really like thinking about that too much."

———

The Mother knew that no amount of magical thinking could bring her son back. She knew this because she knew exactly how long he had been gone. She knew because she did not have the choice to forget. "It's been one thousand and seventy-nine days since the murder," she said. "I count every day. I will count every day for the rest of my life."

Her son was killed on February 14, 2018, Valentine's Day, when a gunman opened fire inside Marjory Stoneman Douglas High School in Parkland, Florida. Her son taught ninth-grade geography and coached the cross-country team. Two other teachers and fourteen students were killed alongside him. It was one of the deadliest school shootings in American history.

The Mother knew it happened because she fought with the county sheriff for access to the security-camera footage from that day. She knew because a court granted her permission to watch the moment her son's life was taken. She knew because the footage showed how he opened the door to his classroom and stepped into the hallway to wave students fleeing the shooter to safety. She knew because, next, the footage showed how before he could lock the door again, the shooter, dressed for a war, fired in his direction. She knew because, next, his blood fell onto the vinyl floor and then her son collapsed. She knew it was real because his body was placed in a mausoleum in Boca Raton, Florida. She knew because her son was not here anymore.

She responded to the loss not by denying it but by doing her best to carry on in a way that would honor her son. She and her husband founded a charity to send disadvantaged children affected by gun violence to summer camp. They lobbied lawmakers for gun safety, which is the term activists prefer to use over the term *gun control*, which they fear feeds into fears stoked by Second Amendment advocates. They tried to make it so that their son's absence from their lives did not mean their lives were empty.

What they could not forget or deny was raised as a question by people who saw in the Parkland shooting an opportunity to promote in bad faith an ideology that would transform the tragedy into content to gen-erate attention and profit through a kind of anti-credibility. Those peo-ple claim to believe many mass shootings are "false flag operations" in which "crisis actors" stage a phony violent attack in order to foment fear of guns so that the government can disarm its citizenry. Once pushed to the fringes of our society, the promoters of such conspiracies have been empowered and mainstreamed over the last decade, in which a fellow conspiracy theorist, or at least someone who convincingly plays one on television to increase his popularity, was elected president thanks, in part, to their support.

The rise of QAnon, a superconspiracy that borrows from popular conspiracies of the last half century to allege an elite global Satanic cult in which world leaders abuse and sacrifice children, invited more for-mer outcasts to Washington, such as an inarticulate and overprocessed blonde congresswoman from Georgia who endorsed and promoted the lie that Parkland was a "false flag" operation. She harassed one of the student survivors of the shooting when he visited Congress to lobby lawmakers.

The Mother is a decent and responsible person. She understood that responding to the congresswoman meant giving her more atten-tion, and that more attention carried the risk of her message reaching more people than it already had, and that among those people reached, some might be persuadable, and they might be persuaded by what the congresswoman had to offer: a reality in which America is not a country where a gunman can stalk the halls of a high school and murder stu-dents and a teacher who sought to protect them. Accounting for this risk, the Mother still believed the best way to stop the spread of a lie is to confront it with the truth. And so on the 1,079th day since her son was murdered, she decided to respond.

"Congresswoman, the shooting where my son was murdered protecting his students was not a 'false flag,'" she said in a statement. "It was not staged. It really happened. Do not trivialize my son's sacrifice to save his students for your own political gain. As [the army's chief counsel] said to [chairman of the] Senate Permanent Subcommittee on Investigations in 1954: 'Until this moment, Senator, I think I never really gauged your cruelty or your recklessness. Have you no sense of decency?' Congresswoman, I ask you the same question. Are you that cruel?" Her voice cracked as she posed questions to me. "What do we need to do? Show her the video? Do I need to take her over to [my son's] mausoleum? Does she need to see how he was shot six times from three feet away?"

––––––––––

SUPERIOR COURT OF THE STATE OF CALIFORNIA

CITY AND COUNTY OF SAN FRANCISCO

Date: November 1, 2022

Time: 1:30 p.m.

Dept: 9

Case No. 22012966

NOTICE OF MOTION AND MOTION TO DETAIN; REQUEST FOR JUDICIAL NOTICE

STATEMENT OF THE FACTS

In the middle of the night, Defendant smashed through a window in a back door of the Pelosi home in search of the Speaker of

the United States House of Representatives, Nancy Pelosi. But
Speaker Pelosi was not home, only her 82-year-old husband,
Paul, who slept upstairs in his pajama top and boxer shorts.

Standing over Mr. Pelosi's bedside just after 2:00 a.m.,
Defendant startled Mr. Pelosi awake by asking "Are you
Paul Pelosi?" Defendant carried a large hammer in his
right hand and several white, plastic zip ties in his left
hand. Defendant then repeated, "Where's Nancy? Where's
Nancy?" Still groggy from being suddenly awoken, Mr. Pelosi
responded, "She's not here." Defendant then demanded,
"Well, when is she going to be back?" "She's in Washington,
she's not going to be back for a couple of days." Defendant
responded, "Okay, well, I'm going to tie you up."

Mr. Pelosi stood up and tried to leave by the elevator
near the bedroom, but Defendant held the door, preventing
Mr. Pelosi from escaping. Mr. Pelosi then returned to the
bedroom, sat on the bed, and asked Defendant why he wanted
to see or talk to Nancy. "Well, she's number two in line for
the presidency, right?" When Mr. Pelosi agreed, Defendant
responded that they are all corrupt and "we've got to take
them all out." When Mr. Pelosi asked if he could call anyone
for Defendant, Defendant ominously responded that it was the
end of the road for Mr. Pelosi.

Still trying to escape from Defendant, Mr. Pelosi asked to
use the bathroom; Defendant allowed him to do so. Mr. Pelosi
stood up and walked to the bathroom where his phone was

charging. *Standing in the bathroom, Mr. Pelosi grabbed his phone, turned it on, called 911, and put the phone on speaker. Watching Mr. Pelosi, Defendant stood about three feet away, still holding the large hammer and the zip ties. During the 911 call itself, Mr. Pelosi said that there was a gentleman there waiting for his wife—Nancy Pelosi—to come back. But Mr. Pelosi said they would have to wait because his wife would not be coming back for about a day. Mr. Pelosi could see Defendant gesturing and heard Defendant tell him to get off the phone. To diffuse the situation, Mr. Pelosi told the dispatcher that he did not need police, fire, or medical assistance. Trying to be calm and discreet while also trying to help dispatch to understand the situation, Mr. Pelosi then asked for the Capitol Police because they are usually at the house protecting his wife. The dispatcher clarified that Mr. Pelosi was calling San Francisco police; Mr. Pelosi said that he understood and then asked someone, "I don't know, what do you think?" Another man responded, "Everything's good." Mr. Pelosi then stated, "Uh, he thinks everything's good. Uh, I've got a problem, but he thinks everything's good."*

When the dispatcher told Mr. Pelosi to call back if he changed his mind, Mr. Pelosi quickly responded, "No, no, no, this gentleman just uh came into the house uh and he wants to wait for my wife to come home." The dispatcher then asked Mr. Pelosi if he knew the person and Mr. Pelosi said that he did not. Mr. Pelosi then said that the man was telling him not to do anything. The dispatcher then asked Mr. Pelosi for his name and address and Mr. Pelosi gave the dispatcher both. Mr. Pelosi then said that the man told him to put the phone down and just do what he says. The dispatcher then asked for the man's name and the man responded, "My name is David." When the dispatcher asked who David is, Mr. Pelosi said, "I don't know," but David said, "I'm a friend of theirs." Mr. Pelosi then confirmed with the dispatcher that he did not know the man. "He's telling me I am being very lazy, so I've gotta to [sic] stop talking to you, okay?" When the dispatcher offered to stay on the line with Mr. Pelosi to make sure everything is okay, Mr. Pelosi said, "No, he wants me to get the hell off the phone." The call ended. Based on her training and what she heard, dispatcher Heather Grives issued an "A" priority well-being check.

After the call, Defendant said that he was tired and needed to sleep; he also told Mr. Pelosi that he had a backpack downstairs with a whole bunch of stuff inside. They proceeded downstairs with Defendant walking behind Mr. Pelosi still holding the large hammer and the zip ties. Turning on the lights, Mr. Pelosi could see where Defendant entered the house; Defendant commented that he had to bash the window several times to break through and enter. Defendant also said that the police would be there any minute; Mr. Pelosi tried to calm Defendant by saying that they would not. But Defendant responded, "I can take you out." Defendant came around to Mr. Pelosi's right with the large hammer upright in his hand. Afraid that Defendant would strike him with that hammer, Mr. Pelosi reached out and put his hand on the handle of the hammer.

Shortly after the initial call, Officers Kolby Wilmes and Kyle Cagney responded to the residence. When Off. Wilmes rang the doorbell, Defendant directed Mr. Pelosi not to open the door. But Mr. Pelosi opened the door with his left hand. As the door opened, the two men stood in the dimly lit foyer facing the officers. Mr. Pelosi nervously but calmly greeted them. When the officer asked what was going on, Defendant smiled and said, "Everything's good" and pulled his hands toward his body. When an officer turned on his flashlight, Defendant could be seen holding the bottom handle of the hammer with one hand and Mr. Pelosi's right arm with the other. Mr. Pelosi had his hand on the top of the handle near the hammer itself. One officer ordered, "Drop the hammer!" At the same time, Defendant raised the hammer and said, "Um, nope." Defendant tried to pull the hammer away from Mr. Pelosi, which twisted Mr. Pelosi's arm back. Simultaneously, Mr. Pelosi pleaded, "Hey, hey, hey!" The officer asked again, "What is going on here?" But Mr. Pelosi could not maintain his grip on the hammer. A second later, Defendant wrenched the hammer away from Mr. Pelosi, immediately stepped back, and lunged at Mr. Pelosi, striking Mr. Pelosi in the head at full force with the hammer, which knocked Mr. Pelosi unconscious. The officers rushed into the house, tackled Defendant, and disarmed him. Mr. Pelosi remained unresponsive for about three minutes, waking up in a pool of his own blood.

While on scene, Off. Wilmes asked Defendant if there were any more suspects. Defendant said that he acted alone;

Defendant then looked at the glass door and said that was
where he broke into the house. Officers later recovered
Defendant's bag outside the damaged glass doors. Inside,
there was another hammer, a laptop, and more bags of zip
ties.

Without any questioning, Defendant told officers and medics
at the scene, "I'm sick of the insane fucking level of lies
coming out of Washington, D.C. I came here to have a little
chat with his wife." Defendant added: "I didn't really want
to hurt him, but you know this was a suicide mission. I'm
not going to stand here and do nothing even if it cost me
my life." "Hurting him was not my goal. I told him before
I attacked him, that he's escalating things, and I will go
through him if I have to."

San Francisco Fire Department Medics responded immediately,
rendered aid to Mr. Pelosi, and transported him to San
Francisco General Hospital. At SFGH, Mr. Pelosi underwent
emergency surgery to repair a skull fracture and serious
injuries to his right arm and hands. Mr. Pelosi remains
hospitalized.

Upon arrest, Defendant admitted that he intended to
enter the home to take Speaker Nancy Pelosi hostage
and, if Speaker Pelosi lied to him, he intended to break
her kneecaps. Seeing Ring security cameras everywhere,
Defendant knew he would be caught on camera. Defendant
was surprised when he found Mr. Pelosi still asleep

*after making some so much [sic] noise to gain entry.
When Mr. Pelosi attempted to enter the elevator near the
bedroom, Defendant held the elevator door, thinking it
would lead to a saferoom. When Mr. Pelosi called 911,
Defendant knew the call was being recorded. But by calling
911, Defendant believed that Mr. Pelosi pushed him into
a corner. Back in the bedroom, Defendant told Mr. Pelosi
that he cannot be stopped; he has other targets. And later
when police arrived, Defendant, not willing to surrender,
yanked the hammer away and hit Mr. Pelosi with full force.
When asked if he had any other plans, Defendant named
several targets, including a local professor, several
prominent state and federal politicians, and relatives of
those state and federal politicians.*

The president was skeptical. "It's weird things going on in that household," he said of the lawmaker's home in San Francisco. "The glass it seems was broken from the inside to the out. So it wasn't a break-in, it was a breakout."

He was not alone. "Paul Pelosi KNEW his attacker and NAMED him in his 911 call," one conservative personality said. Others claimed that in the 911 call, he referred to the attacker as "his friend." Theories developed that the lawmaker's husband and his attacker might be in a homosexual relationship, supported by a report from a local television station, later retracted, that the attacker was in his underwear when police arrived. "They're still pretending it wasn't Paul Pelosi's gay lover," one activist remarked. A

Republican congressman from Louisiana referred to the attacker as a "male prostitute." The South African tech billionaire and mayor of the digital town square promoted the theories and suggested the plot might be connected to the 2016 Democratic nominee. "There is a tiny possibility there might be more to this story than meets the eye," he said. By these accounts, the hammer might have been a tool for a depraved sexual encounter and not a weapon for a political attack. A Republican congresswoman from New York shared an image of hammers aimed at the pride flag. The president's son shared an image of the hammer wielded as a sex toy. "Dear fact checkers this has nothing at all to do with anything going on in the news and simply posting a cartoon of what appears to be an altered South Park scene," he wrote. The victim of the attack, meanwhile, remained in the intensive care unit.

The recording of the emergency call did not support any of the allegations made, and video released by law enforcement did not support the theory of a *breakout*. Speaking to the FBI, the attacker admitted that he broke into the home. "There is absolutely no evidence that Mr. Pelosi knew this man. As a matter of fact, the evidence indicates the exact opposite," the San Francisco police chief said.

In Beachwood Canyon, Canadian flags fly outside the mid-century homes underneath the Hollywood sign. A friend in the neighborhood told me they went up after Election Day. At first I did not understand and then I understood and I still did not understand.

Men love gossip so much that they created intelligence agencies.

—An account called bimbopilled

The Personality was on the phone, in one breath directing his driver to Mar-a-Lago, where he had been summoned for some kind of emergency he could not disclose, and in the next breath responding to my question—Did he trust the Bodyguard?—with a chuckle.

He said, dryly, "Do I trust the sinister billionaire with his own intelligence agency?" Whether the Bodyguard was a billionaire was unconfirmed and for my purposes irrelevant. *Sinister* was the characterization that concerned me. The Personality said that he liked the Bodyguard and—not just because but in part because he had invited him to his island—he thought he seemed like a good guy. Such invitations tend to sweeten impressions, if only so much. "But *trust?*" he asked. He did not think he could go that far.

The Personality said I needed to be very careful. It was his daughter's birthday, and he did not mean to sound paternalistic, but we were the same age, and I really needed to understand how serious he was when he said that I needed to be careful. He referred to *they* and by *they* he meant the Politician and anyone working for or aligned with him. *They* were not going to kill me, he assured me, though that was not reassuring at all, as it had not occurred to me that I was at any risk of being killed by anyone other than the man I did not marry. *They* were not going to kill me, he clarified, but *they* were dangerous.

It is always spy vs. spy with the Personality, like he lives inside a seventies paranoia thriller, and I suppose he does. I suppose I do now, too.

He asked if I was dating anyone and I paused because I did not like that question being posed at all and then I said no and he said that he asked because in his view, I needed to be protected by someone close to me, and I needed to tell such a person everything, in part so that *they* would not drive me insane, which he said *they* would do intentionally, and in part as an insurance policy. I spent all my time alone now. I was alone on desolate trails each day. Did anyone know where I was? Besides of course the Bodyguard, who the Personality said I should assume knew all. I needed to understand: I was, in all likelihood, being watched. If ever I felt alone, that was a trick of my mind. I should assume that I was rarely if ever alone.

Paranoia always animated the Personality, and I always found his paranoia to be contagious.

On this afternoon, he was spooked already. Spooked in particular by what he had just heard about some of the president's advisers.

The good thing about the president was that he was suggestible, and the bad thing about the president was that he was suggestible, and on either side of his suggestibility, what that meant in practice for anyone with special influence was that they possessed more power than they could fully understand, more of an opportunity to shape the course of the administration, pen the chapter of history, and that was all good when it was good, but it made it so that you really had to worry all the time about who you were surrounding yourself with and what their intentions were, because traditional barriers were not in place, and you could, unwittingly, serve as a trapdoor through which nefarious actors entered the chambers of power.

The Personality wanted to know what I had heard. I had heard the same things he had heard. Always, it is a red flag when people seem to "come out of nowhere." He was panicked. He felt responsible. He was trying to not insult the Politician, as if he thought it would insult me if he insulted him, and so he gently suggested that the Politician, as the conveyor of ideas, the "performer"—which he quickly added did not mean he was a phony, lest that suggestion insult me, too—was unfortunately vulnerable to the influence of evil outsiders with agendas. He was already sure the Politician was "corruptible," he said, and he mentioned the matter of Israel, not for the first time.

He had raised the subject one year earlier. I was on the other coast in Miami. It was morning still but the Edition had stopped serving breakfast and further into South Beach the day was progressing, and a crowd formed around a lizard, a big one, a few feet long, silvery blue and orange, with a beard. He did not move much. People crouched down to gawk and take his photo. I wondered if he understood all the fuss, understood his status as curiosity, or if it felt to him that a tribe was encircling, that his capture was imminent. His capture must have always felt imminent. It always was. Eventually he made his way up a tree and I hoped he could stay there. This monstrous little creature. Cute actually. Needing God's love like anybody. Not that I would touch him. Down a few blocks it was more like noon now and a grackle, another late riser, found a worm. An inspirational figure, to my eye. I ordered breakfast.

Afterward, on the phone with the Personality, it took about forty-five minutes into the conversation for me to understand that what he was saying the entire time was that the Politician had been blackmailed by Israel. With the Personality, it often came back to Israel, something I forgot during my periods of retreat from reporting on the kinds of things, or now being involved in the kinds of things, that led me to ask the Personality for help.

But back to the matter of the Bodyguard. I asked how sinister he meant when he said *sinister*. He paused and then he said, "I mean, how big is your imagination?"

The Personality told his driver to pull up by the big guy in a gray polo shirt with the big gun, and the driver said, "I have [the Personality] here," and then there was a lot of background noise, and another voice said, closer, "Who are you here to see?" And the Personality said, "Uhhmm, Donald Trump."

In Wisconsin, at Green Lake, police said a man faked his own death. When I read this I smiled. He was free.

The sea is a desert of waves,
A wilderness of water.

—Langston Hughes

On the Pacific Coast Highway, the sun on the hill moments earlier seemed a hallucination. The trick of the fog. Near Sycamore Cove, it was dark, and the RVs waved their flags, the California and the Gadsden. I thought of the battle, the grizzly bear and the rattlesnake, thought that my money would be on the rattlesnake. Then I had another thought, sudden and urgent, a silent siren. I had to turn around. I did not know why, but I had to turn around right now. I did not question it. I pulled off the road, cut the wheel, and headed back, headed south. I made it up the hill to confirm the sunshine. Then I saw the news. Near Point Mugu, where I had been headed, a crash.

One dead.

––––––––

A former White House official said that she was scared. "The sheriff reached out to me and wants to talk about a safety plan for me because [the FBI director] has an enemies list that seems to be making the rounds here. What world are we living in?" I asked if she was okay. What else do you ask? "I mean, I'm okay but I'd be lying if I said I wasn't nervous. It just takes one wacko person out there to think that killing me would be some service to Trump, and think that Trump would pardon them like he did all those January sixth people," she said.

––––––––

DONALD TRUMP: [The future vice president] was, you know, not doing so well, and now he's doing great, and he's winning, and when I endorsed him he went to first place almost immediately and it's been good.

OLIVIA NUZZI: You ever read his book?

DONALD TRUMP: Uh, I have, yes. I have, actually.

OLIVIA NUZZI: You read *Hillbilly Elegy*?

DONALD TRUMP: I did. Long while ago, when it came out.

OLIVIA NUZZI: What did you think of it?

DONALD TRUMP: I thought it was, uhhh, an opinion, a strong opinion, and he understands a big segment of the voting population, I understood that right at the beginning. I think he understood a faction of people that was a pretty big group. It was an interesting book.

"I felt very good about 2020," the president was saying. It was now four years later, and we were at his Palm Beach estate, and he was, still, unwilling to admit defeat. He raised a spate of excuses: the pandemic, "a lot of bad things going on," "the legislatures," and so on. "I felt very good about 2016," he said. "I feel even better here."

I mentioned that night in 2016. He did not, despite what he said, feel very good about his chances then. He did not believe he would win. No one around him believed he would win. For days prior, senior members of his own campaign staff with careers to preserve went so far as to begin spinning for themselves in private, in attempts to make it known that what was about to happen was due to forces—to *the* force, *his* force—outside of their control. "You did look very surprised that night, though. I remember the look on your face in Midtown," I said. "You mean when I won?" the president said. "Yeah, I just remember—" He cut in. "You were there, right?" he asked. "I was and I remember—" He cut in again. "I remember the beginning of the evening they said I had a ninety-seven percent chance of losing and as the evening went along it went from ninety-seven to ninety-three to ninety-one to eighty-five. Remember that famous needle? It flipped, and by the end of the evening, they had no chance of winning. It was an amazing evening. It was perhaps one of the most amazing evenings in the history of our country."

"Do you remember the movie *The Candidate* with Robert Redford?" I asked. "Yes," the president said. The mention of Redford seemed to please him. "At the end, when he wins, he says to his aide, 'What do we do now?' And he has this panicked look," I said. "Yes," the president said. "You looked like him—" And here the president straightened up in his chair at this comparison to Redford. He seemed to be absorbing the magnitude of such a compliment—"You looked a little worried," I said, completing the thought. In an instant the president returned to his more slouched position and the hopeful look dissolved from his face. "I tell you, if there was a surprise, it was only because the media said that I could not win," he said.

THE FORMER AIDE: He was my life, 24/7. He dominated it. I was too emotionally attached to him. But that's what he does. I don't think any of us are terminally unique to him. There was me, there was the next one, and then the next one, and the next one. For a time I think he did like me, but once it was over, I was gone.

OLIVIA NUZZI: Can you tell me more about being emotionally attached to him?

THE FORMER AIDE: I always wanted to work in politics. My parents became Republicans in '88, voted for [the former CIA director]. We were talk radio people. I was a *National Review* person. I loved politics and I wanted to be involved in politics. Being a part of it—I used to really care about that. That's one thing about Donald you have to respect: He stays in. He stays in whatever game it is. Like, I can't. I've lost the enthusiasm for it. Even if I hadn't been fired by him, I've lost the interest for it. It's the same day-to-day and you can't fight the last war. But do you see how the people that aren't smart do well?

OLIVIA NUZZI: But in terms of your attachment to him—

THE FORMER AIDE: I respect his business. I like his branding, the way he was able to market himself. I was always interested in what I saw of him in the news. What's he doing there? What's he doing now? I liked his style. He was one of the top New Yorkers to me and I was interested in those types of New Yorkers. There are people in New York who are interested in artists, singers, Broadway people. I was interested in characters. And then when I was working for him, he actually appreciated that it was such a small-knit crew. He appreciated my opinions, appreciated my work, appreciated my dedication to him, and he would tell me that we had a very tight relationship, and he would tell me things that didn't involve politics, things about his world, or he would have me get involved in other stuff, whatever it was.

OLIVIA NUZZI: Did you feel like a son?

THE FORMER AIDE: Not like a son but like a confidant.

OLIVIA NUZZI: And then you were discarded.

THE FORMER AIDE: He decided that I was old news. He liked [a rival staffer] more than me. I used to feel like, *What do you mean you liked [the rival staffer] more than me? Why? How? Oh my God.* I feel like a girl, like my heart was broken. And now I ended up thinking, *You like that guy more than me? That's a reflection on you, not on me.*

OLIVIA NUZZI: You are close with your father, right?

THE FORMER AIDE: I am, my whole family.

OLIVIA NUZZI: I'm curious, was the president still a paternal figure in your mind? Did he represent something that was not satisfied by your father?

THE FORMER AIDE: I hate to use this term because Trump has ruined it, but my dad is just a killer. You don't see him coming. Trump, he is in your face telling you he's coming. My dad is stealth. Trump was louder and flashier and I guess I responded to that because it was easy to understand.

OLIVIA NUZZI: I imagine that in some way you loved him, the president.

THE FORMER AIDE: I shouldn't have, but yeah. He's a disloyal asshole.

OLIVIA NUZZI: So when you were fired it wasn't just this professional hurt, or pure ego. You were hurt.

THE FORMER AIDE: I believe in karma. I don't know what that says about Donald now, because if karma was real he'd be in jail, but at a different time in my life I did so many things to people and hurt them and I believe that this was the payback, the punishment from God.

The president raised the subject of Iran, whose government had plotted to kill him, according to a recent report. "You sure you want to be doing this right now?" He looked around the living room of his estate, his eyebrows raised. "Because you may be taken out, too," he said.

I asked if he was preoccupied with the fact that people wanted him dead. "I always think about it," he said, "because, you know, you read about it, you say, 'Wow, that happened to this one and that one and that one . . .' It's a very dangerous thing. I mean, look, this is a very dangerous profession, being president, and especially if you're a certain type, you know, you want things done and you want strong security for the country. You know, you have different types of people, but being president is a very dangerous profession. If you look back, and if you look back at forty-six and you look at the number of assassinations, there's no profession like that in terms of attempts, certainly in terms of attempts and in terms of results, it's a very dangerous line of work. I don't think about that. I don't like to think about it."

A pickup truck, its back window plastered with right-wing stickers, carried a MAKE AMERICA GREAT AGAIN flag that waved in the wind. The elderly man behind the wheel hung a left into a neighborhood in western Malibu.

A few hours later, in Ojai, my eyes found a passing torso wrapped in a Blue Lives Matter slogan.

A man and a woman on the street held signs for a ceasefire: STOP ARMING ISRAEL. A few feet away, three others, a man and two women, held Israeli and American flags, and signs to free the hostages: BRING THEM

HOME. As I walked by, one of the women in the pro-Israel faction said—and this surprised me—"Jared Kushner? Criminal!"

The discourse, right and left, is filled with people remarking on the same thing: Displays of support for the president in new places. West Hollywood. The West Village.

The Politician's Bodyguard posed a question: "Would you really want to go back to a year ago?" I figured he was just being nice and it was meant to be rhetorical, so I did not bother him with the response that screamed out in my mind: *Of course I would want to go back to a year ago.* I could not bear to think about it for more than a few seconds, this notion of a year ago, because I could not breathe when that which was impossible occurred to taunt me.

In Malibu, I hit the gas in my white Mustang, while in my mind, the engine of the white Mustang I drove through the country a year ago revved.

One thousand nine hundred and fifty-four miles, from the Pacific to the Gulf, where people live and work. Where they commute between Mexico and the United States like they commute between New Jersey and New York, passing through a security checkpoint as they would a toll outside the Holland Tunnel. Where you may look in the distance to mountains and valleys and ask where one country ends and the other begins. Where you may start to wonder about the nature of such distinctions, about the nature of separateness, about the nature of self, about borders between men, between man and state, between civilization and disorder. Where you may appreciate just how young a species we are and how tribal. If you have never stood on the banks of the Rio Grande in Texas or the Colorado River in Arizona, if you have never come face-to-face with the wall, thirty feet high, that looms multiples higher in our national psyche, if you have never put your hand through its steel tines and reached into Mexico, if you have never thrown away your bubble gum in Juárez because you cannot chew gum and walk into the United States at the same time, per the signage at Customs, the boundary between countries can seem ominous and alien, an uninhabitable liminal space somewhere between the end of America and the end of the earth.

It rained all week in the desert. I would have told you then, in the winter of 2024, that I was not afraid of anything except for noises in the dark, which meant I was afraid of everything I could not see. I would have told you that because that is what I believed to be true. I slept little.

I parked in the mud outside the senior citizen center, next to the big SUV that chauffeured the MAGA General and his entourage to the event. I had been worried about being trapped in such an SUV with the MAGA General and his entourage for the two-hour journey from Phoenix. I do not like to be trapped. If there is a campaign bus or a plane, I will not get on it, even if getting on it guarantees better access to a subject, a more complete and easier story to tell. I need space from the story. I need a two-hour drive up a canyon with my mind my only passenger. I hate to be a passenger, captive to someone else's whims, captive to a source or subject, forced to filter the world through my perception of their own.

A lot of people say God's Country, and I guess what they mean depends on what they believe God is. When I say God's Country, I mean the big sky. I mean the country that reminds you that you are small. I pulled off to the side of the road to stand before an American flag the length of a city bus, staked in the dirt on a wet hilltop, near a billboard for a personal injury attorney. It fought to untangle itself from a knot. This flag was not much of a dancer. It felt wrong to watch it sort itself out. I sped off. The sky darkened as I drove the last few miles and by the time I got there the lot was full, which was how I came to park in the mud.

Inside, old ladies, listening to the MAGA General speak about the sins of immigration and the biblical stakes of the election and the virtues of the Republican running for the United States Senate who had been a Failed Candidate for various offices in the state twice already, stopped me to tell me how pretty I was. *Oh, thank you. So are you.* I always say that. I usually mean it at least a little, but I always say it in a way that is false, a performance of the kind of femininity that these women valorize. It always goes over well.

I never volunteer why I am there, but I will admit it if I am asked. Most of the time, nobody asks. And most of the time, when they do ask, they are indifferent to or pleased by the answer. For the last few years, no reporters have seemed to show up in places like this. Not even local ones, I guess because private equity firms keep buying local papers and gutting them. Which is beginning to feel like a conspiracy. One reporter does not seem like much of a threat. Plus, the way I look seems to suggest to people something about my intentions. They assume I am one of them, and they thank me, having not learned anything about me at all, because, they say, we need people in my profession who will tell the truth.

I wonder if any of these women are the ones who write to tell me I am the fake news and should be hanged for sedition or who call me a cunt.

The Failed Candidate's press aide said she had a gift for me. I eyed this promise warily. Anywhere she goes where she may interface with the press, the Failed Candidate is trailed closely by her second husband, a cinematographer who films every encounter that may potentially make good content for her branding exercise.

In her office the day before, he hovered near my face as I absorbed the oddness of the staged room, with two dining chairs closely arranged across from each other, their blah beige fabric cast in a yellowish glow by the large professional light positioned to the side, to ensure the Failed Candidate would look as attractive as possible during our exchange. The bigger the light, the softer the lighting. This is something you internalize after several decades in local television news, which is how the Failed Candidate became a household name in this media market.

The gift turned out to be her book, inscribed in her loopy handwriting: "Olivia, Make journalism great again!—[The Failed Candidate]."

She had not found a way to campaign for office, arguing that although the presidency was stolen from Donald Trump and the governorship was stolen from her, people should go ahead and show up to vote again. If the elections are rigged, if Arizona is where they are rigged especially, why bother? She strained to reconcile these oppositional ideas. The MAGA General, nothing if not a good sloganeer, helped her out. He told the crowd they would need to "outvote the fraud." Clever, concise.

When the MAGA General got fired from the White House, he trained his fire on the rest of the world, taking a private jet that God Knows Who was paying for from Teterboro to European countries where the far right was ascendant. I told him he was the Phil Spector of telegenic far-right female candidates across the globe. "The wall of sound has never been stronger," he said. He thought the Failed Candidate could sing, but when she appeared onstage, he winced.

One woman in the crowd grabbed the mic to ask a question. She explained that she is a psychotherapist. The MAGA General asked if he could give her the president's phone number and everybody laughed. It was not that people did not think he was crazy. It was that they rather liked that about him. He was crazy on their behalf.

I slipped out the back door into the rain. The MAGA General's SUV was speeding off, up the hill and into the parking lot and down the road. I hit gas and went nowhere. I accelerated, kicking up rocks and mud. I accelerated again. I tried to back up, to turn to the left, to turn to the right. I hit the gas, and the Mustang growled. The car slid backward, further downhill. It was a dark dark, a moonless sky. It occurred to me that I did not know exactly where I was. An hour or so from Sedona. The map would not load. My phone was hot. It had not been working right all day. A hacking, maybe, or just time to buy a new phone.

The forecast promised snow. I figured it would all be fine because it usually is, because I am in fact very fortunate, and inconveniences need not inspire terror when you have money to spare, like most Americans do not, like my parents never did. Sometimes, when I feel calm as I am faced with the consequences of something careless I have done, like parking a rented sports car in the mud on a hill in the desert during a storm, a flash of guilt zaps across my body, burning my chest and pausing briefly in my throat. I looked at the gas gauge. Half-full. I did not like to let it get too low, because it reminded me of my mother, calling to tell me she was out of money again and was driving around with the fuel light on because she could not afford to get gas. I always sent money. I never visited.

The parking lot was thinning out. I started up the muddy hill for help. I knew I would find help. I was not worried. I have an angel on my shoulder. *I do not know that I believe in angels.* That is what I would say if you asked me. I would venture to complicate the idea of angels. What I would not say is that the veil is thin over my shoulder and that is where the angel is perched.

It was no surprise to me then that the first people I encountered in the parking lot were three officers from the Yavapai County Sheriff's Office. They were eager to assist me. They laughed and joked. They laughed at my California plates, and they laughed as they pointed out that the car was a few feet from backing into a pond, news to me and my poor eyesight, even worse in the dark. I made a joke in poor taste about Chappaquiddick, and they laughed and said they were so happy that young ladies like me knew their political history.

They cleared rocks from the stretch of mud behind the back tires. If their plan worked, the car would jump forward, and the tires would spit the rocks out like bullets. They told me to watch from the safety of the hill. I was wearing Prada. Two of the officers crouched in the red lights and pushed the car while one of them revved the engine. The Mustang heaved. It shot out of its rut, moving as a fawn quickly and unsteadily up the hill. The officers cheered themselves. I thanked them. I went on my way, windows down to air out the interior of the car, which now reeked of mud and manure. The rain hit my face. I did not mind.

The next morning, I drove away from the storm back to the border. The sun was shining. All day, the people there talked about pedophiles trafficking children in from Mexico, and the people listening nodded. The details were gory and depraved, the stuff of FBI sting chat rooms. The tone was righteous, the displays religious. Somebody staged a crucifixion on the back of a pickup truck. They carved the face off Jesus and replaced it with a mirror, BECAUSE NOBODY TRULY UNDERSTANDS UNTIL IT'S THEM. A DJ, wearing an American-flag-patterned blazer, spun a pop song that went like this: "Trump won and you know it! Trump won and you know it! The fake news will never show it! Trump won and you know it!" I had to admit, it was catchy.

They were waiting for a trucker convoy. A few days earlier, thousands of truckers were said to have started a journey from Virginia Beach, and they were stopping along the way in Florida and Mississippi and Texas, and they would all meet in Yuma, ground zero for what they believed was the theft of the last presidential election.

I lingered near a golf cart turned float made of plywood and red, white, and blue tinsel. A group of elderly people sat on folding chairs nearby, and we got to talking, and the women fled, and the men stayed, and a man named Gary told me, though he was really shouting down the gravel path in the direction of his wife, who was walking away, that his wife has always understood and not cared about the fact that he loves to be around beautiful young women. Gary wore big dark sunglasses that made him look like a fly and one of those tan windbreakers like my grandfather wore. He looked like him, I thought. They shared a mean expression.

Grandpa Tony. Everyone hated him. In Korea, he had been hit in the face with a piece of shrapnel that deformed his nose. He left his family for a sixteen-year-old. My father was the oldest of four. He told me once, smoking a Marlboro Red on the porch, that he would go out on foot and search the streets of Williamsburg for Tony's Cadillac. When he found it, outside a bar, usually, or a woman's house, he would beat the car with his fists until it was dented. My father's entire life could be understood as a rejection of his father's entire life. My brother and I, we begged him to leave our mother. If he would not leave, could we find him a girlfriend? I wanted so badly for him to be loved as he loved or just to be cared for. He refused.

Gary smiled. He had a question, he said. He wanted me to tell him what the Democratic nominee, the incumbent president, had ever done for the country. *I dunno*, I said. *But he would probably say something about infrastructure.* That was not what Gary wanted. Gary wanted to know what I would say he had ever done for the country. Could I name a single thing? It is a trap, to engage in political debate in a place like this, to serve as representative for the liberal media elites. *I had never thought about it*, I said.

Gary waved over a younger man in a red polo shirt and when he arrived he asked me for a business card. I did not carry those. He asked to see my press credential. He held it up and put his phone to his ear. "We got a reporter here," he told the person on the other line. "Yeah. From *New York* magazine." I realized at that moment that I was, near as I could tell, the only reporter present at this event. I figured I would be on my way to Vegas soon enough, as it seemed that I was about to be kicked out. This was fine by me. I was used to being kicked out and I wanted to drive in the daylight. I do not like to waste the desert on the dark.

A small man ambled over to the float in a cowboy hat. Red polo shirt introduced him. He was the guy on the other end of the call. They were ready for their interview now, they said. I had not asked for one. We all stepped up onto the float. The trio sat down on the benches. I stood over them one row in front. Suddenly I was very aware of my whiteness, my blondness, my height. I felt like I was on stilts. The men were all Hispanic. They told me they were the whistleblowers, the ones from a right-wing propaganda film called *2000 Mules*. They had been fucked over by *The New York Times*, they said, but they volunteered that they trusted I would not fuck them over. They asked me if I had seen the film, and I lied and I said that I had because I did not want to listen to them explain the film to me. I was the fake news media, fake privately.

The votes had been stolen from Donald Trump, they said. They had proved it. It was around this time that I began to wonder where the trucker convoy was.

The saloon mostly operated as a wedding venue now, the owner told me, but she and her husband were honored to open it up to help save the union. Demonstrators had planted a nylon forest, hundreds of flags staked into the dirt. DON'T TREAD ON ME, the *Playboy* logo, ALL ABOARD THE TRUMP TRAIN, the Monster Energy logo, FUCK BIDEN, PROUD AMERICAN CHRISTIAN, the Confederate battle flag, DONALD TRUMP: MAKING AMERICA GREAT AGAIN! and JOE AND THE HO GOTTA GO. The American flags had been bastardized to feature the president's face or slogans about the virtues of law enforcement or some combination of the president's face and Christ on the Cross.

There were no truckers anyplace that I could see, just some pickups and sedans and SUVs and minivans and four-wheelers and motorcycles, parked all along the narrow street, the saloon on one side, standing alone, and the farmlands of the Yuma Valley on the other. The narrative of the Republican border gothic, the scene of the Democratic border pastoral. A patchwork of strip malls, reservations, charming houses, and 230,000 acres of what they call desert agriculture, irrigated by the Colorado and tended to by fifteen thousand migrant workers who cross the border from Mexico each morning and cross back at the end of the day. So that in winter you can order the Bibb lettuce at a restaurant in New York for twenty-three dollars, or the cost of an hour and a half of manual labor here. The sun was shining. At the horizon, the gravitational border painted a Rothko where the verdant fields met the clear blue sky.

Per the schedule, the trucker convoy would arrive in two parts. The first was set to roll through at 3 p.m. and the second at 6 p.m. But something fishy had been going on. The truckers had sent out a warning about infiltration by the Feds, stating that no trucks should stop in Eagle Pass, a small Texas town on the Rio Grande, because it was a setup. It was January 6 on wheels.

I had first traveled to Eagle Pass a year ago, or maybe it was two years now, after a national guardsman had waded into the river to save a drowning migrant. The river did not let him go. He was a kid. Early twenties. The governor had seemed so pleased by his death, for it confirmed everything he wanted the country to understand about his views on the border crisis. He smiled when he appeared on the right-wing network. I remember, in my Houston hotel room, I shut off the television.

In Yuma, rumors circulated in the crowd about where the truckers might now be. A hundred and twenty miles out, someone heard. Two hundred miles. Fifty-eight very specific miles. By 7 p.m., not a single truck had rolled through. The sun had set but it was not yet dark. I thought I had some daylight left for my drive west. I waited a little longer for the trucks. Or just for a truck. Any truck. It was cold now and I waited in the Mustang, which no longer smelled, or where I could no longer notice the smell.

People were leaving now, packing their flags and folding chairs into their trunks. The remaining crowd of optimists moved from the saloon to line the street in anticipation of the convoy's arrival. I waited a while longer. I took more Adderall. Still no truckers. Darkness fell about five minutes after I peeled off onto the highway.

VERA PAPISOVA: Where are you right now?

OLIVIA NUZZI: I'm on Thompson and Houston, and the [forty-sixth] president's motorcade is blocking Houston. The White House is fucking up my day and I'm not even in Washington.

VERA PAPISOVA: The president literally is tracking you right now.

OLIVIA NUZZI: There are not that many scenarios in life where people routinely express paranoia that the White House is out to get them. One is if you are a White House reporter and another is if you are schizophrenic. It's always a little challenging to maintain your grip on consensus reality in this line of work.

VERA PAPISOVA: How would you like to be credited and how can I describe your career up until this point?

OLIVIA NUZZI: The first one is easier. You can say I'm the Washington correspondent for *New York* magazine. I've been their Washington correspondent since Trump was inaugurated.

VERA PAPISOVA: Okay, you don't have to describe your career, but how would you describe your expertise?

OLIVIA NUZZI: My expertise? I wouldn't, is the answer. I wouldn't characterize it that way in general. Um. I don't know. If I describe what I do to people, I say I cover American politics, I write sort of character studies of people seeking or wielding or influencing political power.

VERA PAPISOVA: I wanted to ask you about burnout. Have you personally been affected by the political burnout that many people are experiencing?

OLIVIA NUZZI: When I accepted the assignment to cover Donald Trump, I didn't know how long it would last. I didn't think about it. It didn't occur to me for a very long time that it might never end. It felt so unwieldy and sprawling. It was this fire hose of information, on average a Watergate every hour. And the way I do things—I wouldn't say I go native, exactly, but I have a kind of Method reporting style. I like to be among the people I'm covering and do my best to understand them as human beings. Eventually, I reached this point where it got to be too much, there was no separation, no place in my life that was not consumed by the project, and I felt like, *I cannot spend every waking moment, I cannot show up to this White House every day, I cannot talk to these people every day.* The gap between consensus reality and their reality became impossible to bridge, it became impossible to communicate, harder and harder to establish any consensus.

VERA PAPISOVA: What did it feel like?

OLIVIA NUZZI: The reason I was good at covering it, in part, is that I was very familiar with the dynamics inside the Trump campaign and Trump White House because it reminded me of when I was a child, growing up in my house. My mother was mentally ill and she was an alcoholic, and there's a lot of secrecy in a house like that, and a lot of shame, and a lot of allowing someone to maintain their reality as a means of peacekeeping. I developed this ability to exist on dual planes, and an ability to mitigate conflict, or operate on a plane above conflict and not be immediately affected by it, in a way that really served me in covering Trump's rise to power, and all the people around him angling for power and proximity to power. By year three of the White House, which was for me year five of covering Trump, I was drained, and my phone would ring, and I would see it was an administration official, and I would think, *I don't care if they're calling to tell me that they're bombing Canada, I am not answering that fucking phone.*

VERA PAPISOVA: What is the hardest thing to convey to people about what happens on the dual political plane?

OLIVIA NUZZI: In your effort to get information that you can use and communicate to the public, you have to maintain relationships with people who you ordinarily would not want to maintain relationships with. You have to find a way to survive and manage strange interpersonal dynamics. The effort to retrieve information from individual people and from institutions is this ugly little puzzle every day. I am for whatever reason good at talking to people who are abhorrent and getting them to explain themselves to me at least a little bit and to trust me and share information with me and to maintain their relationship with me after I write something honest about them or about something they have shared with me. It is a high-wire act, a form of diplomacy.

———————

A reporter called to confirm a biographical detail: My father was among the workers who died from exposure to toxins at the World Trade Center after the attacks on September 11, 2001. "Who said that?" I asked. There was an organization, the reporter said, that kept track of the deaths, and his name was on their list.

The list to which the reporter referred was known to me. I had come across it once while researching the Department of Sanitation. I told the reporter that while I would like to claim for my father some kind of heroism in death, and while I figured his time at the site that he called *Gotham* had not helped matters any more than the Marlboro Reds, or his stubborn commitment to his marriage, I had no reason to believe his work at Ground Zero contributed in any direct way to him not being here now. It seemed to me a function of algorithm, a trick of the search engine, that he had been swept into this plot of a digital graveyard due to keywords in his obituary. His death was for the organization more faceless data. Another body to prove the point. The point was sound. The data suspect.

A name is a term. A death is a number. I could understand it best this way. He was born in New York City in 1955 and given the name John, the fifth most popular name for boys that year. He was raised on Ainslie Street in Williamsburg, the oldest in what would become a family of three sons and one daughter. He died on December 20, 2015, State File Number 20150068846, per the "certificate of death," bureaucratic confirmation without which I might never be sure he was gone. "Domestic Status: Married," "Manner of Death: Natural," "Cause of Death: Cardiac arrest; Respiratory failure; Gastrointestinal bleed; Cirrhosis of liver." She was born in New York City on February 12, 1962, and given the name Kelly, less common, the thirty-eighth most popular name for girls that year. She was raised in Queens, I never knew where, with a pink horse named Strawberry, for "Strawberry Fields Forever." She died on February 24, 2021, State File Number 2021040769. No manner or cause of death was listed. It had been a combination of alcoholism and a weakened immune system from treatment for metastatic breast cancer, itself a result, in all statistical likelihood, of alcoholism. I could understand it best this way, in terms of statistics. According to the Centers for Disease Control and Prevention, 95,000 deaths in America were "alcohol-related" in 2015. Such deaths ticked up precipitously. By 2021, 108,791 fell into the category. I could understand it this way, too, in terms of categories. Isolation and despair accompanied the working-class sprawl to the suburbs. The collapse of institutions at the most macro level and the decadent consumerism of the post-9/11 period drove the isolated and despaired further away from community, from spirituality, and drove some of them, drove her, to madness.

In the few photos she kept from her childhood, she was tan with long dark hair and green eyes. She looked like America, I thought, always with her horse. She had been a surprise, born to older parents, her mother an entrepreneur who according to lore had arrived alone on a ship to New York from England when she was twelve and worked in the kitchens of diners in the outer boroughs, which is why she knew how to cook, why I know how to cook, though I never do; her grandfather, a bit actor in silent films with a pet monkey who leapt from his shoulder around the house; her father, dead before she was two years old; her stepfather, a kind man whom she said she nevertheless rejected. The sixties and the women's movement had passed right by Queens. She wanted to be an oceanographer because of Jacques Cousteau. Instead she became a catalogue model, mostly swimsuits and wedding gowns, and an underage creature of Studio 54 and Xenon. She was twenty-four when she married my father, twenty-six when she had my brother, and thirty-one when she had me.

She was always the way she was, that was what the few people who knew her long enough to know said. The way she was, an uneven and explosive personality with an emotional range in primary colors. There was anger and there was sadness and much less often there was elation. There was nothing else. The alcohol corroded her simpler, dissolved the barrier between stability and madness, until it became almost irrelevant, whether she was intoxicated. As madness conquered her, the specter of madness and addiction rolled in. At my apartment on Christopher Street in the Village I kept a jar of cocaine, untouched; to observe it there on the table served as proof of an iron will, proof that I could be of them but not like them.

I lived in the nighttime. At night there was no one else. At night there was peace.

From the front porch I heard laughter. It was 3 a.m. I moved my ear to the window. Laughter, I was certain. Three a.m.

Inside, I walked down the long hallway. The door to my mother's bedroom was locked. I knocked. My mother answered. It was dark and she was cast in shadow. I thought she was on the phone. That is what it sounded like. When she came into the light I saw that she was holding a stuffed animal, a little dog that looked like my Jack Russell terrier. They were talking, it seemed, laughing together, though I could not hear the other side, could never know what she heard. I backed away and shut the door and ran to the other side of the house to wake my father. I told him about the laughter and the stuffed animal. He raised his eyebrows. No beat had he ever missed. He assumed one of his recurring characters, a God-fearing Puerto Rican woman. "Ay, Santa Maria Magdalena, don't let it be true!" he said, before he collapsed in faux distress, hand on his heart. We laughed.

The hospital had been so loud. Doors swung open and shut. People rushed through the halls in scrubs that whooshed, wheeled carts that rattled, sent alerts that buzzed and pinged and beeped. The hospital had grown louder and louder. An orchestra of emergency, the rushing, whooshing, swinging open and shut, conducted to a crescendo. Then he was dead and it was quiet. The quietest quiet I had ever heard.

In the hall I fell to the floor with his youngest brother, the baby like me. A big man with a big voice and the head of a wolf tattooed on his calf, cool and pure of a heart even bigger than he was. He was my age when his mother died, he said. He would come every day to the house on Ainslie and he would open the door and he would yell, "Ma!" And then she died, at sixty, hardly anyone in our family lived past sixty, and for months after, he would come every day to the house on Ainslie and he would open the door and he would yell, "Ma!"

The quiet now, as the quiet that fell on the earth in the middle of the night when snow began to fall. It was a few days before Christmas. Christmas would not arrive.

The raccoon could not believe his luck. A block of cotton candy, all his. In the viral footage, his pride apparent, he carried the sugary loot to the puddle. He put it down. *Poof.* In less than a second, it dissolved in the water, as if it had never existed. But it had existed. Right there within his paws. He had just seen it, had just held it. The raccoon did not understand. He grasped at the water. Where had it gone? He brought his nose to the surface and looked down. He waded deeper to search. He moved his arms through the water. Nothing. There was no trace of the object. There was just what he remembered.

The sea was a kind of blue that I was sure I had not seen before. I like to be here, on this ambivalent earth, because each day I wake with every reason to believe I may see something I am sure I have not seen before. On this morning, the tide rolling in crystalline barrels, the sun flashing green and silver; a bed of opals, a field of liquid light. It could kill me. It might try. I may not mind. I have not yet seen that, either. Though I hope it will be a while longer, hope for more time to see all that I might still see for the first time.

It is a human right to consider the elements in this manner and record their features. For as long as our species has had the ability to perform this exercise, we have tried our best to explain all that we see, and everyone has equal claim to take a stab. It is my first time here, in this form at least, and yours, too. There is only what Rebecca Elson termed "a responsibility to awe." I for one have noticed a pattern. I have noticed a few. One, all the world and all we have observed beyond it adheres to pattern, through the bud of the rose into our flesh, our veins, veins of leaves, of rivers, the neurons of our brains a maze as the knife-turn planetary pathway sprawl of the cosmos. Everywhere, God repeats Himself, makes Himself clear, forgives us time to see the truth, to speak His name. Two, the second-to-last gasp is all ecstasy. The eve of destruction is the most beautiful moment you will ever waste. I stared into the sea and found the sky.

All this time later it is a shared memory, the sky that morning. Would I still know that in isolation, had I not been conditioned to pluck the image from my mind, to freeze the frame, to contribute what I saw of the cloudlessness to the cloud of our great American memory? I can see it now. Blue. A blue blue. A blue that makes itself clear. A blue I saw then for the first time and never saw again. Not exactly. Not like that.

I had expected to leave school early that day with my mother, as I did a few times per week. She would drive me to a studio in SoHo or a theater in Midtown, and I would pose for a Polaroid or I would read sides, and then we would drive home. I did not particularly enjoy posing for Polaroids or reading sides but I did enjoy leaving school early. I hated to be trapped anyplace, then as now, most of all a classroom.

EDDIE PEPITONE: I never book commercials because I'm too angry, and the commercial world is that ridiculous, like, "Honey, how'd you get the shirts so fresh?" . . . The world is falling to shit, but the biggest thing is, "How'd you get—" So I'm always improvising, like, "Honey! Honey! How'd you get the shirts so fresh! I mean, one out of three people are in jail these days! People are stabbing each other for food not half a block away from this audition! Yet you get the shirt fresh! How do you fuckin' do it?"

Due to a similar disposition that prevented me from reciting lines such as "More Ovaltine, please!" or "Only on Nickelodeon!" in a believable manner, I found my theatrical services were seldom desired and when they were it was to appear in my natural pale and sullen state in advertisements for cold medicine. I was good at faking sick. If I was home sick, I could get in my mother's way. I could not stop her from drinking but I could throw obstacles in her path. She might become enraged over this, and I might pay for it, but a somewhat sober rage was safer than a drunken one. I monitored her mood and balance. The most dangerous state was moderate intoxication. That was when she was active. When she might have ideas and attempt to execute them, execute me. If she reached this point, I got out of her path and recalibrated my strategy to enable her to drink until she passed out. In that event, to manage the rest of the day and night all I had to do was stay very quiet and check her breathing once in a while. I was the only one she never hit on purpose. This made me bolder than my brother or father could afford to be. I faked sick as often as possible. I positioned myself between her and her targets.

On the blue morning I had dressed in a more considered and colorful way than I ordinarily would, in a green shirt stamped by a yellow flower and my hair braided with little green ribbons. I thought of this as dressing up as a regular child, *playing the child.* As I waited to escape, an exodus began. Child after child plucked from the classroom. Nearly every child except me. I asked for the hall pass and roamed around the building. In a room near the principal's office I found a few teachers huddled together watching the television, their hands covering their mouths. The sand-colored smoke, the blue sky. The adults did not notice me in the doorway. Even then, like a ghost.

When she arrived, my mother did not know that anything had happened in New York. She did not know that the bridges and tunnels were closed. She melted over the steering wheel. The first time I saw the work of Salvador Dalí, I was startled. He had painted my mother, I thought, in her ethanol warp. I was used to this sight. I was used to this dilemma. First, how to exit the parking lot of the school without detection by an adult who might raise the alarm, a source of constant paranoia, though no adult had ever raised so much as a question. Second, how to travel the two miles home without dying, or without killing someone else. The terrorism variable presented a third challenge. My mother ignored my objections and swerved up the parkway. There were no other cars headed north.

I fixed my stare on the horizon, slowed my breath, and imagined light. I talked to angels. I figured they had sent me here. I figured they would not take me out so soon. I told them I trusted they knew what they were doing when they made their assignment. Still, I wanted to check in, to make sure they were with me here in the car with the madwoman, that they had not forgotten about my deployment. This was how I survived, talking to angels. At the police barricade, the officer looked at my mother with a puzzled expression. He leaned into her window to peer at me in the back of the car. She backed up, turned onto the median, and swerved south.

Sally Quinn taught me about labyrinths. In Washington, I would walk from my house on Twenty-Eighth Street to her house on N Street, and she would emerge platinum in the doorway, and together we would go down to the Potomac, where over the river was a labyrinth paved in stone. At the mouth of the path, she told me, you state your intention. As you wind your way through, you meditate on that intention. When you emerge, it is to new clarity.

South on the Pacific Coast Highway, to Sunset, to the trailhead in the Palisades. This loop became what I thought of as a western labyrinth. I loved the variety of architecture in Los Angeles, loved that the imagination shared by its citizens seemed to manifest through the incongruent aesthetics in the residential neighborhoods. The mid-century marvel right next to the Mediterranean villa, the Art Deco angles colliding with the Greek columns or the soft edges of the Tudor cottages next door. There was always something to look to with wonder, with amusement, no shortage of character drawn into the terrain by a population that seemed to believe that reality can be, a lot of the time, anyway, just what you decide, that the fragile world can hold your desires for a little while and within them allow you to live as you please.

What at first visit struck me as the *Truman Show* quality of the Palisades came to charm, and at night when I thought Malibu too desolate and too conquered by the coyotes to walk alone, I would instead wind through the sidewalks there, where I found some kind of clarity around every corner.

The rumor of wind. The power out. Everywhere, I saw fire.

In Pismo, the mounds of sand and sea figs, white and green and pink, the shock of yellow, the Brazilian buttercups, and the bright blue surf in the shadow of the Santa Lucias, in shape and pattern and palette, the land of Oz or Dr. Seuss or Milton Glaser. In the grove of eucalyptus trees I watched the monarch butterflies migrate. *Danaus plexippus.* The orange flash of their burning flight prompted a physiological flight response. Movement paused, chest tightened, breath held. As though I should next expect smoke, sirens.

Back in Malibu around 1 a.m., I talked to a friend, a longtime adviser to the president, who could not sleep in New York, and as she told me about her plans to travel to Washington in a few hours and attend a dinner for the new attorney general that night, a flame shot up over the hills to the south. The deep blue night, the charcoal ridge of earth, the slash of blood orange. I leapt from bed and ran out the door onto the deck. I focused my eyes. It was still, the flame, even as it seemed to grow taller. I climbed down from the deck and walked through the yard, past the lemon trees. The flame rose higher and higher until it revealed itself as not a flame at all but a slice of moon. I exhaled. Still I eyed the trick crescent with suspicion as it moved in the sky until dawn.

Fresh Kills was a 2,200-acre landfill in western Staten Island. By the year my father was born, it was the largest such facility in the world. It was here that 1.6 million tons of rubble from the fallen towers arrived for forensic analysis, sorting, and final rest. Of items recovered by thousands of Department of Sanitation personnel who worked over a period of ten months, beginning in September and ending the following July: fifty-four thousand personal artifacts, fourteen hundred vehicles, close to eighty thousand dollars in domestic and foreign currency. Three hundred people were identified in the four thousand shards of human remains found at the site. The rest of the rubble was placed within a forty-acre plot; the medical examiner said that it was all but certain the rubble contained the undiscovered pieces of people murdered on the blue morning.

I recall my father was gone for a long time. When he returned, he brought with him what looked like big pale rocks. Pieces of the towers. He put them on the mantel over the fireplace.

———

The spark, the flame, the rumor fulfilled. The labyrinth on fire. The Palisades Fire.

10:30 a.m., ten acres burning.

10:50 a.m., twenty acres burning.

The winds returned at what was described by officials as a "hurricane force" of eighty miles per hour. It had been in Southern California not just a drought but the driest nine-month period in recorded history. Billions of dollars to fund fleets of hundreds of fire trucks and aircraft and thousands of responders, plus the thousands more volunteers and furloughed prisoners paid as little as one dollar an hour for their labor, up against our more flammable world.

2 p.m., seven hundred acres burning.

3 p.m., one thousand three hundred acres burning.

Past hairpin turns down canyon roads to the shore, firefighters threw up barriers, knocked on the car windows of people as they tried to flee, advised that there would not be time for traffic jams near the highway. Wildfire is a sprinter; flames grow as fast as three acres a second. Wildfire wins every race. Survival would require quick acceptance here. Escapees would need to abandon their cars, their belongings, and exit the disaster on foot.

Wives prepared. Husbands forgot. What they recalled, mostly, was the "good-generic" day before the burning began. "I had a bowl of apples," one man said. "I gave her some apples." His wife closed her eyes and smiled. "He gave me some apples."

By nightfall, the winds had grounded the helicopters. The fire swelled.

12:30 a.m., three thousand acres burning.

9 a.m., five thousand acres burning.

11:45 a.m., twelve thousand acres burning.

1:30 p.m., sixteen thousand acres burning.

New fires broke out elsewhere, everywhere. In the Hollywood Hills near Runyon. In Altadena. North in Ventura. South in Orange. All of Southern California, painted orange. The wealthy summoned private fire departments. The poor found their emergency alerts delayed by hours. Of the eighty-eight cities that make up Los Angeles County, thirty-nine have the official designation "Very High Fire Hazard Severity Zones." From the 405, the whole place in flames. At a distance what appears a cinematic apocalypse or dystopian war is, up close, a bunch of eyes stinging, lungs infected, lives disrupted, homeless displaced, memories destroyed, children terrorized, parents helpless and then distracted by calls to inept insurance companies.

Over the fire, a drone collided with an aircraft, boring a hole through its wing.

Six thousand structures burned to the ground.

Ten people burned to death.

One hundred and five thousand people evacuated.

Five hundred homes destroyed.

Forty miles northeast in Altadena, the Eaton Fire killed eighteen people and tore through ten thousand structures; churches and temples, restaurants, schools, and close to five thousand homes, half of all Black households in neighborhoods that became, after the Civil Rights Act and Fair Housing Act, a haven for a Black population squeezed out of parts of Los Angeles by redlining still enforced unofficially once legally dismantled by the prohibition on race-based discrimination.

The air was toxic, the ground a heap of rubble growing larger.

9 p.m., twenty thousand acres burning.

8 a.m., twenty-two thousand acres burning.

4 p.m., twenty-four thousand acres burning.

Through the burned-open door of the burned-down house, a dolphin leaps out of the sea. Perverse, that the great fire break-in made available the view. Malibu, population thirteen thousand, twenty-one miles of coastline. All that is left is the doorframe, the spiral staircase, the chimney. On a house that still stands, a neon sign at the entrance reads, 21036 THE PARTY'S HERE. Good times ghost. Bad times crash. I look down at the crashing swell. Alone at the after-party, a kind of honeymoon in hell. I am on the list, a bit of grave misfortune. I am in the *New York Post*, even worse. The ink is black, the pages yellow. Everything, some kind of lie. What of doubt? Scientists cannot see the soul. That does not mean much to me. The soul sees scientists all the same. Another house, 21300, flayed open to the fireplace, the filing cabinet. The debris of my life litters the planet. My mistakes, harassment, humiliation: fishwrap, recycling in a best-case scenario, and in any case the mechanism by which more dyes and chemicals are delivered to the atmosphere, another sin to which I am a party. The party, here. I can hardly remember what it was to shut the world out. A television newscaster stands before the rubble. Artificial light on her hair, a radioactive kind of yellow. She fixes her gaze on the eye of the camera and goes live. Behind her the bones of someone's birthdays,

Sundays, dinners, showers; just a backdrop now, a set piece, a *great shot.*

"Are you alone?" the Bodyguard asked. I was alone, I said. "Good. I'm alone, too," he said. "[The Politician] called earlier and asked if I knew how you are doing." The Politician, by now the Secretary, had called others recently with similar questions. I thought it was a stupid thing to do, to involve others. It was just like the Politician to be stupid in such a manner. The Bodyguard continued on. "He wanted to tell you that he's very sorry, and he wanted to express recognition, he said, 'That this has also been very difficult for Olivia, and gratitude for everything she has done to help me,' and he said he feels bad about and is sorry in particular—and I didn't know about this, but he said that you would know what he was referring to—for the times that, uh, evidently there had been some times when he yelled at you."

When he yelled, the soft flame of his voice roared a lithium fire, sparked anger that sparked anger and torched everything in its path. He yelled himself foreign. The man who yelled was not the man I thought I knew. The man who yelled was the man others had told me to fear.

"What am I supposed to do with this?" I asked the Bodyguard. I liked the Bodyguard. I liked him long before I knew him, because I liked his writing, and I liked him even though I knew that he was managing me, even as he insisted that he was not managing me, and I liked him even when he communicated on behalf of the Politician things that I knew to be false. He was, on balance, smart and perceptive and calm and strategic, and with the exception of the occasions when the Personality told me that I should be scared of him, the Bodyguard made me less scared. Because I liked him, my tone when I asked that question, *What am I supposed to do with this?*, was sharper than I would have liked. "Well, nothing. Just, well, he's sorry," the Bodyguard said. "I told him to let me handle this. I need you to read between the lines."

———

Soon after the call with the Bodyguard, I was lying on the lawn of Saint Augustine grass at the little house at Zuma, watching a red-tailed hawk move through the fog. Then I heard it. That distinct electric hum. At the hedges, a drone hovered at eye level to meet my gaze. It stared straight at me for a while. Then it moved left. Then it moved right. Then it pushed forward across the grass and paused. It stayed there, still, over my head. It drifted lower. It was proud, aggressive, bigger than the drones I had seen, or that had seen me, near the driveway, the biggest predator in the sky.

"That's not subtle," the Personality said. "The point may be to make you paranoid." He asked if I wanted him to send me a shotgun.

———

In the days before the confirmation hearings, I slept so little that lines bent, and time skipped ahead and slipped back, and soft sounds startled while the voices of those who addressed me, even face-to-face, did not come through completely or on time. I was in some sense in the next room, or out the door, or underwater.

I would come to, and I would realize that someone had been talking for a long while, talking right at me, and talking in a manner that seemed to suggest they had been talking for long enough that they must be very far into a story, and I would search for clues, trying to recall what the jumping-off point had been. Surely I had heard it at the time. Surely it had landed someplace in my mind. Must be there still, recoverable, if only I could locate it. *What was he saying?* Oh yes, he was talking about the Broadway production, or the off-Broadway production. Or no, about the theater in Washington named for the Politician's family that was now a battleground for cultural and political warfare. But by now he seemed to be talking mostly about union health insurance, and the press, and the FBI, and for reasons even less clear, communism.

All my hours being waking hours, my time was concerned mostly with inputs that I hoped would form an informational dam to halt the river of my thoughts. I spent the days analyzing different translations of *The Divine Comedy*. I hired an Italian tutor, from Lake Como but living now for mysterious reasons in Nicaragua, so that I could try to understand the source material myself, which he found to be a ridiculous idea, though he said he would do his best to help. I spent the night pacing the house listening to lectures and audiobooks: Nikola Tesla's theory about human advancement, and a gambling addict's memoir, and a time capsule about anxiety related to terrorism in the wake of 9/11 written by the Bodyguard, and a history of the rivalry between Edwin Thomas Booth, a great actor, and John Wilkes Booth, a bad actor before he was a bad actor, and some Nietzsche for levity.

During this period I found that I could not formulate my usual prayers. Around where my heart must still be, the tide of blood ripped and curled; from here, drowning, I would try to speak my petition. Could I maintain enough grace to pray only selflessly? Could I want only that which was selfless? If I was not sure then I said no prayer at all. Often, I said no prayer at all.

I had not eaten for a long while and that combined with not sleeping in a long while made me strange and scared and one night, around 3 a.m., I fled out the back door and drove up the coast, up past Santa Barbara, where around four thirty the only establishment open was a diner, and I was very cold in this period all the time, and I found it to be a warm place, and I sat there drinking bad coffee in bad light and picking at average pancakes.

The diner played Billy Joel and a homeless man and an old woman filled two other tables and it stayed that way until, just before sunrise, some teenagers arrived and entertained loudly subjects ranging from macros and seed oils to details of the prior night's acid trip, and they did not know they were anyplace near Santa Barbara, they thought they were in another part of California altogether, and one of them was planning to go for a run later in the morning and another said he would go home to sleep, and the girl said things like, *No cap, bro*, and I found them to be a lovely presence.

Rain rolled in. The cloud-darkened sky made it so there was not much to distinguish between night and day. I lost track of whether and when I had slept, how many nights ago exactly, whether two days had passed or three or four. As the senators entered the chamber, I prayed that the Politician would be protected, prayed that God would use him as a force for good, and in that way prayed, too, for myself, for my own redemption. Most of all I prayed for the country.

I woke to my phone ringing. Without thinking, I answered. An unfamiliar voice. A reporter, she said, with a tabloid. I did not speak. I had forgotten, in the dark, the dark comedy of errors that had led me here.

"Is this Olivia?" she asked.

"... *Yes* ..." I said.

I said this in an uncertain way, not as though I was uncertain of whether I should answer but as though I was uncertain of the answer. The reporter went on.

"I wanted to see if you had any comment about [the Politician's] confirmation," she said.

I did not speak. If I hung up, she could use that. She could infer whatever she wanted. She could write the action as a response to the events in Washington about which she had posed her question and not the event in my ear of her having posed the question.

"Hello?" she said.

She could use a silence, too. I had used silences. Had inferred from silences. With each second the odds of that increased. How many seconds had it been already? I had to say something. I tried to think fast, but a supercut was barreling across my consciousness, every time over the years, when I was on the other side of an exchange such as this, when I had been screamed at or hung up on or had a door slammed in my face or an insult hurled in my direction. I squeezed my eyes shut.

"I'm not speaking to the press," I said.

I hung up. I turned the phrase over and over.

I'm not speaking to the press. I had spoken it so easily. Spoken of not speaking.

I'm not speaking to the press. But I am the press? I was. I am not.

I'm not speaking to the press. I am not speaking and I am not the press.

I'm not speaking to the press. I am not speaking to myself.

———

Ahead, I clocked a cop car. It was dusk and the sky was pink and the tar valley between the mountains and the sea was otherwise empty and so this cop was, to my mind, an even less welcome presence than any cop on any road would ordinarily be. Except, that is, for the occasions when I am being followed out of a gas station through some desolate stretch of country, in which case I long to see a cop, one of the many minor hypocrisies I engage in on the road; when I am on foot, drivers are my enemy, while as a driver, I regard pedestrians and above all cyclists as hostile troops, and so on.

I slowed down to observe the speed limit. Close to it, anyway. As I neared the vehicle, I noticed the lettering under its taillights. Green. The same shade of green as the lettering on vehicles manned by Border Patrol. I was almost to Ventura County, two hundred miles or so north of Tijuana. Border Patrol would not be this far up the coast, would they?

Democratic senators voted to approve the construction of seven hundred miles of fencing in 2006. Comprehensive immigration reform remained an elusive goal for both parties, but the ideological disagreements that killed bipartisan negotiations time and again were about the interior of the country, not the line that determined where its exterior began. The conservative Right routinely denounced these proposals as "amnesty," the labor Left as wage suppression for American workers.

Meanwhile, Republicans were losing the popular vote in presidential elections and party leadership increasingly thought messaging on immigration was to blame. The 2012 Republican nominee said undocumented immigrants should "self-deport," and after his defeat, the Republican National Committee concluded that the future of the party would depend on its ability to "carefully craft a tone that takes into consideration the unique perspective of the Hispanic community."

The modern border crisis arrived two years later, in 2014, when migrants fleeing violence and poverty in Central America began crossing the Rio Grande in record numbers, sometimes more than four thousand a day. The administration of the forty-fourth president, which would deport more undocumented immigrants than any to that point in history, called in backup for an overwhelmed Border Patrol and constructed a new processing center, where detainees were separated by metal fencing, young men in one area, mothers and small children in another, families in another. Migrants called it the dog kennel, *la perrera*. It was condemned even by the far-right media, for whom opposition to the Black president was a greater priority than opposition to the brown immigrants.

Then, on June 16, 2015, Donald Trump rode the escalator into the atrium of his high-rise to announce that he was running for president because the American people were getting ripped off by their leaders and the country was less safe and less prosperous as a result. "When Mexico sends its people, they're not sending their best. They're not sending you. They're not sending you. They're sending people that have lots of problems, and they're bringing those problems with us. They're bringing drugs. They're bringing crime. They're rapists and some, I assume, are good people," he said. It wasn't just Mexico, he added. It was "South and Latin America," and "probably" it was "the Middle East," too. But it was Mexico that he promised to address first and most forcefully. And it was the wall itself that he identified as the symbol of American security and wealth, his very own Lady Liberty in reverse. "So just to sum up, I would do various things very quickly," he said. "I would build a great wall, and nobody builds walls better than me, believe me, and I'll build them very inexpensively. I will build a great, great wall on our southern border, and I will have Mexico pay for that wall." The

Trump era of American politics had begun, and the very concept of border security was claimed as an extension of the Trump brand. It always came back to real estate.

Upon his return to office, the president had directed incredible manpower to execute his plans for mass deportations of undocumented immigrants throughout the country. His secretary of Homeland Security was a woman with no law enforcement experience who had been governor of a state fourteen hundred miles from the southern border, and since she assumed office, her central activity was the creation of propaganda in which she posed, animated by a kind of sexual fervor and sadistic spirit of retribution, her head festooned with hair extensions and face inflated with criminal imprecision by cosmetic fillers, alongside the hordes of shackled men that as a matter of policy the administration called *illegals*. The president had campaigned on the promise of a purge of such people, and she was seeing to it, and more important than that, she was making sure she was seen seeing to it. It was not impossible that optics-focused policing edicts might send Border Patrol very far from the southern border; the message from the administration, after all, was that the country would be safe only so long as no *illegals* were safe. That was implicit in the slogan Make America Safe Again, which came in the chant after the better-known slogan Make America Great Again.

Still, nowhere in America had I ever seen a Border Patrol sedan. In California and Arizona and Texas, they rolled by, as far as I could recall, exclusively in SUVs and pickups. Curious, I sped up.

This vehicle was not from a fleet deployed by Homeland Security or any other branch of federal law enforcement. Nor was it from the Los Angeles County Police Department or the Ventura County Police Department. The green letters spelled out a different kind of body entirely:

BOOTY PATROL. On the side of the car, an illustration of a peach was rendered in the style of a sheriff's badge.

Immigration and Customs Enforcement arrived to raid Los Angeles, and demonstrators arrived to protest the detention of undocumented immigrants downtown. ICE called in the FBI, and as the police response grew militarized, the scene grew violent. Tear gas and rubber bullets fired into the crowd. Molotov cocktails fired from the crowd.

The president summoned the National Guard. The defense secretary mobilized a full battalion of five hundred marines stationed 145 miles east in the Mojave Desert oasis Twentynine Palms. In response, the governor sued the administration. "This is a manufactured crisis. He is creating fear and terror to take over a state militia and violate the U.S. Constitution. The illegal order he signed could allow him to send the military into ANY STATE HE WISHES. Every governor—red or blue—should reject this outrageous overreach. There's a lot of hyperbole out there. This isn't that. This is an unmistakable step toward authoritarianism that threatens the foundation of our republic. We cannot let it stand," he said. The president said he would arrest the governor, given the authority. The governor dared him to do it. A representative for ICE made a statement: "Troops on the ground in Los Angeles are providing perimeter and personnel protection for our facilities and officers who are out on daily enforcement operations. They are providing security at federal facilities."

A form of civil unrest played in the discourse as levity: On the scanner, the Los Angeles Police Department made a request to shut down a service that summons driverless, autonomous vehicles: "People keep calling them and then lighting them on fire." Of the development, someone remarked, "I love LA."

At the White House, the scale of the American flags swelled.

Down in Tijuana, a man drove a white GMC pickup truck with a Mexican flag looped around the rearview mirror. The back window was a collage of stickers: Infowars, LET'S GO BRANDON, the Blue Lives Matter flag, and so on. A sign of distress in the form of the backward American flag waved from the gas cap. When the driver cut me off, trash flew out of the bed of the truck.

Nearby, a vehicle from Bulldog Towing dragged a mangled Border Patrol SUV across the pavement.

As a body rots, the face starts to smile.
—Dr. Yasser al-Kassem, assistant head of the Forensic Science
department at al-Mujtahid Hospital in Damascus

To identify hundreds of bodies from the prisons opened up after the former president of Syria lost power, al-Kassem asks families for photos in which the missing are smiling. The former president of Syria, whose regime made people who smiled into bodies.

————

The protester was being shouted down, shouted over, by a tall man whose figure cast a shadow on him where he sat in the lawn chair on the sidewalk. The protester did not shout back, did not rise up. He let the noise and the anger wash right over him. After a few minutes the tall man wore himself out. He stormed off. The protester remained just as he was, unbothered in the lawn chair with a serene look on his face.

When we spoke I learned he was hard of hearing, and maybe that helped, but it seemed more that his identification as a peace activist applied far beyond ideas about government-waged or -sanctioned barbarism.

He had been living in Malibu a few years, in Point Dume. He did not like it here, he said, because there was too much money and not much soul and it was hard to feel comfortable, to discern any community around him with which to engage, and so he was the solitary man in the lawn chair, a sight of relief or curiosity or provocation to passersby, depending on their views.

He was retired now from the career he said he stumbled into in which he had been a producer and director of "everything" from *Miami Vice* to *Friends*. He was from Los Angeles but he had been living in New York with an actor, and he tagged along to an audition for *Hope Is the Thing with Feathers*, and was offered two jobs: a small acting part or the role of assistant director. The AD gig paid five dollars more per week, so he became the AD. Then the director got sick, so he became the director. Then some years later, after stints directing here and there, and all the while he was active in the antiwar movement, which meant he knew Jane Fonda, knew her pretty well, and she was putting together a cabaret to protest Vietnam, and she needed a director, and so he became the cabaret director, and then she asked him to direct a film related to the project, and he said "Sure," and that was how he became a screen director. All of his life followed him saying "Sure" to offers, is what it sounded like.

He was distraught over the results of the election, although no candidate had been good on the issue of the war in the Middle East, he said. He worried about what the president would do. That was the nature of presidents, in his experience: You worried what they would do. This president, with his idiosyncrasies and volatility, was an extreme cause for worry but he was just a new plot point on an old power spectrum.

This protest was like all the others he had waged for half a century, he said, though he did not distinguish between protests. The way he saw it, he had been putting on one long antiwar demonstration the whole time. The wars changed; opposition to war did not. He had been coming to the farmers market every Sunday since October 7, 2023, he said, and when I asked if he would be back next Sunday, he said he would be back every Sunday until the war stopped, and so I said, "Well, then, I will see you next Sunday," and I had not intended to make a grim joke about the world when I said this, but as the words escaped my lips I realized that I had, and he laughed a sad laugh and he said, "Yeah, I will see you next Sunday."

There are cathedrals everywhere for those with the eyes to see.
—Dr. Jordan B. Peterson, referring in the specific to the reflection
of sunlight through the plastic facets of an Evian bottle

The president was showing off a friend. He was another businessman, a billionaire from Israel. He had arrived in America with just $250 to his name, the president said, and through sheer will and wit he had made himself here, made a fortune in entertainment and an oddball collection of investments.

The president was dazzled by this tale of success, and as he spun it for me in the living room at Mar-a-Lago, he gestured to the businessman and smiled a wide smile. The businessman could not have been taller than five foot four, and the president looked down to beam the smile right at him. "Amazing, it's amazing," the president said.

For all the focus on his finicky tastes and hard-to-please nature, it was true that it was not hard to impress the president. He liked doers. It did not matter much what exactly was being done. And there was, still, nothing as impressive to the president as wealth, visible and tangible, and creation—of structure, product, and most of all of self. He was awed by anyone who, like him, had made a self of themselves so consequential that all the world had to accept the terms. He was extra awed by those who made themselves by themselves. For all the focus on his overtly sensitive ego—and it was true, he was egotistical and so sensitive it seemed at times unimaginable that he could make it through a single day as a person in the world, never mind as leader of the for-now-still-free one—he was never withholding of praise for those who did something he did not, so long as those people did not withhold praise for him. As always, if you liked the president, he loved you in return. "Isn't it *amazing?*" he asked me.

Before he had segued into this spate of compliments for the businessman, we were talking about his rallies, about him taking me to a rally out west. I had been by then to so many rallies in so many states over so many years that they had long ago blurred into a kaleidoscope of red and red and red and red and blue and white, of hats and flesh and flags and fistfights and fast food and rhinestones, a borderless mass with one heart beating very fast, dancing to "Y.M.C.A." and chanting about the border wall, chanting for or against the rule of law, the scenes stretched and pulled apart and apart and apart and apart. Even on the floor of a rally, I might have to remind myself where we were, what city, in what context, in what year. Dubuque, 2023; Hartford, 2016; Manchester, 2015; Carson City, 2020; Biloxi, 2016; Orlando, 2019; Fredericksburg, 2016; Long Island, 2016; Casper, 2022; Harrisburg, 2017; Des Moines, 2020; Cedar Rapids, 2017; Harrisburg, 2024; Cincinnati, 2016; Hickory, 2020; Boca Raton, 2016. On and on like that. Ten years of this narrow palette of colors, and a score of hits and incantations, and the scorpion and the frog, and the oral anti-history told by the star at the center of it all. He was the only quality never in doubt; this was true even when he was shot at. There was the country itself and there was the president. Little else reliably mattered. He was the beginning and end of his own point.

The businessman did not go to the rallies. "He doesn't like them," the president told me. He laughed. This did not appear to bother the president at all. "Why not?" I asked, directing my attention down to his guest. The businessman bulged his eyes cartoonishly and erupted in an emphatic cranial gesture of disapproval, shaking his head from side to side in such a vigorous manner that it looked as though he might take flight right through the gold-leafed ceiling. "*No, no, no, no, no,*" he said. His Israeli accent was heavy. "I don't like to go."

The president raised his eyebrows, extended his hands, palms up, and shrugged. "They make him uncomfortable," he said. What can you do? The businessman leaned over and lowered his voice to a whisper. "He hypnotizes the people," he said. He nodded his head in the direction of the president.

———

On the blue morning, 2,753 people died in the Twin Towers, 147 from Monmouth County. From Mount Mitchill, the highest point on the Atlantic coast, the buildings could be seen as they burned, fell. In the weeks after, when my father was gone at Ground Zero, the rituals of patriotism intruded in new ways. Each morning, over the sound system at River Plaza Elementary School, the Pledge of Allegiance was followed by the Lee Greenwood ballad "God Bless the USA."

I would not hear the song again for a long time.

———

The chimes of terror, of war. The sound of Lee Greenwood flooded the arena. On the floor, I looked up. Time folded, overlapped, stretched, pulled apart and apart and apart and apart.

The first five minutes of the first MAGA rally, in Des Moines hours after the formal declaration of Donald Trump's campaign, were devoted to mocking another politician over what the candidate said was his insufficient wealth. He retold the story of how his comments on the matter had ricocheted through the media; the Gucci store in the lobby of

Trump Tower was worth more than the man, he said. He distracted himself with a tangent about the primo location of the store and how it proved his real estate acumen.

He turned to the subject of American foreign policy misadventures and the mistakes of the forty-fourth president. His Big Idea, which he predicted the other candidates, "those lightweights," would soon adopt, would be, "you go into each one of these things"—the "four or five major major oil hubs"—"and you blast the hell out of them. You just take them over . . . *You kill the devil at the head. You kill the devil at the head.*" The great sin of America's wars in the Middle East, he said, was "We got nothing!"

For the next rally, a few days later in Manchester, the animating feud was with a Republican interest group. "It's all money, it's all corruption . . . the lobbyists, the donors, the special interests . . . I don't need anybody's money," he said. On foreign policy, his platform served two purposes: criticism of the status quo and book promotion. "We don't know what the *art of the deal* is," he said.

In Phoenix, the crowds began to find him. "So this began as five hundred people in a ballroom in Phoenix and the hotel called us up and they said please don't do it here, we're going to be swamped, it's going to destroy the building—it's been amazing! And outside, sadly, we have thousands of people that can't get in, so you know real estate," he said.

He talked here about corporate blowback to his announcement speech, the *sending rapists* of it all, and he talked about reality television, "We had a tremendous success," he said of his own program. The network on which it aired, he said, "renewed" the program. "See: I give up a lot. You're gonna see how much money I made when I do my filing. Seriously, it's very lucrative—you know, when you have a big television show, you're, like, a movie star, you get a lot of money," he said. The network went so far as to beg him to return for another season, he said, "Which is good, 'cause I always wanna be loved, you know? . . . I told them, I can't. I want to make America great again."

It was not until Alabama that the *MAGA rally* registered with the small campaign staff as a phenomenon.

By the time he was as good as nominated by the Republican Party, he had refined the stagecraft of these events. Where he had once entered to the nasal howl of Neil Young, a Canadian, "Rockin' in the Free World," or to the theme song for his terrestrial reality television show, "For the Love of Money," and always exited, a bit of comic genius, to the Stones, "You Can't Always Get What You Want," he now walked onstage to Greenwood and performed a slo-mo survey of the crowd, waving and nodding, his face an expression, depending on the mood of the day and the light, of satisfaction or gratitude or solemnity.

———

Ten years later, the Bible would be subsumed by the president's brand with Greenwood's assistance. For $59.99, plus shipping and tax, he sold the God Bless the USA Bible: the King James Bible, plus a page printed with the chorus of "God Bless the USA," written by hand, plus the Constitution, the Bill of Rights, the Declaration of Independence, and the Pledge of Allegiance. For the Presidential Edition Bible, the First Lady Edition Bible, the Vice Presidential Edition Bible, the Platinum Edition Bible, the Golden Age Edition Bible, the Inauguration Day Edition Bible, the Veteran Edition Bible, and the Patriot Edition Bible, the cost was steeper, $99.99, plus shipping and tax. The President Donald J. Trump Signature Edition Bible, advertised as, "Limited

Edition," "Less Than 200 available," "While Supplies Last," "Each Bible Contains President Donald J. Trump's Hand-Signed Signature," goes for $1,000, plus shipping and tax.

"All Americans need a Bible in their home, and I have many. It's my favorite book," the president said. "It's a lot of people's favorite book."

I spun the globe in the year 2003. I was surprised to find Iraq was not next to Afghanistan, where I expected it would be, based on what I heard of the new war, the additional war. At the same time, the rituals of patriotism remained an intrusion. My brother came home with a report from school. The *French fries* in the cafeteria were now called something else: *freedom fries*. He laughed as he told me this. I recall I did not understand the joke.

The French president had declined to back the war in Iraq. "For us, war is always the proof of failure and the worst of solutions, so everything must be done to avoid it," he said, and for his wisdom he was protested by American lawmakers, among them a Republican congressman from North Carolina. In his district, the owner of a restaurant, Cubbie's, took a cue from World War I, when Americans renamed German foods to express anti-German sentiment, with mixed results: *Sauerkraut* became, for a time, *liberty cabbage* and *frankfurter* became, for good, *hot dog*. The restaurant owner posted a sign in the window of his establishment: "Because of Cubbie's support for our troops, we no longer serve *French fries*. We now serve *freedom fries*." The congressman brought the issue to the attention of the Committee on House Administration, which manages the congressional cafeteria. It caught on. Which did not impress the French. "We are at a very serious moment dealing with very serious issues and we are not focusing on the name you give to pota-toes," the embassy said in a statement.

Speaking to the writer Eve Peyser in 2018, the congressman re-sponsible for the ordeal said that, looking back, he was not impressed, either. "I didn't believe any of it but I asked no questions," he told her. "When I had to make a decision, in my heart, I regret it, but I'll be hon-est with you, I was too concerned about getting reelected." He regretted his support for the war, too. "We think we can change the world, but certain parts of the world don't want to be changed. My understanding of what I had done in the Iraq war in not being strong enough to vote my conscience has probably been an evolution of where I am now."

The House changed *freedom fries* back to *French fries* in 2006 without ceremony. The Iraq War would continue for so long that its name would change, too, one of the Forever Wars, as Dexter Filkins termed the American invasions of the Middle East. By 2011, when the war officially concluded, 40,000 service members were wounded and 4,500 were dead; thousands more, unclaimed in official tolls, would die by suicide. Less certain are the statistics about civilians killed; estimates range from 150,000 to more than 1 million.

The chairman of the FCC wore a lapel pin in the distinct shape of the president's head.

The celluloid pin-back button was patented in the late nineteenth cen-tury, which heralded the age of campaign advertisement delivered via lapel, and the flag pin emerged as a Right-coded mandala in Washington amid the Vietnam War, when Republicans in Congress poked them through their suits to communicate opposition to antiwar activists. Robert Redford wore one in *The Candidate*, which inspired the chief of staff to the thirty-seventh president to suggest that he do the same. He liked the idea and he asked his White House aides to wear them, too. From there the flag pin became a common part of political dress and then, after 2001, a mandatory one. Politicians who balked at the expectation to accessorize in this manner were met with swift condemnation. The senator who would become the forty-fourth president said, during his campaign, "Shortly after 9/11, particularly because as we're talking about the Iraq War, that became a substitute for, I think, true patriotism, which is speaking out on issues that are of importance to our national security, I decided I won't wear that pin on my chest; instead I'm gonna try to tell the American people what I believe will make this country great, and hopefully that will be a testimony to my patriotism." Outrage ensued, as it does. "I think he's disrespecting the American flag," one partisan pundit said. "It's almost a form of protest," said another. "They just hate the flag," said another. "Put on the pin!" another demanded.

The fifty flags at the Washington Monument flew at half-staff. The War Hero, the senior senator from Arizona, had died, and in accordance with protocol, to honor his life and his service, flags were lowered at government structures across the country.

The War Hero had been shot down in Vietnam. He was captured by the enemy, and when he would not renounce the United States, he was tortured. He had been beaten so badly that for the rest of his life his arms moved in a stiff way; he could not lift them over his head. The president, who had dodged the Vietnam draft by crying "bone spurs," an affliction to which military-age sons of rich families seemed especially vulnerable, had feuded with him over the years. The War Hero did not bend to his dominance, and represented, in that way, a challenge to his dominance, a barrier to notions of reality as the president sought to draw it into being. He said the War Hero was "not a war hero," and that his capture by hostile troops had been a failure. "I prefer people who don't get captured," he said. In the Senate, the War Hero cut a lonely path of defense against the president. When he died, the president cut a lonely path of dissent as elsewhere the War Hero was honored.

For two days, the president refused to comply with protocol about the flag at the White House. Senior members of the administration tried to intervene. The vice president. The chief of staff, whose own son had been killed in his service to the country. Still the president refused. Senior White House officials tried to convince him to release himself of the burden of statesmanship and allow instead for aides to direct the official response to the death. He refused that, too. As he saw it, his Washington and his America should not be affected by the absence of a man whom he did not like. A White House spokesman told the press "I'm not commenting on that" because, he said, he did not work "in flag world."

In his final statement, published after his death, the War Hero got the last word that would ever matter:

We are citizens of the world's greatest republic, a nation of ideals, not blood and soil. We are blessed and are a blessing to humanity when we uphold and advance those ideals at home and in the world. We have helped liberate more people from tyranny and poverty than ever before in history. We have acquired great wealth and power in the process.

We weaken our greatness when we confuse our nationalism with tribal rivalries that have sown resentment and hatred and violence in all the corners of the globe. We weaken it when we hide behind walls, rather than tear them down, when we doubt the power of our ideals, rather than trust them to be the great force for change they have always been.

We were half through the day when the flag lowered on the White House lawn. "Despite our differences on policy and politics, I respect [the War Hero's] service to our country and, in his honor, have signed a proclamation to fly the flag of the United States at half-staff until the day of his interment," the president said, finally, in a statement.

The War Hero had anticipated the president would not handle his death well and so he fired at him another insult or gesture of mercy, depending on the light. Among his requests for his funeral was the matter of the guest list: the president was not invited.

The president wanted to sign some hats for me and Isabelle Brourman, who had been painting his portrait in the living room while we talked. "Have you ever drawn?" she asked him. The president looked up from the red hat. "You know, I know myself. I know what I'm good at. I've never been good with a paintbrush in my hand," he said, "but if I'm in a room, I know what should be moved and what should stay." Isabelle nodded. "So you're a conceiver in the third dimension," she said. The president smiled at the sound of that word, *conceiver*. "I'm a conceiver!" he said. "I like that, a conceiver!"

OLIVIA NUZZI: What do you dream about?

DONALD TRUMP: Nothing, things. Things happen, and you'll go to bed, you close your eyes, and, you know, you could be thinking about a subject that you never thought about, or you haven't thought about in years, or something that hasn't happened, or you're not involved, and so it's very interesting. It's an interesting question, though, because usually you don't remember, like, the details of it, but you remember the concepts.

OLIVIA NUZZI: At Mar-a-Lago, we had been talking about this idea of you as a kind of artist. Isabelle used the word *conceiver*. I recalled this scene, you were sitting down to film a documentary, and in thirty seconds, you reconfigured the whole shot, and you made it look so much better. Yet you only changed a few things. Do you always think visually?

DONALD TRUMP: I think I do. I've always designed things that worked. You know, I mean, my jobs work, my real estate things worked. I have very successful buildings. I have very successful clubs. A lot of imagination goes into those things. I've always thought of myself as being actually very—I don't talk about it, I'm talking to you, probably for the first time, certainly, with any writer, I talk to some people, but some people tell me exactly what you just said, but no, I'm a very visual person, and I'm, you know, I'm very much that way inclined.

OLIVIA NUZZI: You had wanted to be in the movie business, right? When you were young?

DONALD TRUMP: I was going to go to Southern California, where they have a great movie school. I don't know if they still do—probably, they did—but I was going to go there. I wanted to be in the movie business. I liked it, and I'll never forget, I was with a friend of mine who was essentially in that business, Broadway and movies and things, and he was having a problem getting a house and a problem with loans and a problem with banks and lots of problems, and he actually looked to me to help him out, and I listened to his problem, and I was able to get him straightened out, and I had a great depth of knowledge on real estate, which is what he was having a problem with, and he said, "Honestly, you shouldn't be in the movie business. You should be in the real estate business." I think I put a lot of that into the real estate business. You know, it's like Trump Tower.

OLIVIA NUZZI: You've said that you brought show business to business.

DONALD TRUMP: I think so. A lot of people—well, not a lot of people have said that, most people don't think that. But I sort of combined the two. I think real estate is a better business, but I sort of put a lot of show business into the real estate business.

OLIVIA NUZZI: Did you know Robert Evans?

DONALD TRUMP: I did.

OLIVIA NUZZI: What was he like?

DONALD TRUMP: I really liked him. Actually, he was a different kind of a guy. He was a different guy. He was a character. He was a great-looking guy. He was better looking than the movie stars.

OLIVIA NUZZI: He was with Ali MacGraw, right?

DONALD TRUMP: Yes, he was. Married her. He was a very, very creative, very creative guy. He was a nice guy, he was always great to me.

OLIVIA NUZZI: I'm curious, can you explain why you keep referencing Hannibal Lecter in your speeches?

DONALD TRUMP: I do that because I'm saying they come in from prisons and jails, and you know, there is a slight difference between a prison and a jail, but they do come in from both, one being a little more severe, and they come in from mental institutions and insane asylums—and that, again, would be more severe, the insane asylum, right? Sometimes I'll define *insane asylum* as being, like, as an example, *Silence of the Lambs*, the late, great Hannibal Lecter. And I'll do it to be fun. You understand that, to be fun, I hope. The problem with sarcasm or, you know, sometimes bringing things into a little lighter air, the problem is that a lot of people either don't get it or they can make you look a little bit bad. You know, when you use sarcasm, they can turn it back at you if they want.

OLIVIA NUZZI: The press can be hyper-literal.

274

DONALD TRUMP: They do it with me a lot. Hannibal Lecter was in *Silence of the Lambs.* You saw the movie, Olivia, right? One of the greats, in your opinion? One of the great movies?

OLIVIA NUZZI: It's not in, like, my top five, but it's a great movie.

DONALD TRUMP: One of the scarier movies. He was a very violent person, I think we could say, to put it mildly. She played great in the role. Anthony Hopkins was incredible. You know, Anthony Hopkins was on *The Tonight Show.* I think it was early. It was a long time ago, when I was doing *The Apprentice*, and he was being praised for doing *The Silence of the Lambs*, and the host said, "What would you consider to be really scary?" He said, "The scariest thing I can think of is being fired on *The Apprentice*." I said, "Wow. Do you believe that?" I was just watching and it was cute, but he's a great actor, but, I use that just as an example, but in a certain way, a kidding example. Then I'll look at someone and say, "He wants to have you over for dinner," you know? Or, "He wants to have you"—I look, I say, "He wants to have you for dinner," meaning, not in the traditional sense, right?

OLIVIA NUZZI: So Hannibal Lecter is a caricature of the worst-case scenario of undocumented—

DONALD TRUMP: —of the people coming in, yes.

OLIVIA NUZZI: Got it.

DONALD TRUMP: The people that are coming—Oh! Wait, is that not clear? Because, you know, I do get asked that, "Why do you bring up Hannibal Lecter?" To me, it's so clear.

OLIVIA NUZZI: You know what I think it is? It's when you say "The late, great," because then there's some confusion about whether you think that he is not a fictional character.

DONALD TRUMP: Maybe, but I say "The late, great" because it's sort of a cool introduction. The late, great Hannibal Lecter, you know, he was so bad. They had him in that glass cage. You couldn't have a pinhole in there, he'd figure out a way to get out, and you know, the genius of it all. But I use that as an example of people who are coming into the country that are in mental institutions, like Hannibal Lecter was in, and it's true. I mean, there are countries, are many countries, not South America, everywhere, they're releasing their prisoners, and they're releasing their people from mental institutions, and terrorists are coming in, and they're coming into our country as we are speaking, and they're coming in in big numbers. Honestly, Olivia, it's really bad. It's really dangerous. You're seeing what's going on in New York, right? With the migrants, with the fighting. I mean, we have fistfights with cops. You know, I've seen cops get shot. I've seen cops—a lot of things happen. When a cop is in the middle of a street fistfighting, you know, in a fistfight with a migrant from Venezuela? It's, like, it's crazy.

OLIVIA NUZZI: I talked to the mayor about this. He has been lobbying the federal government for relief with the migrants who have arrived there. What is the role for the federal government as it relates to cities managing migrants?

DONALD TRUMP: [The mayor] has been one of the people that is willing to speak out about what's happening. He's got close to a hundred thousand people. And I'm amazed that the city can afford it. They're spending billions of dollars, and it's inconceivable that the city has the money, because the city hasn't had the money to do small things. And you know, where do they get that kind of money? And the federal government? Well, first of all, they shouldn't be here, and you know, they're being lured here, lured here with healthcare and Medicare for All and Social Security and school, you know, they're going to schools and they don't speak any language. They're sitting in schools and they're taking the seats of kids that have been there, you know, of citizens of the country. It's, the whole thing is, it doesn't make sense. It doesn't make sense. But, so you spoke to [the mayor] about it. Are you friendly with him?

OLIVIA NUZZI: I was just interviewing him.

DONALD TRUMP: Well, in all fairness to him, he's one of the few that complains about it, you know, because a lot of them don't complain and he does complain about it.

OLIVIA NUZZI: Will you commit to provide federal relief to cities like New York that are dealing with that?

DONALD TRUMP: I would, I would, but then I'm also committed to getting to and starting with the very criminal element and the very bad dangerous element, getting them out of our country immediately. So we have to do that.

OLIVIA NUZZI: What's the mechanism for something like that? I know you were talking about [the thirty-fourth president].

DONALD TRUMP: The local police know everything. They know their middle names. They know everything about them, where they came from, what country, everything else, you have to rely on them. I was with local police today up in Michigan, the sheriffs, in this case, they know everything about it.

OLIVIA NUZZI: So you would have DHS—

DONALD TRUMP: —*They* know. DHS, ICE, Border Patrol to a lesser extent, you know, once you get to the border, but they would be dealing and they would do a great job. They know everything about them. They can tell you everything about them. They know. They have to live with them.

———

The South African tech billionaire spent hundreds of millions of dollars to support the president, and on the day he was sworn back into office, the South African tech billionaire appeared at a rally in Washington to celebrate. He thanked the crowd for having made the same choice he had made, to stand behind the president at what he called "a fork in the road of human civilization." He was all head, the South African tech billionaire, a roaming consciousness. The autonomous vehicle of his body looked soft and rubbery under his dark clothes. His physicality was rubbery, too. He moved with certain imprecision and on what appeared a delay. But now his motion seemed synced to the beat of his intentions: his fist pressed first to his chest, then his arm shot upward at a rigid angle. A salute, unmistakable, in the manner of the Third Reich. He had not meant it as such a salute, he said later. His assertion was echoed by many actors in our age of insincerity.

His mother posted on the digital town square that he owns to praise the prototype of a fully self-driving electric vehicle called the Cybercab, her son's innovation. "The most insane thing is, you sit in a seat and there is no steering wheel nor foot pedals. It takes a while to enjoy just sitting as if you're in your lounge, while driving to your destination," she said. The ambition of transhumanists is that the shift to autonomous-and-artificial-everything will prompt swift adaptations to conveniences that will not register as a shift away from human autonomy and intelligence.

In California, the lithium in the batteries of his electric cars had burned the fires hotter, had bled into the earth, the atmosphere. How many men cleaning up the wreckage, I wondered, would be away from home for a long time, would return with some piece of what was lost that represented their service, would be swept, one day, into the plot of a digital graveyard?

A few weeks later, I drove down the jagged canyon road to the water and noticed the grass aglow on the hillside. I looked up. Across the sky, a looping salute of blue and green and pink and purple clouds. I pulled off into the dirt. In this valley, the sense of the uncanny valley: the primal alert that activates human suspicion of nonhuman phenomena. The loop of clouds in too-saturated colors appeared to suggest the election of an alien pope, maybe, or the occasion of some cartoon genie gender reveal. A rocket launch, it turned out, by the South African tech billionaire.

"I have this thing called PeaceFeed. It blocks any references to Donald Trump or [the South African tech billionaire]. Look at what *The New York Times* looks like."

The man spun his screen around so I could observe the effects of this technology. Ninety percent of the newspaper was rendered in focus so soft that it was just a blur of black and white and splotches of color.

"I have genuinely no idea what's going on in the world. It's spectacular," he said.

'are u ok' im literally a forest fire and i am the fire and i am the forest and i am the witness watching it.

—An account called fringeffect

From my rotting body,
flowers shall grow
and I am in them,
and that is
eternity.

—Edvard Munch

Quentin Tarantino imagines that Sharon Tate lives. In his ninth film, *Once Upon a Time in . . . Hollywood,* the Manson murders are rendered slapstick, the violent siege on Cielo Drive gone haywire to a greater good, the murderers murdering themselves, a stunt man and an afterthought of spaghetti Westerns made savior and star with the assistance of an acid cigarette and a flamethrower. When the night is through, Tate opens the door on a new day in an America in which the sixties did not end in a pool of her blood.

Dan Bern imagines that Marilyn Monroe marries Henry Miller instead of Arthur Miller. In "Marilyn," a song he wrote in the early 1990s while living in Los Angeles, he figures her existence would have been in that event a more whimsical and less burdened affair. The bulk of Monroe's estate had been left to her acting coach, and when he died, it was inherited by his second wife, who licensed her image with liberal abandon. At the time Bern was in the city with which she was most associated in the American imagination, "she was everywhere," he told me, and he could not help but contemplate her life and its material end. In the song, he croons, "Marilyn Monroe didn't marry Henry Miller, but if she did he'd've taken her to Paris," "she'd've smoked a lot of opium," "she'd've dyed her hair blue," "they'd've fucked every day," "she'd've felt like a woman, not like a photograph in a magazine," "and okay, maybe she'd've died the same anyway, but if she did she'd've had more fun."

Pamela Anderson is celebrated because she deserves celebration. She is celebrated, too, because she survived to represent the second half of the life that Monroe did not get to live. Through Pamela, we see ourselves redeemed.

We kill. We forget our fervor. We did not mean it. We spin tales of creative justice. We look for salvation. We try as best we can to take it back.

The man who would be assassinated was concerned about assassinations. It had been sixty-one years since the last American president was shot and killed. It had been fifty-six years since the last presidential candidate was shot and killed. It had been forty-six years since the last federal lawmaker was shot and killed. You could talk yourself calm with such data. You could do your best to refuse the data that argued concern was a rational response to violent threats against members of Congress that had swelled in the seven-year period from when the president was sworn into office, in which US Capitol Police recorded 4,500 threats, to this third general election in which he was the Republican presidential candidate, in which they recorded 9,500. You could do your best to forget that the Capitol Police had been beaten by the mob that threatened to hang the vice president. Or that the president himself had raised gun violence as a lighthearted rhetorical device in his earliest campaign. "I could stand in the middle of Fifth Avenue and shoot somebody, and I wouldn't lose any voters, okay?" he said. He was correct in spirit even if he never tested the premise on the specifics.

The man who would be assassinated knew that the country could not be understood through data alone. He knew, in fact, better than most that the application of science had limits in the realms of human behavior, that American politics reflected American moods, that such moods swung volatile, and that the American mood right then, in Arizona in March 2024, was more volatile than it had felt at any time in his thirty years of life.

With solemn respect, the man who would be assassinated introduced the MAGA General. The MAGA General looked satisfied. He was an adviser to the president who had become a kind of philosophical influencer for a terminally online faction of the MAGA base. "The forces aligned against us are only getting more serious and more severe," he told the man who would be assassinated, "and when I say there's no middle ground, there's no middle ground. One side's gonna win here, and one side's gonna lose." The macho language of war is pervasive in politics, but the MAGA General, a Navy veteran who looks like the Skipper of the Underworld, seemed to really mean it. Under the thumb of the elite ruling class, the country was going to shit, he said, and that was by design. And with MAGA "ascendant" once again, the elites were "panicked" and "desperate," scrambling to weaponize the nation's powerful institutions against movement leaders to strike fear in the hearts of the congregation. "They are converging the Central Bank, the lords of easy money on Wall Street, the tech oligarchs, the national security apparatus, the legal apparatus," the MAGA General said. He anticipated high drama in the election. "This next year, you're going to see things you've never seen in your life—in any country—to try to stop this movement."

"Including assassination attempts?" the man who would be assassinated asked.

The MAGA General thought so and cited as proof a *Washington Post* column that compared the president to Julius Caesar. The column was a green light flashing at anyone inclined to try. "I've also heard from some donors that there's been loose talk in Democratic social settings, Republican social settings, that they're tossing out the concept of assassination, figuring out if they can decapitate our movement."

The man who would be assassinated agreed. "It's a dog whistle," he said.

The man who would be assassinated lived in a state of constant fear, he added, that he would wake up one morning soon to news that "they've done it," that the president had been assassinated.

This was not the stuff of conspiracy theories or unfounded anxieties. This was the stuff he felt. The same way he felt, in 2016, before many leaders of the conservative movement could feel it, before they were prepared to support the president, that the rise of the president was inevitable, and that good things would come to those who did not wait to accept it. For his ability to feel, to accept, and to act, he had been repaid in so many ways; his organization was popular with the masses and influential at the top. A conversation with him was a requirement for those who wished to vault to the top themselves. Listening to him was a requirement for those who wished to understand the movement that had so shaped the country, so defined its mood, for a period so long that it was by now an era. But was it the end or the beginning of one? By now what the man who would be assassinated had felt early and felt all along was a force felt by all even if they could not agree on whether what was felt was good or bad. It was beyond rightdoing or wrongdoing, far afield of any idea at all beyond the visceral reality, now undeniable, that this was big, and that big was hard to argue with, because in our politics big had long ago replaced good.

The message from the man who would be assassinated was that messengers of the national mood, working as he was sure they were in service to God, would need to use their gifts of communication as a kind of shield against the intervention of the bullet. He felt this as surely as he felt everything else about which he was proven right. "The way we prevent it, besides having actually loyal people around Trump, is we have to call the bluff and say, 'They're going to try to kill Trump,' and that might scare them enough to stop it. Because what I've found is, if you can broadcast the play before it happens, you've got a fifty-fifty shot that they don't do it. Fifty-fifty."

Still, those odds were not so great that they assured America would be made great again. "Is there any other way to prevent them from—I mean, let's just say it bluntly—we are dealing with people who say he's literally Hitler. They spy on him. There is only so much more. Seven hundred years in prison. There are thirteen thousand people here," he said. They would all need to be vigilant. They would all need to accept what he felt and to admit they could feel it, too.

"It is not a profound new concept that you go take out the person you don't like," the man who would be assassinated said.

The MAGA General was a showier and more cynical creature. He interjected with a note of optimism. The people listening would be, after all, skeptical of voting by mail, more so after the last election when, amid the coronavirus pandemic, the president had lost after he told his supporters it was unsafe to vote by mail because more votes were stolen that way. It was unwise strategy to tell those same voters now that the country itself was unsafe, that mortal danger lurked, that assassination was imminent. Even if they killed the president, the MAGA General said, he would not be dead. The president was the idea that registered viscerally, the unkillable force that they felt. They had made him immortal.

Eighteen months later, back in Arizona, the senior leaders of the federal government sat behind thick glass as if for sale. Their presence was intended as a show of strength. The set, a labyrinth of security compromises, formed instead an installation of weakness.

The president had dodged the bullet that flew toward his life. As a matter of rhetoric, he had leaned on this idea of himself as the shield metaphorical throughout the trials, the *witch hunt*, that made him a felon and then made him the president once more. As he campaigned in between dates at the criminal court, he said, "They're not coming after me. They're coming after you. I'm just standing in their way." The man who would be assassinated was assassinated. In the country founded on radically evolved ideals of freedom of speech and expression, enshrined in law, that make it the place where violence is the least necessary and least justifiable means of dissent, an assassin had cut him off with a bullet in his throat. Footage of the moment he was murdered flew by in the endless scroll; I watched as he was hit and as he fell while the blood fell from his flesh. The next thing I saw was an image of a sitcom actor from the eighties holding a trout and smoking a cigar. The next thing I saw was a half-naked woman. The next thing I saw was a joke about the assassination of the man who had been assassinated.

The Personality had a rifle by his side. He believed that it was Israel. Another hired a defense contractor whose predecessor's involvement in war crimes in the 2000s had generated such negative publicity that they had changed their name. Another determined to listen to her intuition even when it interfered with her work responsibilities. Another was open to theories popular among neoconservatives interested in justification for a war with Iran that the assassination had been carried out by Iran. In the discourse every aspect of the event was picked apart. Every facet of the man who had been assassinated was seized upon. People who had not known him or had barely known him called him their close friend, their best friend, their brother, their soulmate. Where there was grief there was attention, validation, and profit. Where there was chaos and fear there were limits to reason and no limits on doubt, on wonder, on conspiracy.

We were the same age. I did not remember when I first met him. He was like a kid from my class, someone who was friends with many of my friends, who had been around as long as I had been around, though I did not see him around much, and did not know him beyond what you might call the green-room level on which you nod and smile and say hello and continue on your own timelines unaffected by the exchange. On the afternoon when I heard his fear, when I witnessed his nerves, I did not yet know what he may have felt. I did not yet know that I would come to consider him the man who would be assassinated. I did not yet believe on some level that his concern for the president was an alarm blaring through his body. That the alarm was intended to warn him.

———

THE DEVIL'S ADVOCATE: The Constitution requires that punishment be not cruel, according to the plain language of the Eighth Amendment. What I've been fighting for in the last decade or so is based upon research that I've done that shows that lethal injection kills people in a way that is quite cruel. This is called *post-conviction death penalty defense.* These are guys who are convicted and who are facing execution. You can make something called an *as applied challenge*, which means that what you're claiming is that the method of execution as applied to you will result in a death that will be cruel, or you could do something called a *facial challenge*, where you're claiming that the technique of execution in anybody would be cruel, but the law also requires that you name a second method. I've been to death row in eight states.

OLIVIA NUZZI: What does success look like if preventing execution altogether is not possible?

THE DEVIL'S ADVOCATE: When it comes to the rightness or wrongness of capital punishment broadly, I guess I'm agnostic. It is hard to get behind American capital punishment because it's so racist and classist.

OLIVIA NUZZI: You're agnostic on the matter?

THE DEVIL'S ADVOCATE: Yeah, kind of. I'm not against it categorically. I'm certainly not for life without parole. In issues like the death penalty, when you're commenting on it, people are listening to you to decide, *What side are you on? Are you an abolitionist or are you a proponent?*

OLIVIA NUZZI: Whether or not you agree with me that one wrongful execution is too many, I guess my question is: Should the state play God?

THE DEVIL'S ADVOCATE: What's funny about the state, of course, is that the same people who very strongly think that the government should stay out of everything are the same people who think the government is authoritative when it comes to executing people.

OLIVIA NUZZI: Well, I'm not talking about hypothetical people. I'm asking you.

THE DEVIL'S ADVOCATE: The classic example to me then would be people like Eichmann. Should Eichmann have been executed? I can certainly see why I would think he might and the value in that. I don't know. Could there have been some other alternative punishment for him that would have been equally valuable and satisfying and would feel like justice? I don't know. Maybe.

OLIVIA NUZZI: Are you an atheist?

THE DEVIL'S ADVOCATE: Yes.

OLIVIA NUZZI: Does certainty about anything unknowable not strike you as ridiculous?

THE DEVIL'S ADVOCATE: Okay, fair. Then let me refine my answer about the existence of God. I would say that it's not knowable. So I would not classify myself again as an atheist. I don't think the evidence is compelling, but nevertheless, it's not knowable. I mean, by nature, faith cannot be disproven. That distinguishes it from science, of course, which can be falsified, but faith can't be falsified, and I have faith in things that I can't see or can't know. In terms of capital punishments, functionally, I think that if I've made any progress, it's because people don't look at me and think, *You're just a crazy abolitionist.* I'm telling them that with the method, their problem is constitutional and technical. Lethal injection was always an impersonation of a medical act that was meant to fool the public. Lethal injection outwardly looks like a mild way of dying, none of it is true. South Carolina now is going to shoot someone in the firing squad.

OLIVIA NUZZI: I think I would take that over being injected.

THE DEVIL'S ADVOCATE: I think the data actually would support that. What I like about the firing squad, if I could say it like that, is that it's honest. Then we can decide, as a public: *Do we like this? Do we think this is what we should be doing or not?* Execution is our civilized version of beating the shit out of someone until they die.

OLIVIA NUZZI: I would take that over the injection, too, I think.

In the atrium of Trump Tower, I reminded myself of the year. It was 2024. Twenty twenty-four. I had been here so many times in so many different periods of our recent history. And most of the people here, I had known them for a third of my life, and the way that only my brother knows what it was to live in our childhood home, to be of our family, only these people, the witnesses and the officials and the reporters, knew what it was to be in the eye of the distortion field as it swept from Manhattan across the country.

Time folded, stretched, turned. I turned on the heel of my pink Gucci stilettos from where I was standing, outside the facade of the Gucci store in the atrium, to face the fabled golden escalator. In my mind the stilettos morphed into the black Prada stilettos I had been wearing the day when I first stepped onto the marble here. I could remember it clearly, what the sun looked like outside, how it shone on the buttons on the uniforms of the doormen. I wore a white angora sweater and I could remember how it felt warm to the touch when I entered the building, because it had been unseasonably warm that day. It was freezing in the lobby, then as now.

That morning, I had met one of the president's aides in the café downstairs. We talked for a long while. She would become over time a close friend. The equivalent, in some ways, to my brother in my childhood home. A vital witness against whose judgment I checked my own perceptions and experiences in my capacity as another American citizen bearing close witness to events, and in my official role as witness, drafting one of the early records of what went on here and later in Washington. That day, she told me that if I stuck around, the candidate would meet with me. It was almost noon by that point, and she said he was still upstairs in his penthouse apartment, but he would come down to his office sometime soon to begin his workday, and he would meet with me then. Quickly and self-consciously and unprompted she offered a clarification: He really started his workday much earlier than he arrived at his office, and when she said *workday* she meant his *official workday*, the day spent in the office. His unofficial workday included certain rituals he liked to observe, like watching television, making phone calls, and so on, and he liked to observe those rituals in his apartment. But he was *always* working, she said. Lest I think otherwise.

A few months before, in one of our last conversations that I could recall, my father had asked me if "this Trump thing" was "for real." For my father, the kind of working-class guy who would ultimately form the so-called *super base* of supporters that helped deliver Trump to the White House, Trump was part of the infrastructure of the history of his city. Not in the sense that he was in real estate, and his mark was scrawled across buildings all over town, but in that he represented how the city and how America had changed in his lifetime, how it had developed in some way away from him. The Greed Is Good eighties looked different to guys like him than it did to guys whose fathers funded their real estate empires. My father considered himself fortunate. He knew a guy, he knew a lot of guys, and he was a guy guys knew, and through a guy he got a good job with good benefits, but that was not enough, and so he worked nights and weekends as a driver and as a security guard at the Garden and the Central Park Boathouse. He knew every block and every alleyway of every borough. He knew the history of seemingly every building, who had lived there, what had been filmed there, if it had been the scene, too, of crimes or other sagas of public interest. And in the same way that he knew these things he knew that Donald Trump was, as he said, "a buffoon" and "full of shit." I called him once from outside the skyscraper, on the sidewalk on Fifty-Seventh Street, when I was covering an early campaign event. Inside I had met a strange character who struck me as the kind of guy a guy like my father would know. I was correct. "Livvybaby!" he said. He always answered my calls that way. One word, *Livvybaby*. My question darkened his mood in an instant. "What the hell are you talking to [the strange character] for?" he shot back in response. He was panicked in a way I would not understand for several years, until the strange character ran for mayor and I was forced to learn more about him. "Be careful!" he said. Always, he said that, but rarely with this much urgency. "God, chill, Dad," I remember saying, in the particular manner of a twenty-two-year-old. "I'm fine."

Was the "Trump thing" for real? I did not know. He did not live to find out. Often I would encounter someone at a rally, a fan or a member of the security team, who would remind me of him, and I would wonder how his views of the president would have evolved. There was a particular way he stood. In the Saul Leiter photograph *Snow* (1960), a working man is seen through a frost-smudged window, standing outside in the slush, peering down at something in his hands. He is absorbed in his task, which is inside his head, but there is purpose and grace in the sharp angle of his body against the elements. He looks present even as he is for the moment elsewhere. He looks like my father.

He had voted for the War Hero in the 2008 election. I overheard him talking to my mother after 9/11. She had voted for the Democrat in 2000, and I did not know who he voted for, but they both agreed that the forty-third president was doing a great job now. And I remember he did not like the thirty-ninth president because he was "a hick" and "a peanut farmer." Rural people always freaked him out. He seemed to hate whoever the mayor of New York was at any given time, but he was impressed by how much the billionaire mayor cleaned up the city even if he made life much more of a hassle for smokers. Sanmen, I was often reminded, really do love to clean up. His politics were not intuitive to me. It did not come up much. He was a union guy and he thought the unions were corrupt. He did not like politicians in general. Who did? They were "all crooks," he would say. And aren't they? Still, I wondered if he would have come around on the president.

All of that flashed in my mind as I paced around the room now, marble and glass and enormous as it had always been. I returned, firmly back in the realm of the pink stilettos, to the year 2024. Twenty twenty-four. He had been dead for nine years. For weeks, it had required effort to believe this. As prosecutors asked a jury to step back in time to the 2016 campaign, all witnesses did the same, and I found myself remembering things I had long ago buried, and communicating with people with whom I once maintained daily or sometimes hourly contact but had not spoken to regularly in years.

The prior weekend, someone at a Washington cocktail party was talking to me, and I knew based on how he was talking to me that I must know him and maybe I knew him pretty well at one point, and the whole time he was talking I was trying to figure out who he was and why I knew him, or why he knew me, and it was not until hours later that I realized he had worked for the vice president and had been a source of mine for much of the duration of the first administration. I had forgotten him entirely.

He was not alone. I had known so few people and then in the span of a few years I had met hundreds of people and then it became the case that sometimes people knew me from my work or public appearances and I had a great deal of trouble keeping track of who I knew and how and why I knew them or whether they were just familiar with an avatar of me and I convinced myself that it was not just rudeness or ineptitude on my part but a normal human response to unusual circumstances, since people had not evolved to know so many other people. We evolved to know our families and a handful of people in our communities and to know those people forever and this was a modern aberration and in fact it was not my fault that my brain had reached capacity and could not process all of this information.

Nice to see you, the very Washington custom, with all the ugliness that implies. I was willing now to accept ugliness for utility, which is one definition of Washington.

That there was a criminal trial seemed not a shock at all. Not exactly. It had felt in some way inevitable, that what started just up the FDR would land everyone here eventually, in a courtroom where, a few floors away, prisoners idled in their cells. Were we not, all of us, captive to the whims of this one figure and to his fate?

———

His felony conviction, his verdict of guilt, reflected back at the country that made him, again, the president.

———

The common wisdom offered by people, people who mean well, and they do mean well, when you have face-planted before the world: *This, too, shall pass.* The phrase does not appear in the Tao Te Ching, Scripture, Talmud, Midrash, Veda, or Quran. The best guess of phraseologists is that it originated from the work of Attar of Nishapur, the Sufi poet, but its first direct references are from the nineteenth century, when it was recorded in Jewish folklore and English poetry and then popularized by Abraham Lincoln during an 1859 speech before the Wisconsin

State Agricultural Society. He related the story of an unnamed eastern monarch who assembled what must be one of the earliest known writers' rooms: "It is said an eastern monarch once charged his wise men to invent him a sentence, to be ever in view, and which should be true and appropriate in all times and situations. They presented him the words, 'And this, too, shall pass away,'" Lincoln said. He was struck by how well the wise men lived up to their characterization. "How much it expresses," he added. "How chastening in the hour of pride. How consoling in the depths of affliction."

I heard the phrase so much throughout the fall, throughout my fall, that it became a part of my act, in which I deflected from inquiry, however charitable the motive, as a defensive effort in self-preservation. It was as though I had lost custody of my exterior to the country. I guarded my interior as best I could.

Question: How are you doing?
Answer: I had not been doing so well, but then I learned something.

Question: Oh? What's that?
Answer: Did you know—
[beat]
—that this, too, shall pass?

I have seen death. This was not that. This was something lesser, something infinitely smaller, something that was a kind of death, okay, but one that called for a period of griefless mourning. It was the death of an idea. An idea of a self. Not of self itself. Not of myself. But of an iteration of myself. It was the great test of the hypothesis of that self, and what it wrought was a verdict: That self, weak, not durable, not real, had failed. It was a self beside myself. I thought of that phrase, *Beside myself.* I thought of a viral joke: *Me to myself: Is she bothering you?* Yes, in fact. More than anyone else ever has.

The public-facing components of an interior-based profession, accountable to the public, always struck absurd. It became an uncomfortable fact of the president's rise that he succeeded in making all political and media actors into actors. He was producer, director, and star of the country, and those who chronicled or engaged with him as a profession found their fortunes attached to his in ways that seemed, even when they were cast officially as his opponents, like a kind of collusion.

It is useful to hear from people anyplace, but the sorts of voters who attend political events—at an Elks Lodge in a blizzard, past the jack-knifed semitrucks keeled over on the highway like bad omen-bones strewn about some cursed forest, or an open field in a far-flung farm town, sun reliably beating heatstroke onto the spectators in the middle of a workday—are atypical in their level of engagement, not representative of Average Voters, and I cannot passively talk to anybody, and I am, being the way I am, going to be invested in what I learn about their mother's cancer and their dog who got hit by the car and—*What is the dog's name? Jinx*—I am going to want to know more about Jinx, and inevitably there is a cat, too, and maybe a goat, and I will need to hear about them, and I will care about what I am told, and it will affect me, and then I will have to field questions, too, about the soap opera storylines and the sins of the press who have *normalized* or *otherized* the president.

The more visible I was at any given time, the more that became an intrusion, because you cannot be a fly on the wall when people would like a picture with the fly, and when the sweet older woman has a grandson in medical school who *Just has the biggest crush on the fly* and *Actually, if the fly does not mind,* she is *Going to call Michael right now, this will just make his day,* and while it rings, while she *Has the fly here,* she will wonder, *How do you stand it, talking to the awful president?* and, *What is his attorney like? He seems drunk, is he drunk?* and the media personalities whose television programs the fly appears on, *Are they as wonderful as they seem?* and—*Oh, Michael! Honey, look! The fly!*

It is a shock to me when I am recognized now by strangers. They ask when I will "come back." They ask me to assess what is happening in Washington: a bit of on-the-spot personalized punditry. Time stretches and folds, the scenes overlap on the single stage, I am pulled apart and apart and apart and apart. What is it that they recognize? I feel confident that I would not recognize me, if I saw me now. Feel that, if the person they recognize were to walk right by, I would not know who she is. I try my best to assume what I recall of her character. I have never wanted to disappoint anyone who takes the time to read what I write, to express what they made of it, good or bad. But it is as though we are discussing someone who died long ago. Someone I hardly remember. Someone I did not know very well to start with. At the mechanic, trapped in my car, the man at my window wanted to know how much longer I would be "gone," and I did not know what to tell him. Forever, I figure. A while, at least. As long as possible and anything less than forever seemed impossible, since she was by now pretty far out, the person to whom he referred, severed entirely from the range of any signal I could send, and I would not send a signal anyhow. I let her go.

Here a woman will tell you that what you need to do is practice grounding, as in walk outside each day without shoes to connect to the earth, and you need to eat dandelions and drink blue algae, and you need to do a heavy-metals detox, and you should never wear sunscreen, and you should put hydrogen in your water, and you should head over to Ojai to see her Reiki guy, though he only works one day a lunar cycle, which makes it tough to get an appointment, and as she is talking you will struggle to maintain eye contact because her artificial breasts seem to intrude into her speech as if their two peaks are a form of punctuation, and while she chatters away, and by now she is onto the subject of goat's milk and she is saying something here about sulfates, you will in one part of your mind conclude she is talking about goat milk soap and in the other part of your mind imagine her breast implants, under her sun-freckled skin, and whether the microplastics in her body are at war with those two bulbs of macroplastics, and if this affects her in profound ways, the stress of this plastics battle, ways that she cannot see but that she is perhaps trying in vain to address with dandelions and hydrogen and once-a-lunar-cycle Reiki healing.

A friend from New York called and he was talking as people in New York do about people in Los Angeles, and I mentioned that as far as I could tell people in Los Angeles do not talk much about people in New York. They are too busy being happy. "That's the difference," he said. "In Los Angeles, people believe that the right combination of sunlight and hiking and supplements and tinctures and breath work will make them happy. Nobody in New York believes they will be happy."

A few blocks away from Trump Tower, at Michael's, Michael himself was at the table telling me and two friends, other members of the media, about the various members of the media seated throughout the restaurant, as though that was somehow unexpected at Michael's, the midday Midtown headquarters of the media. My phone rang. It was the president. "Is it gonna be a nice story?" he asked me. It would be a good story, I said. "Okay," he said. For someone defined by his sensitive ego, he was at odd intervals and more often than not resilient when it came to the tenor of his media coverage, at least as it related to me. "If it's not, we'll try again next time," he said.

A Washington Republican wove through packs of tourists on the Mall and considered, as he now often did, karmic retribution. "If you were a samurai back in the day, you had only been born a samurai because of what you had done in a past life—it determined how you were reborn," he said.

At that moment I was having a problem with ants, common in Malibu. They march in with the spring and summer, and they do not heed polite urging to leave. "I really don't like killing them," I said. It made me feel like a tyrant when I obliterated them in a chemical attack, so I determined I should only kill, if I must, through manual means, since it seemed the less cowardly thing to do. "Then I think, *I believe that every living thing is conscious, but could there possibly be this many extra conscious beings in my home? Could there be so many souls?* And then I think, *Are they condemned to live as ants, to die this way?*" The Washington Republican liked this theory. "They were Nazis in a past life," he said. "Am I doing exactly what I'm supposed to be doing, killing the ants?" I asked. "Yes, you're on solid ground killing ants. They're people who were bad in a past life," he said. "Every murderer or genocidal maniac thinks some version of that," I said. "I feel like that would be really nice, but unfortunately, I think once you die, it's horrible. Right now, a second ago, someone on this earth just died, and we're all still here going about our lives, and one day that will be your turn or my turn to do that, and everyone else will just go about their lives, and that kind of fucks me up. It's both profound narcissism but also humbling to say, the world is not spinning for you and one day everything will go black for you and everyone else will keep going. The only things you ever experience are through your two eyes, but that fundamentally doesn't matter. You are not essential to the well-being of the world even though you are essential to your own well-being," he said.

The Washington Republican had never been the sort of guy you could accuse of always looking on the bright side of life. He was not a depressive. He was not even a bummer. He just had a fundamental pessimism, and it was that which allowed him to work for so long in Republican politics and government even as his party became disfigured beyond recognition in ways that he found reprehensible.

OLIVIA NUZZI: When you think about the butterfly effect, the tiny little things that led to you being saved—without illegal immigrants crossing over that border, there would be no chart; without that chart, there would be nothing for you to turn your head to look at—do you feel in any way, I guess, grateful?

DONALD TRUMP: Nobody's asked me that question. I always say I love that chart. I know, I think illegal immigrants saved my life. That's very interesting. Somebody else told me that. I said, in a way, I think you're right. I mean immigration, immigration saved my life, or I could say illegal immigrants saved my life, well, I wouldn't be, look—look, if I didn't have that chart, I wouldn't have been looking over there. It's the only chart I really put up. I put that chart up because it's so vivid. It's done by Border Patrol. It's all certified stuff. And, you know, you see the numbers very well. Then it goes like a rocket ship up. That's very interesting. I don't know if I can answer that question.

At the Mar-a-Lago gift shop, an item advertised on the Father's Day gift guide "FOR THE BOSS DAD." The 45-47 Flag Tie, "100% Silk, Made in America, Vineyard Vines, TRUMP logo," per the sales description. "Show your patriotism with a classic flag silk tie. Proudly made in America. 100% silk adds style and texture, making it a head-turning accessory for a day in the office or a night on the town. Arrives beautifully wrapped in a complimentary Vineyard Vines gift box. Available in 5 colors." The item, which sells for $120, may be purchased with a coordinated Trump Flag Tie Clip ($32): "Elevate your style and match your look to your business acumen with the Trump flag tie clip. Small but impactful, adding a tie clip to your look signifies a man of distinguished style, professionalism, and respect for our country."

———————

I do not recall what a plane ought to look like in the night sky, whether it should move fast or slow, if it should appear to remain in one place for very long, if it should ever move in circles or up and down as if drawing a heart rate. I can hardly say. Nobody cares anymore. The drones are a distant unsolved memory. Any aircraft that does not fall from the sky seems a friendly one now. We are an adaptable species. Normal is a state to which we arrive as soon as we can. We define its borders on the way.

———————

In the bluffs, a few feet over my head, a lattice of blades let out a thin electric hum. At the trailhead stood a young man with long hair pulled back and muscles that strained his shirt. He held a remote in one hand and waved at me with the other. I nodded. At least there was an explanation for one of the devices.

On the path, the ash in the air burned my nose when I inhaled. My eyes watered. I looked down away from the wind and there scattered in patches on the burned earth were hundreds of little green flags of triumph. About five weeks since the fire. Embers of death, sparks of life.

The electric hum lifted my attention again to the sky. While at night the machine is a false star, in the day it is a decoy bird of prey.

On the cloudless horizon, the drone accelerates like the red-tailed hawk, launched by the hand of God from nothing right into the fabric of everything. The red-tailed hawk moves, hulking yet graceful. It treads the air and scans the ground, hovers for so long you start to wonder if it may be stuck, caught in some invisible web or a patch of sky that sticks to its feathers like a glue trap.

In an instant then it pushes forward. It does not soar. Soaring is for eagles. Instead it zips as a razor, slicing into the side of the atmosphere a line long and steady, and the line spells out the word of God, and the word says that you are not alone, and by this God is not quite clear in His intent, whether by that He means to offer reassurance or to issue a threat.

About the Author

Olivia Nuzzi is the West Coast editor of *Vanity Fair*. From 2017 to 2024, she was the Washington correspondent for *New York* magazine. She lives in Malibu.